The Politics of Globalization

The Politics of Globalization

GAINING PERSPECTIVE, ASSESSING CONSEQUENCES

Mark R. Brawley

broadview press

NATIONAL LIBRARY OF CANADA CATALOGUING IN PUBLICATION DATA

Brawley, Mark R. (Mark Randal), 1960-
The politics of globalization: gaining perspective, assessing consequences/Mark R. Brawley.

Includes bibliographical references and index.
ISBN 1-55111-280-9

1. Globalization—Political aspects. 2. International relations.
3. World politics—21st century. I. Title.

JZ1318.B72 2002   327.09'051   C2002-904768-4

BROADVIEW PRESS, LTD. is an independent, international publishing house, incorporated in 1985. Broadview believes in shared ownership, both with its employees and with the general public; since the year 2000 Broadview shares have traded publicly on the Toronto Venture Exchange under the symbol BDP.

We welcome comments and suggestions regarding any aspect of our publications–please feel free to contact us at the addresses below or at broadview@broadviewpress.com. Broadview Press gratefully acknowledges the support of the Ministry of Canadian Heritage through the Book Publishing Industry Development Program.

North America
Post Office Box 1243,
Peterborough, Ontario, Canada K9J 7H5

3576 California Road,
Orchard Park, New York, USA 14127
TEL (705) 743-8990; FAX (705) 743-8353

EMAIL customerservice@broadviewpress.com

UK, Ireland and continental Europe
Thomas Lyster Ltd.
Units 3 & 4a, Old Boundary Way,
Burscough Rd, Ormskirk, Lancashire L39 2YW
TEL (1695) 575112; FAX (1695) 570120; E-MAIL
EMAIL books@tlyster.co.uk

Australia and New Zealand
UNIREPS University of New South Wales
Sydney, NSW 2052
TEL 61 2 9664099; FAX 61 2 9664520
EMAIL infopress@unsw.edu.au

Cover design by Liz Broes, Black Eye Design.
Typeset by Liz Broes, Black Eye Design.

Printed in Canada

10 9 8 7 6 5 4 3

For Mathieu

Contents

Acknowledgements

I would like to thank my colleagues and students at McGill and Harvard, whose ideas influenced some of my choices in writing this book. I benefited from the atmosphere in the McGill Political Science Department, and among the members of the Université de Montréal/McGill Research Group in International Security, and of Harvard's Weatherhead Center for International Affairs. In 2001 I taught a course titled American Foreign Economic Policy and Globalization in Harvard's Department of Government, which proved a valuable testing ground for some sections of the manuscript. I also owe an intellectual debt to Lawrence Broz, on whose course outline I drew heavily. I would like to thank Michael Harrison for being patient with me while I restructured elements, and missed deadlines. I would like to thank two anonymous reviewers for helpful suggestions, as well as Richard and Laurna Tallman for improving the quality and clarity of the text. I would like to thank my wife and children especially, for bearing with me during the writing and research as I put the finishing touches on the manuscript, instead of spending warm July days at the park.

Mark R. Brawley
Montreal

1 | Defining Globalization

This textbook focuses on the politics generated by globalization. Globalization has garnered much scholarly attention of late, but often discussions only confuse students newly introduced to these issues. On the one hand, academics studying globalization usually centre their analyses on particular limited aspects of a more general phenomenon or set of processes. These scholars follow disciplinary boundaries. While it is all supposed to be about "globalization," the diversity and disparities in this emerging literature can leave the reader quite bewildered. Not only are there legitimate debates about what globalization *means*, producing some perplexities, but many of these definitions are specific to a single academic discipline, or even more narrowly, they are specific to an issue-area or sub-field within a discipline. Since disciplinary boundaries separate subjects of study, definitions that follow these boundaries naturally may look quite different. All of this confusion can occur even before we enter into debates about whether globalization is actually occurring!

There are those who come at the issue of globalization from a more journalistic perspective. These authors tend to be interested in general observations, and are somewhat loose in their use of the term "globalization." This slipperiness may be convenient for the authors, but doesn't lead to greater clarity in the minds of readers. Moreover, overly glib or general definitions get mixed together with the overly narrow ones — ensuring that many people talk past each other when the subject comes up in conversation! A proliferation of meanings merely confounds public discussions as well as baffles students first learning about this subject. The initial goal of this chapter, then, is to guide readers through some of these definitions, arguments, and studies to illuminate the political issues at stake. Here, globalization is treated as a set of processes having many facets. This may aid readers in sifting through the somewhat chaotic literature, but we will also continue to observe disciplinary boundaries. Therefore, while we still have to pay attention to how globalization might be defined within specific domains, we are going to interpret this literature in terms of how it informs our analyses of politics.

Coming to Grips with the Concept

Globalization is a term we hear repeatedly these days, and for most of us, it already carries some vague meaning. While there is little consensus on a precise definition,[1] globalization usually refers to a multi-dimensional process whereby markets, firms, production, and national financial systems are integrated on a global scale. This definition, however, emphasizes the economic aspects of globalization. Globalization in other areas of life, such as communications, might be having ramifications in non-economic areas too, as in cultural affairs—and these can have a subsequent political consequence. Therefore, while this book stresses the political consequences associated with globalization of the world's economy, these will not be the only globalizing processes considered.

Yet, which of these processes are new? Which are not new, but have reached new levels of intensity? How do the former differ from processes that have been at work for some time? How do these changes compare with periods of sweeping economic change in the past? Different scholars from different disciplines answer such questions in quite different ways. This leaves us with a dizzying array of possible definitions for the term "globalization," even before we address our chief political questions. Let's see if we can reach into this cauldron, and pull out some useful ideas before turning to the more pressing political issues: Will globalizing processes gather momentum, or will a political backlash arise?

CONSIDERING SOME POSSIBLE DEFINITIONS

Though the idea of globalization has received widespread attention only in the last decade, there are already many different—sometimes incompatible—definitions offered in the literature. Professors can make their careers by pioneering new areas, which may explain why many academics have so quickly gravitated to the subject of globalization. Creativity is rewarded highly among scholars; academics are enticed not only to take on new fields, but also continually to develop new theories. They have a tendency, furthermore, to tinker with definitions, thereby allowing pet theories greater tractability; hence the many different ideas and theories floated so quickly. We should approach many of these definitions with circumspection.

Of course, there are also legitimate reasons why definitions would vary widely. Disciplinary boundaries exist for a reason. Each discipline in the social sciences prioritizes different phenomena. Sociologists, economists, and historians worry about slightly different things—though their subjects also overlap. Political scientists worry about political outcomes. While it should be no surprise that different definitions of globalization surface in different academic fields, our concerns are with the political aspects of these different meanings. Since many definitions of globalization hint at the different aspects involved in the processes people are interested in, disciplinary boundaries are blurred. This can be both a blessing and a hindrance.

We'll start with some of the definitions focusing on economic tendencies, since these are quite prevalent. We will then look at some of the definitions emphasizing technological or cultural dimensions of globalization before turning our attention to other concerns.

The Organization for Economic Cooperation and Development (OECD) defines globalization as a process "by which markets and production in different countries are becoming increasingly interdependent due to dynamics of trade in goods and services and then flows of capital and technology." To see whether globalization is occurring, one would look at *the volume of trade*: ratios of trade to output, levels of foreign investment, subcontracting and licensing agreements across borders, cross-border mergers and acquisitions, international joint ventures or inter-firm agreements, and so on.[2] We will examine some of these specific economic figures in later chapters.

Economist Ronald W. Jones has argued that globalization is more than just the rising volume of international trade. The amount of goods and services traded, compared to national incomes, has certainly risen; but just as important, according to Jones, is that the *nature of goods being traded* has changed. Intermediate goods make up more and more of the goods crossing borders. This reflects the increasing importance of vertical transnational production processes also being fragmented due to increased international specialization and corporate strategies that emphasize outsourcing. Lower transportation and communication costs, plus the increased opportunities to engage in international investment and trade, accelerate this trend.[3]

Richard Rosecrance narrows the economic changes even further, equating globalization to *the movement of the factors of production from one economy to another.*[4] This may overlap with the definitions just provided, but its specificity accentuates more recent changes in the international economy. On the other hand, as we will show later on, one factor of production—labour—is *less* internationally mobile now than a century ago.

Louis Pauly observes that emphasizing capital has become a trend in the literature, the single factor of production most mobile internationally. When "pressed for examples of what the term [globalization] means, the mind now turns automatically to the image of more integrated financial markets, through which international capital flows ever more fluidly."[5] Statistics back up this image, as later chapters will illustrate.

Jeremy Brecher and Tim Costello distinguish between globalization in trade and globalization in capital markets. They point out that globalizing trends in capital markets are much more recent—such trends represent something relatively new and very different. Brecher and Costello relate these new trends to greater corporate wealth, higher unemployment, and declines in real wages, public services, working conditions, and environmental standards.[6] Their arguments connecting the two will be explored throughout this book. Brecher and Costello view capital mobility as the principal villain in the political economic drama. Capital mobility, rather than increasing trade, labor flows, or other changes, is the root of a very destructive globalization they fear is unfolding.

There are those who leave the specifics open-ended. Globalization can refer to "high levels of cross-border flows," including labor migration, trade, communication, transport of goods, and other items.[7] While vague, this is probably the definition that fits most closely with popular conceptions. A favourite theme in the economic version of globalization focuses on national markets coming together. Hans-Peter Martin and Harald Schumann define globalization in terms of the creation of a global market. In their view, advances in communication, combined with falling transportation costs and unrestricted trade are creating a single world market.[8] As the title of their book suggests, this integration of markets may pose a serious threat to established social and political practices. Most people who have been exposed to literature on globalization have this sort of causal pattern in mind: government policies are being undermined or challenged by economic changes, which in turn are shaped by new technologies.

One focus on markets projected from the left of the political spectrum, as in Martin and Schumann's work, emphasizes that economic forces are overriding other interests due to increasingly powerful international market processes. From more Marxian roots, for example, Ankie Hoogvelt describes globalization as:

> a new social architecture of cross-border human interactions. It breaks down the old international division of labour and the associated hierarchy of rich and poor countries. In this process the integrity of the national territorial state as a more or less coherent political economy is eroded, and the functions of the state become re-organized to adjust domestic economic and social policies to fit the exigencies of the global market and global capitalist accumulation.[9]

In other words, she is noting that the expansive phase of world capitalism (its development of a global reach) is over. With no new economic areas to penetrate, capitalism is changing in character. Capitalism can continue to develop only by deepening in various countries and regions.[10] As economic conditions change, the role of the state also changes.

While not all who study globalization would agree with this assessment, or even with the more general point suggested about the relationship between the growth in international economic ties and changes in government policies, most agree that this is the popular perception of globalization and its impact. Several economists and political scientists challenge this connection by looking more closely at the evidence. For instance, Canadian economist Bill Watson writes: "The race to the bottom—the idea that ever-deepening economic integration, or 'globalization,' as it is more popularly known, will cause all the world's countries to become more and more alike in their tax rates, regulation, and public spending—is as close to an article of faith as can be found in the otherwise mainly unbelieving 1990s."[11] As will become clearer in the next chapter, Watson and others claim that the statistics suggest this imagery is false.

Some economists note that it is hard to untangle the international dimensions of what people are talking about from other processes going on. According to John-ren Chen, Richard Hule, and Herbert Stocker, although "globalization seems to imply increasing internationalization and new chances, it is often associated with fears of mass unemployment, deindustrialization [sic] and social unrest." They add that "One basic reason for this atmosphere of uncertainty is the complexity of the process of globalization. It involves economic as well as political and sociological aspects, which can be expected to change the everyday world."[12]

Chen, Hule, and Stocker settle on defining globalization as "a process of increasing international economic activities." Yet they try to make this more specific by discussing how to measure "increasing international economic activities." This process is characterized by "increasing liberalization of international trade for goods and services and of international capital movement (both financial and direct investment), while cross border labour movement is still strictly restricted."[13] This stands in some contrast to other definitions by recognizing some limits to economic globalization. Those limits reflect policy choices, therefore suggesting that political decisions open the door for globalizing processes. Politics may play a role in the introduction of globalization, just as globalization will have political consequences.

The political theme is propounded by Ethan Kapstein, when he argues that too often definitions of globalization stress the economic over all else.

> In most of the popular and journalistic accounts of "globalization," the emphasis is usually placed on the allegedly deterministic forces of technical change that are now creating a world without borders. These analyses miss a central point: that globalization is fundamentally a *political* phenomenon. It did not arise "naturally," but rather was the product of policy decisions taken after World War II among the Western allies.[14]

Instead of seeing economics as the determinant of politics, Kapstein emphasizes the role of politics in underpinning various economic practices. Political decisions may create globalizing processes, in economics or elsewhere. This position is seconded by other political scientists, such as Eric Helleiner. Helleiner downplays the role of technological change in explaining globalizing trends in finance. Instead, he points out the important role political decisions played in fostering such movements.[15] Helleiner and Kapstein agree, as do other political scientists, that while technology or economic opportunities clearly shape policy choices, politics determines which policy options are actually chosen. Of course, policies are chosen without knowing what their real implications may turn out to be. Politics can be critical, therefore, in the choice of policies; but once implemented the policies may generate economic outcomes that feed back into politics in some surprising ways. That brings us back to the most pressing political question surrounding globalization: Will recent trends build support for further globalizing processes, or will they generate a political backlash against globalization?

DEFINITIONS OF GLOBALIZATION THAT DO NOT PRIORITIZE ECONOMICS

To appreciate fully the political consequences of globalization it is necessary to go beyond definitions stressing only economic processes. Other types of change can come into play, sometimes by themselves, sometimes alongside economic processes. *According to Eleonore Kofman and Gillian Youngs, globalization refers to a state of mind*: it "relates as much to a way of thinking about the world as it does to a description of the dynamics of political and economic relations within it."[16] If people begin to conceive of their place in society or in politics in global terms, political outcomes will be different from before.

Others stress how *the decreasing importance of distance* is having a dramatic impact on various facets of life. Roland Robertson, writing from a sociological perspective, describes globalization as referring "both to the compression of the world and the intensification of the consciousness of the world." Along similar lines, Anthony Giddens defines globalization as "intensification of worldwide social relations which link distant localities in such a way that local happenings are shaped by events occurring many miles away and vice-versa." David Harvey, another sociologist, writes that globalization has caused "an intense phase of time-space compression that has had a dis-orienting and disruptive impact upon political-economic practices, the balance of class power, as well as upon cultural and social life."[17]

Along these same lines, other academics (who are neither economists nor political scientists) also have emphasized the connection between technological advances and changing spatial relations. Saskia Sassen, author of two widely read books on globalization, stresses the changes wrought on everyday life in big cities. In her words,

> Economic globalization has mostly been represented in terms of duality of national-global where the global gains power and advantages

at the expense of the national. And it has largely been conceptualized in terms of the internationalization of capital and then only the upper circuits of capital, notably finance. Introducing cities into an analysis of economic globalization allows us to reconceptualize processes of economic globalization as concrete economic complexes situated in specific places.[18]

While she is motivated by concerns and issues in urban planning, Sassen shows how globalizing processes affect the concerns in her specific discipline, yet these concerns spill over into, or have ramifications for, other matters cogent to political science. In particular, these concerns relate to *how people identify themselves politically. Globalizing changes of this sort shape politics.*

Alan Harding and Patrick Le Galè also note that the overwhelming majority of academic literature on globalization has focused on the changing nature or role of the nation-state. They ask instead how other levels of government will be affected by globalizing processes. Power can be shifted down to lower levels of government in response to globalization, and *the politics generated by globalization can be felt across the spectrum of government bodies and agencies.*[19]

Another European, *Michael Zürn*, has written that the key processes at work are really of interest to us precisely because they are *decreasing the powers of the state.* Yet he prefers to talk about these as "denationalizing" processes, rather than as globalization. This is because Zürn would argue that most of these processes are not really global in character. Many of the processes at work are merely regional, or affect only the most economically advanced countries.[20]

Finally, we have the sort of definition that combines the different pushes and pulls described by these other explications. *Henry Teune and Zdravko Mlinar define globalization as changes in "two separate domains*: (1) one in which territorial diffusion of things, people and ideas occurs and (2) another, in which different parts of the world gradually become interdependent. Which is why globalization contradictorily indicates the world becoming concomitantly bigger and smaller."[21] This is an interesting way to think about globalization, for it notes that the phenomenon is made up of several different changes, which combined lead to differing consequences.

Journalist Thomas Friedman has provided a definition or description of globalization that draws on academic literature. He describes *globalization as an "international system—the dominant international system that replaced the Cold War system.*" By system, he is referring to the mix of international structure (the distribution of capabilities among states and other actors) and the rules and norms governing how these actors interact.[22] Whereas the Iron Curtain and the hotline between Washington and Moscow symbolized the bipolar division of states, and the dominance of the two superpowers, the images representing globalization are an integration of economies and communication via the Internet. This description leaves us with such questions as: Which processes are really undermining the power of the state? Is power merely being shifted to other levels of government? Could it be that some processes are strengthening the power of the state?

COMPETING CONCEPTS

Like Zürn, many object to the term globalization, and prefer to speak in terms of older concepts such as *interdependence, economic integration,* or *internationalization.* Take, for example, the definition used by editors Helen Milner and Robert Keohane in their *Internationalization and Domestic Politics*: "Internationalization ... refers to the processes generated by underlying shifts in transaction costs that produce observable flows of goods, services, and capital."[23] They add that according to this definition, they can trace a recent upsurge in activity. As they explain, internationalization is really about shifts in the opportunities and constraints actors within society face, including the government itself. It may not change their preferences, but it does alter the means these actors select to pursue their goals. Since transaction costs are affected by both technologies and government policies, it is possible to combine some of the forces suspected of driving globalization in the earlier definitions.

It is also important to say a little about what globalization *does not* mean. Most authors would point out that globalization means more than just interdependence.[24] It also must mean something different from other existing terms, such as Westernization or modernization.[25] There are those, however, who argue that globalization refers to a homogenization of cultures; for whatever reasons, people feel national differences are being eliminated. People may blame this on corporate policies, economic pressures emanating from the market, or cultural imperialism; hence, many observers feel the emerging global culture is not one created by adding together different cultures, but is rather a reflection of American culture. Others dispute such claims, arguing instead that the U.S., Canada, and other countries are becoming increasingly multi-cultural in character.

Since this text is especially for students of political science, it is important that we understand how globalizing processes in other areas affect politics. Thus, we examine the phenomenon of globalization through the lenses of two sub-fields within political science: international relations and comparative politics. We need to be prepared to cast a critical eye on the various definitions given above if we are to address the veracity of many of the claims concerning globalization, and if we are to evaluate these definitions for their utility in comprehending political changes.

The definitions covered so far often describe a similar sort of chain reaction that comes from a single source. Changes in underlying technology create the opportunity to increase ties across national-political boundaries. Not all the arguments examined in later chapters focus on the same sorts of causal variables. Certainly they do not all see political causes of globalization. Many focus solely on economic aspects of globalization; others focus entirely on technological change. However, the only reasons we are examining them here is to learn whether these changes have altered politics. Have they changed the way people conduct their political lives, political agenda, or how political outcomes are reached?

The Politics Globalization Can Spark

By enhancing and increasing the number of ties between people of different countries, globalization can be thought of as a phenomenon primarily economic and cultural in character, though it has technological sources as well. One of the themes underlying many of the definitions above is that certain practices seem to be escaping from political control or oversight. In particular, this tension is placed in terms of markets growing larger and more powerful than governments; it may be an old theme in international political economy, but it has a fresh urgency. As Martin and Schumann, two critics of globalizing trends, put it in 1998, "the foremost task of democratic politicians on the threshold of the next century will be to restore the state and the primacy of politics over economics."[26]

On the other hand, globalization can also be thought of as the result of adopting particular government policies, meaning we can view it as ultimately political in character if we wish. Economic transactions can only take place over national boundaries if states concede permission to engage in such activities, according to some. If we observe an increase in international economic intercourse, it is largely because states have permitted this change—the trends can be traced back to specific policy decisions.

We still need to examine the economic changes at work, to understand what political consequences result.

Yet this leaves us with a tough question. If a state chooses to alter its regulations, is that a sign of the weakening of the state? The answer may rest on the way one responds to a second question. To what extent have states accelerated or supported globalization?[27] If states' policies were pivotal for the spread of globalization, it may appear possible for states to reverse some of these decisions in the future—globalization may not be a permanent feature of life in the twenty-first century after all. I shall argue that the outcome will depend on political competition and political decisions. Thus, understanding globalization means analyzing interests both within and outside of specific countries, and getting a better sense of how political conflicts concerning globalization are being resolved. Only then can we hope to understand whether globalizing trends will be supported further or whether a backlash will halt or reverse such changes.

There are those who see globalization as driven primarily by advances in technology. Improvements in communications and transportation, in particular, have allowed economic actors to escape governmental control. When the costs of communication and transportation decline, we should see more actors taking advantage of opportunities to conduct business at greater distances. Importantly, specific traits of the new technologies make it harder for governments to monitor and regulate these activities. In these views, globalization is the result of deterministic processes and will be next to impossible to reverse.

Let us now turn to three specific ways in which globalizing trends can be identified and discussed. These trends each can be seen as reshaping how domestic and international politics take place. First is economic globalization; underlying economic globalization are changes in technology. These technological changes can be further subdivided as improvements in communication and advances in transportation. Finally, I will also briefly discuss globalizing trends in cultural areas, before highlighting aspects of the political background in which all these trends are proceeding.

WHY WE STRESS ECONOMIC PROCESSES IN GLOBALIZATION

Globalization is often viewed as first and foremost an economic process. There are several reasons for this. First, we typically practice political economy by using economic models to establish who the relevant actors are, as well as to calculate their interests. We then load that information into models of politics to understand how these various actors will use their power to shape policy decisions or outcomes more generally. An examination of globalization defined in purely economic terms would help us understand who would support globalization in the future, as well as who might challenge these changes. Second, the economic aspects of globalization are easily observed. Economists have established a greater consensus within their discipline on how to measure many of their concepts, again making it easier to establish whether some of these changes have occurred. Third, economics is also infused with Liberal ideas and normative arguments that stress the advantages of unleashing markets. Economists often see a more direct stake in their world-view and interpretations of globalization than we find in other disciplines. In the words of one concerned writer, "There is no activity more intrinsically globalizing than trade, no ideology less interested in nations than capitalism, no challenge to frontiers more audacious than the market."[28]

Not only are economists in greater agreement on what core concepts mean (and how to measure them), the economics discipline is more mathematically oriented than several of the other social sciences. This makes it easier for economists to turn to statistical measures to chart those changes we would consider as signs of the advance of globalization. That several possible indicators exist does not mean all the data have been gathered, but at least there is fairly wide agreement on what to look for. Contrast this to some other disciplines, such as sociology, or urban planning. Just what globalization means in cultural terms or in comprehension of spatial relations, or how to measure the processes one might observe there, is much more contentious.

Of course, even when the economic data may be on hand, we may still maintain reservations about its accuracy. Economists who have looked more closely at how government statistics are generated in many countries will readily sound the warnings. World Bank and other institutions report large sets of data that are potentially inaccurate. Much of the data is generated using slightly different methods, which can skew comparisons. Also, when considering trans-border activities, the data often underestimate large volumes of trade or money crossing borders illegally.[29]

Even with a greater agreement on what globalization might entail and how one might measure these processes, economists continue to debate several claims about globalization. One major source of disagreement concerns whether or not globalization is a new phenomenon. Economic historians correctly point out that most of the indicators used to claim that today's national economies are highly integrated also imply that similar claims must be made about the pre-World War I world. While these issues will be dealt with in detail later, it is worth noting that this can be valuable for conducting analyses and projecting findings into the future. In particular globalizing processes were considered socially and economic disruptive, and sparked political backlashes in many places. It would therefore be valuable to examine those periods to uncover some of the political consequences associated with earlier episodes of globalization.

There is a debate over whether the set of economic changes currently going on are really comparable to those that occurred in the nineteenth century. In those days, capital did flow across borders in prodigious amounts (and comparably high amounts), as did trade. However, there are some significant differences between the two periods. Labour migrated over borders at high levels during the late nineteenth century; also, there was open land for both capital and labor to travel to. How might these differences show up in the political consequences of globalization? In the conduct of domestic or international politics? Before turning to past evidence, we need to get a better handle on just what the competing theoretical claims are, so that we will know what to look for in the historical record.

We should remain cognizant that some readers think too much can be made of the statistical measures economists rely on. This can be especially important for examining the political consequences of globalization, for it may not matter so much whether globalization has actually occurred or not. Instead, what is critical is that *the choice* to partake in globalization exists. The *threat* of increasing international economic activities may be enough to alter political outcomes. If one is interested in the disciplining of domestic activities by global markets, the mere threat of foreign competition, or even monitoring by foreign actors may change behaviour with important consequences.[30] The economic indicators that show how far globalization has proceeded may only be useful for placing decisions into the current context—throwing light on what opportunities other states may be forgoing as well as showing what some states have chosen to exploit.

TECHNOLOGICAL PROCESSES IN GLOBALIZATION

Underlying our notions of the economics of globalization are changes in two other areas. After all, economists tend to assume that people exploit economic opportunities whenever they discover them. This would lead them to argue that something other than changes have created new opportunities for international economic intercourse. Milner and Keohane observed that the two logical areas to look for such changes would be technological advances and policy changes. Each of these could be driven by very separate factors, though they could also interact. Before we look at policy changes we will consider the ways in which new technology could foster the economic processes of globalization.

Technology plays an important role in promoting changes in economic activities by altering the costs of various choices. Advances in the technology of production, for instance, can lower the costs of providing certain goods or services. This may occur through gaining a better understanding of how to manufacture the good, or how to generate a service. (An example of the latter would be when an engineer creates a software application to be used in an entirely new area, such as evaluating insurance claims or writing out medical dosages.) Changes in production technology may make a good available to a wider market. Reducing the size of products may also have an effect on the ability to transport goods longer distances at a reasonable rate.

Another way to think about these changes is to consider how digitization of cultural products such as music or movies (originally as CDs or DVDs), can reduce the transportation charges to nil—once someone has invested in the computer or receiving equipment necessary. Thus one of the largest expenses for distribution of movies to theaters across the country, or indeed across the world, has been producing numerous copies of the film, and then shipping these copies everywhere at once. However, in the near future, these movies could be "shipped" to theaters via satellite transmission or secure optical fiber lines, at much reduced cost.

Rosecrance takes this thinking one step further. He argues that since technology is the key factor driving such changes, that international competition between states will in the future boil down to educational differences. Here is his line of argument: "As information becomes an increasing component of GDP, the weight of exports and the products of national income grows lighter—easier to carry and transmit—because their knowledge component is higher. At the ultimate stage competition among nations will be competition among educational systems, for the most productive and richest countries will be those with the best education and training."[31] But this can have a very positive effect, in Rosecrance's view, for "[a]s countries strive to improve their human resources in worldwide competition, they will also concurrently improve their own societies."

Those who see technology as the driving force for globalization more generally, typically think of it as an unstoppable force. Technology is treated as the proverbial "genie out of the bottle." It will progress whether individuals or governments like it or not. As it progresses, communication over borders will increase, transportation costs will fall, transnational economic ties will rise in volume and value, cultures will change as a result, and so on.

There are those who challenge the notion that technology is unstoppable. Henry Teune and Zdravko Mlinar characterize arguments about globalization that rest entirely on technological change as "facile."[32] All technologies have some form of substitute, or can be improved on in time. This makes it difficult to predict the specific impact of a single innovation. As an example, they discuss fax machines. Wire services had used the technology for years to transmit pictures; only later were these same techniques widely used to send regular copy from office to office. As Teune and Mlinar ask, "What are the social forces that explain these technologies and their use?"

Let's take a closer look at how technological advances would be channeled through changes in transportation and communication. Then we will examine the degree of policy choice that states or political actors might retain in the face of these changes. Only then can we better grasp the full chain of events linking these concepts together.

CHANGES IN TRANSPORTATION AND GLOBALIZATION

According to the causal chain above, technological advances can have a powerful influence in several ways on decisions to undertake international economic activities. Most obviously, advances in technology can reduce transportation costs. New aircraft, for instance, are often more fuel-efficient than their predecessors, require less maintenance, can carry more freight, and travel longer distances. All these advances in performance can reduce the costs associated with shipping people or goods by air.

Nowadays, the declining cost of transportation, and the increased speed at which goods can be transported, has allowed some African countries to export goods one would have thought impossible only a few decades ago. People in European cities can buy fresh flowers shipped from southern Africa, for example. The speed with which flowers can be delivered is critical, for they do not remain fresh for long.

Technology can also make the goods themselves lighter and smaller, and therefore easier to transport. The reduced size of goods, such as personal electronic equipment or computers, certainly makes it easier to ship these goods long distances. Other items, conversely, may not be so easy to transport; HDTV screens, for example, are large and fragile, as well as expensive. They may not be good items to ship long distances. The

25

Internet has reduced the cost of shipping digital information to remarkably low levels while disseminating digitized products at extremely high speed. Compare the cost of printing and shipping a textbook like this around the world, with the price it would cost simply to post it on the Internet. On the other hand, control over copyrights and intellectual property more broadly limit how commerce takes place on the Web. Still, to cite Rosecrance, "We are entering a world in which the most important resources are the least tangible...."[33]

Much more mundane instances of technological improvements have already had a profound impact on levels of international trade. Perhaps the best example here would be the spread of containerization in the post-World War II period. By placing goods in large sea containers of roughly uniform shapes and sizes, containerization reduced the amount of time spent loading and unloading ships. Huge cranes specially built to lift, manoeuvre, and stack containers can empty and then freshly load a large ship in remarkably small amounts of time. If ships spend less time in port, they can spend more time in transit, thus shortening the amount of time it takes to transport goods, allowing the shippers to charge less. A freighter can now make a transit of the Pacific in less than a month, yet hit major ports in China, Japan, Canada, and the United States.[34]

Containerization also affects the linkages between forms of sea and land transport. Containers lifted from a ship's hold can be placed directly onto rail cars or flatbed trucks achieving dramatic savings in costs and time from previous practices. Indeed, we must remember that in most respects, the old adage is true: *time is money*. Anytime resources sit idle they are usually not generating income. Thus, one of the main insights into how technology impacts international economic exchange is that improvements in technology increase the speed of transactions, reducing the impact of distance.

Along these same lines, technological advances that translate into improvements in communication often are considered to be the spark to globalization. It does no good to transport goods over borders more quickly if there aren't consumers waiting to purchase those goods. Information on the availability of markets is important if foreigners are going to seize these opportunities as they arise. Similarly, a freighter full of containers can only exploit the speed of unloading if there are forms of land transport or storage space near the docks waiting to accept the containers it offloads, *and* there is outgoing cargo ready to take on board. Communications are critical for organizing these activities.

These decisions are even more critical when we move from simply transporting goods across borders to organizing the production of goods in many separate countries. Imagine how difficult it is to organize the production of sophisticated machinery where various components must match within very limited tolerances. Then imagine trying to ensure components match when they are produced in entirely different parts of the globe. (Curiously, one of the best examples here would come from textiles, where international agreements govern the distribution of the production of various types of garments. Forcing the production of different types of clothing into different countries makes it harder for Third-World producers to capture certain parts of the market in Europe and the United States, such as colour-co-ordinated outfits. If imported pants can only be made in a handful of economically developing countries, and tops can only be produced in a completely different set of countries, manufacturers will have a difficult time ensuring that, say, pants from Guatemala match in colour and texture the tops made in Pakistan. This production can be integrated only because samples can be shipped rapidly, consistently, and cheaply, and because people can also travel just as rapidly and easily to oversee the dispersed production.)

Unfortunately it is a bit difficult to understand just when an improvement in communication becomes pivotal. After all, the first great advance in communication technology came with the advent of the telegraph. Later forms of technology, such as teletype and the telephone, undoubtedly helped speed up the most necessary flows of information. What is added with teleconferencing? Satellite transmissions? The Internet? We may not understand the limits of the Internet yet, simply because we don't yet understand the limits of digitization of products.

In fact, there are good historical analogues to the examples cited above. Extensions of the telegraph lines did have an impact on the economies of states. Advances in sailing techniques and ship design helped improve the shipping and reduce the costs of bulky commodities in the seventeenth century; the development of railroads and steam-powered ships changed the global markets for grain in dramatic fashion in the late nineteenth century. Some are easier to recognize than others—suggesting that certain types of advances in technology are much more likely to influence globalization in the current period than others.

GLOBALIZING PROCESSES IN COMMUNICATION AND CULTURE

Advances in technology affecting the production and dissemination of cultural products are at the root of most arguments about cultural globalization. A common observation is that cultural homogenization seems to be taking place. Wherever one goes, a lot of the same products and images can be found. It used to be that when one traveled abroad, you would expect to find very different cuisine served, different clothes worn. People from different countries could often be identified by their various styles of clothing or footwear, long before they betrayed their national identity by speaking. Today global brands exist in many basic products.

Sociologists have in recent years begun to talk about changes in cultural arrangements affected by globalization. Roland Robertson, argues that globalization at the cultural level has now begun, sparked by advances in technology. Technological improvements result in the "compression of the world." This phrase is meant to describe how we now know much more about what is happening all over the world, soon after events occur. This knowledge affects the way we think, but especially the way we think of ourselves. Robertson argues that a global consciousness is being formed.[35] Similarly, Harvey has described a "space-time compression," which leads to redefinition of relations and a reorganization of power.

Anthony Giddens has claimed that space has less meaning, since its relationship to time has been drastically altered. He writes of the "virtual annihilation of space through time" thanks to advances in technology. This allows for the reorganization of society—imagined communities can now be constructed, where they would have been impossible in the past. Here we might consider how events in other countries are broadcast to us very quickly, affecting how we react to them. In the 1970s, the genocidal policies of governments in Uganda and Cambodia were perpetuated some time before they were reported in the Western press. Even then, we were provided graphic descriptions in print, with few photos. In the 1990s, similar events in Bosnia and Rwanda were aired much more rapidly and with the immediacy of more photographic images. And pictures can be much more powerful than words.[36]

A major concern regarding the globalization of culture is that economic factors impose uniformity across states. The culture being spread around the globe is generated by corporate products and corporate decisions.

Benjamin Barber states this perspective succinctly: "A culture of advertising, software, Hollywood movies, MTV, theme parks, and shopping malls hooped together by the virtual nexus of the information superhighway closes down free spaces, such a culture is unquestionably in the process of forging a global *something*: but whatever it is, that something is not democratic."[37] Barber goes on to conclude with the idea that the market can—indeed must—be balanced by activities of the government.

In effect, Barber and others see technological change, usually through changing economic patterns, altering cultural practices or public consciousness. These in turn may be reshaping politics. They may spark a political counter to globalizing trends, as Barber suggests, or they may create further pressures for globalization to continue.

EMPHASIZING POLITICAL FACTORS IN THE BACKGROUND TO GLOBALIZING CHANGES

Several purely political factors may be influencing the way in which globalizing processes are proceeding. The end of the Cold War changed the nature of international affairs, for instance. Not only has the bipolar structure of international security affairs ended, but this reshapes the way a variety of international institutions work. Many have expected the UN and other international organizations to function much better; they were partially paralyzed by the superpower rivalry from the 1950s through the 1980s.

The superpower rivalry was fueled by ideological differences between the Soviet bloc and the West. The ideological differences not only formed the basis for difficulties between the U.S. and Soviet Union, they also spilled over into broader political relations. Many developing countries sought to generate economic development through state intervention in the economy, along the lines pioneered by the Soviets. American difficulties with many Third-World governments were imbued with ideological content. Those ideological differences have largely disappeared.

In international political economic affairs, the end of the ideological rivalry together with the experiences of the 1980s led to the "Washington consensus." To the economically developing countries, the 1980s brought the debt crisis and in that sense a development crisis. The countries that weathered the 1980s well were the East Asian "tigers." These countries had actively embraced the international economy—their successful industrialization seemed to settle much of the debate over the best sort of development strategy. Dependency theory, with its Marxists roots, had predicted that those economically less-developed states that willingly engaged in the international economy would be harmed in their inter- actions—they would be least likely to industrialize, for instance. Yet by the end of the 1980s, it was clear that countries such as Taiwan and South Korea had done quite well economically, as opposed to those who had kept the international economy at arm's length.

The Washington consensus could be defined as agreeing to reverse import-substitution industrialization policies: open up to interna- tional trade and capital flows, privatize state-owned enterprises, and subscribe to capitalism's precepts on markets. Powerful actors on the international scene promote this consensus. Not only might it include some powerful states, but also multilateral international agencies (such as the IMF and World Bank), global corporations, the WTO, regional arrangements (such as NAFTA and the EU), and others. All of these transnational forces are pressuring nation-states to conform to certain practices. Some writers go so far as to equate this with a new form of imperialism.[38]

At closer examination, it became clear that the East Asian countries were employing strategies that did embrace markets, but these strategies did not necessarily mean accepting purely market-driven outcomes. These countries were intervening in their economies through a variety of policies. In fact, government policies were critical for pushing or help- ing domestic actors to engage in international transactions. Without government incentives, firms within several countries, including South Korea and Taiwan, would probably never have successfully produced export items in the 1960s or 1970s. Moreover, the financial crises these countries experienced in the 1990s have discredited much of the inter- national advice they had apparently followed.

The point of this discussion has not been to judge these policies, so much as to illustrate that broad political changes in the international system have helped shape the character and speed of globalizing trends. Ideas encouraging an opening up to the international economy became much more widespread after the Cold War ended. International organiza- tions promoting such ideas wielded great power in this environment, as no competing ideas have found much widespread appeal.

Identifying the Political Consequences of Globalization

In the next chapters, we will come to grips with arguments about changes driven by international trends in the way domestic policy comes out, the way international relations are conducted, and the ways in which the two interact. New dynamics are possible in all three areas. Yet the possibilities for change have to be tempered with the possibilities for continuity. Some insightful comments can be gleaned from R.B.J. Walker's observations on James Rosenau's book, *Along the Foreign-Domestic Frontier*. Rosenau is interested in talking about the new tensions found along this "frontier." But Walker rightly questions whether the importance of this boundary is really all that new.

> The crucial flaw is the belief that the contradictions of the modern international system have only recently come to be resolved on this complex Frontier rather than in either domestic or international politics. In fact, the contradictions of modern politics have long been resolved, both in practice and in principle, on just such a boundary. The claims of the modern state depend precisely on its ability to resolve all the fundamental contradictions of modern life that arise from the dividing line between itself and others.... This need also explains why modern disciplines of scholarship have been organized so that we rarely talk about the dangerous edges—the awful discriminations between us and them—that constitute our spheres of domestic comfort and external distress.[39]

In short, Walker is urging us to not take the international/domestic distinction as given. We need to open up our minds to other ways of thinking about the world, or the other ways it could be organized politically.

We shall try to do this by discussing globalization in terms of both international and domestic politics. As Milner and Keohane have put it, this is a necessary step for anyone interested in the issues to hand:

> For social scientists, internationalization of the world economy should sound the death-knell to the anachronistic divisions, institutionalized in universities, between "comparative politics" and "international relations." Cross-national comparisons are meaningless without placing the countries being compared in the context of a common world political economy within which they

operate. Likewise, theories of international relations that treat all countries as fundamentally similar provide only limited insight into the variations in policy and institutional change. Neither comparative politics nor international relations can be coherently understood without aid from the other.[40]

There is nothing exceedingly novel about the sort of feedback that links these two, but it remains a challenge to consider the wide range of issues that arise during the comparisons. We can only answer our chief questions about whether support for globalization will build, or whether opposition will arise, by dealing with domestic and international connections.

NOTES

1 See, for instance, the articles of Kosuke Shimizu, Craig Murphy, and Jonathon R. Strand, in the *Mershon International Studies Review* 40, Supp. 2 (Oct. 1996).

2 Cited by Herbert Stocker in "Globalization and International Convergence in Incomes," in John-ren Chen, ed., *Economic Effects of Globalization* (Aldershot, UK: Ashgate, 1998), 103.

3 Ronald W. Jones, "Private Interests and Government Policy in a Global World," *Tinbergen Institute Discussion Paper* TI2000-051/2, 1.

4 Richard Rosecrance, *The Rise of the Virtual State* (New York: Basic Books, 1999), 77.

5 Louis Pauly, *Who Elected the Bankers?* (Ithaca, NY: Cornell University Press, 1997), 1.

6 Jeremy Brecher and Tim Costello, *Global Village or Global Pillage* (Boston: South End Press, 1994), 4.

7 Peter Katzenstein, Robert Keohane, and Stephen Krasner, "International Organization and the Study of World Politics," *International Organization* 52, 4 (Autumn 1998): 669.

8 Hans-Peter Martin and Harald Schumann, *The Global Trap: Globalization and the Assault on Prosperity and Democracy*, trans. Patrick Camiller (Montreal: Black Rose Books, 1998), 5.

9 Ankie Hoogvelt, *Globalization and the Postcolonial World* (Baltimore: Johns Hopkins University Press, 1997), 67.

10 Ibid., 115, 122.

11 This is the opening line of the preface to his book on the subject. See William Watson, *Globalization and the Meaning of Canadian Life* (Toronto: University of Toronto Press, 1998), ix.

12 John-ren Chen, Richard Hule, and Herbert Stocker, "Introduction," in Chen, ed., *Economic Effects of Globalization*, 1.

13 Ibid., 2.

14 Ethan Kapstein, *Sharing the Wealth* (New York: W.W. Norton, 1999), 17.

15 Eric Helleiner, *States and the Re-emergence of Global Finance* (Ithaca, NY: Cornell University Press, 1994).

16 Eleonore Kofman and Gillian Youngs, "Introduction: Globalization—the Second Wave," in Kofman and Youngs, eds., *Globalization: Theory and Practice*, 117.

17 These definitions are reviewed and discussed by Marc Williams in "Rethinking Sovereignty," in Kofman and Youngs, eds., *Globalization: Theory and Practice*, 117.

18 Saskia Sassen, *Globalization and Its Discontents* (New York: New Press, 1998), xix.

19 Alan Harding and Patrick Le Galè, "Globalization, Urban Change and Urban Politics in Britain and France," in Harding and Le Galè, eds., *The Limits of Globalization: Cases and Arguments* (London: Routledge, 1997), 189-92.

20 Micahel Zürn, *Regieren jenseits des Nationalstaates, Globalisierung und Denationalisierung als Chance* (Frankfurt: Suhrkamp, 1998).

21 Henry Teune and Zdravko Mlinar, "The Developmental Logic of Globalization," in José V. Ciprut, ed., *The Art of the Feud* (Westport, CT: Praeger, 2000), 106.

22 Thomas Friedman, *The Lexus and the Olive Tree* (New York: Anchor Books, 2000), 7-16.

23 Helen Milner and Robert Keohane, "Internationalization and Domestic Politics: An Introduction," in Milner and Keohane, eds., *Internationalization and Domestic Politics* (Cambridge: Cambridge University Press, 1996), 4.

24 Williams, "Rethinking Sovereignty," 119.

25 Alan Scott, "Globalization: Social Process or Political Rhetoric?" in Alan Scott, ed., *The Limits of Globalization: Cases and Arguments* (London: Routledge, 1997), 3.

26 Martin and Schumann, *The Global Trap*, 11.

27 Hoogvelt, *Globalization and the Postcolonial World*, Ch. 7.

28 Benjamin R. Barber, *Jihad vs. McWorld* (New York: Ballantine Books, 1995), 23.

29 Tom Naylor has written several books and numerous articles on this subject.

30 This point is made by Hoogvelt, *Globalization and the Postcolonial World*, 122.

31 Rosecrance, *The Rise of the Virtual State*, xv.

32 Teune and Mlinar, "The Developmental Logic of Globalization," 106.

33 Rosecrance, *The Rise of the Virtual State*, 3.

34 See Richard Rosecrance, *The Rise of the Trading State* (New York: Basic Books, 1989).

35 For a brief summary of these sociologists' views, see Hoogvelt, *Globalization and the Postcolonial World*, 117-21.

36 A few weeks before Operation Allied Force, I saw journalists' footage of Serbian police moving into a Kosovar village; they were riding in armoured cars I recognized as those seized from the Dutch battalion charged with protecting the UN "safe haven" of Srbrenica. If crimes had been committed at Srbrenica, one could reasonably suspect that crimes would soon be occurring in Kosovo.

37 Barber, *Jihad vs. McWorld*, 276.

38 See, for example, Philip McMichael, "The New Colonialism: Global Regulation and the Restructuring of the Interstate System," in David A. Smith and Jozsef Böröcz, eds., *A New World Order?* (Westport, CT: Praeger, 1995), 37.

39 R.B.J. Walker, "The Elusive Study of Global Change," *Mershon International Studies Review* 42, 2 (Nov. 1998): 328.

40 Milner and Keohane, "Internationalization and Domestic Politics: A Conclusion," in Milner and Keohane, eds., *Internationalization and Domestic Politics*, 257.

2 | Theoretical Lenses for Viewing Globalization

We will begin our examination of globalization by looking at how established approaches in international political economy treat these issues. These will provide us with guidelines concerning not only the processes of globalization, but also who would support its continuation, who would oppose it, and how these various competing interests will clash in coming years. In the following chapter we will look at several specific aspects of globalization to lay out descriptions of the competing points of view, and then in Chapter 4 we will examine specific indicators to determine whether or not globalization is occurring—or rather, to what extent current trends conform to the various definitions provided in the preceding chapter.

As long ago as 1968, Richard Cooper had made the point that domestic policy and foreign policy were too intertwined to study separately. Some of our traditional approaches in international relations obscure these relationships, however. Others focus quite intently on the interplay of domestic and international forces. Because the assumptions they use are different, these traditional approaches suggest very different interactions are at work in globalization. They also lead to different predictions concerning the political reactions to globalization in the near future.

Traditional Perspectives on Globalization

Theories or approaches are supposed to provide us with several types of information. They are supposed to help us describe what we have already observed; understand why current or past events have occurred; and assist us in making predictions about what will happen in the future. Finally, by providing some insights into why things in the past occurred, and some understanding about what is likely to happen in the future, they can help us formulate better policies for attaining control over our destiny.[1] Some theories also contain a normative element—what we should want the future to look like. The normative element—or lack thereof—is what makes us think about these theories in more familiar political terms, such as radical or conservative. Yet, as many have noted, writers from both the left and the right of the political spectrum criticize globalization.[2] We will want to think about how these various approaches help or hurt us towards an understanding of how globalizing processes will be politicized in the future, and to help us come to grips with our choices about the future.

GLOBALIZATION AS PROGRESS: A CLASSICAL LIBERAL'S VIEW OF MARKETS

In the opinion of Paul Hirst and Grahame Thompson, "Globalization realizes the ideals of mid-nineteenth century free trade liberals."[3] Nineteenth-century liberals thought of the state as untrustworthy, especially in economic policies. In most countries in the eighteenth century (and well into the nineteenth), the state had maintained mercantilist policies. Mercantilism was aimed at maintaining a positive balance of payments internationally. Mercantilism also was attractive to governments as a source of taxes. To attain these ends, the state exercised tight control over any and all connections with international markets.

Classical liberals, such as Adam Smith and David Ricardo, attacked mercantilist thinking. They viewed the market as one of the best means to allocate wealth in society. Mercantilism promoted favouritism by government, with wealth buying political favours, and political favours providing an excellent source of wealth. The political system was corrupt, and the economic increase was held back, the early liberals charged. If markets were unleashed from political restrictions, the ill political side effects would be reduced and the country's wealth would increase. If people were allowed to trade with whomever they wished, even with foreigners, the gains from economic specialization would create additional wealth for society as a whole.

Important in their views was the role of voluntary action. Individuals, interested in their own narrow interests, would pursue wealth. That their unco-ordinated, individual actions, through markets characterized by competition, would lead to social welfare was Adam Smith's contribution in discussing the working of "the invisible hand" of competitive market forces. In these terms, globalization should be a good thing.

International integration of markets should deliver economic rewards in terms of increased opportunities to make money. The gains from increased competition should be an important source of continued growth. International economic openness might even be associated with less political favouritism in the economy, since competitiveness has to be pursued so intently. For instance, mercantilism created market restrictions that translated into special privileges for many producers—part of why Adam Smith and the early liberals attacked these policies.

This is an overly positive picture of economic globalization. Liberals expect globalizing processes to be accepted positively by most people. The opponents to globalization should be those same sorts of people who resisted liberalization of markets in the early nineteenth century: those who either dished out political favours, or those who received the political favours. Since most people were excluded from such favours, we would expect most people to prefer to liberalize the economy. Yet globalization is not popular everywhere.

If we break down the liberal arguments into component parts, we can come up with some interesting insights. For liberals, opening up a country's economy to international competition delivers to it political and economic benefits. This is how they would describe past periods of history, as well as the current period. When barriers between economies were raised, everyone suffered economic losses. They would predict that, since economic increases are popular, that pressures to continue with globalization will continue, especially now that so many countries are democracies. Normatively, liberals would expect globalization to have positive effects.

There are several ways to challenge this view. Many question whether further integration of national markets is yielding any positive results. For instance, Martin and Schumann claim prosperity through trade is an "unfulfilled promise." They assess NAFTA in a negative light, arguing the "promised blessings are nowhere in sight."[4] This sounds similar to Ross Perot's expectation that NAFTA would lead to a "giant sucking sound" as the United States lost jobs and investment to Mexico. Yet, overall, statistics suggest that trade and wealth are positively correlated.

Is free trade popular? Some see pressures developing for political attacks on markets in the economically developed countries. This is driven, in the liberal view, by the adjustment process that occurs as specialization proceeds. Moreover, in the richest countries, the benefits from trade may be positive for the country as whole, but liberals would also readily agree that trade redistributes income within the country. Some people will not be made better off by trade. In the rich countries, labour is relatively scarce. Being in short supply, it can command a higher price than it would otherwise (relative to capital as an input). Liberalizing trade means getting imports from countries where labour is relatively abundant—and therefore relatively cheap. Trade makes it appear that labour is no longer so scarce. Labour's wages will fall, unless it increases its skills.

Of course, the same dynamic driving competition in trade and where the benefits accumulate goes on elsewhere. For countries with many unskilled labourers but not much capital, free trade opens up the possibility of importing cheaper goods made in countries where capital is relatively abundant; but also of exporting goods made largely from labour to places where labour is relatively scarce. This should alter positively the returns to labour and capital in these poorer countries. Economist Paul Krugman has argued that long-term productivity growth in the economically developing countries will naturally drive wages up in those countries in the long-run. As they develop, their ability to offer cheap wages to undercut the wages offered by firms based in the industrialized countries will lessen. This prediction is supported by previous historical events.[5] It already characterizes the competition observed in some sectors, for example, where the wages paid in Korea or Brazil are too high to remain competitive against firms based in Indonesia or Vietnam.

Some view this pattern and are quite worried. If wages for low-skilled workers around the world are going to converge, workers in the wealthy countries should be worried. Everything depends on your perspective. Those workers probably will have their earnings reduced, while workers in the rest of the world will have their earnings increased. Workers need to be concerned, therefore, about improving their education and skills, so as to become more productive. Unfortunately, other factors determine the productivity of labour, not just skill level.

Even the purely economic aspects of Liberal theories have been challenged. The keystone to the Liberal perspective is that freeing up trade delivers economic benefits for society as a whole. This is based on the theory of comparative advantage. Some today argue that comparative advantage is no longer at work in international economic exchange. Absolute advantage holds instead. This view is based on the fact that most trade occurs between the industrialized countries, and involves the same sorts of goods crossing boundaries. If trade is based on absolute advantage, the effect of markets (and more importantly of market integration) is to drive all prices down. Since wage rates are the price of labour, this too is being driven down.[6]

Should labour in North American and Europe fear globalization? The pay levels of less-skilled workers in the industrialized countries have come under pressure from a variety of angles. In the U.S., for instance, the transition to a service economy (and away from manufacturing) has put pressure on the rise of wages. High levels of immigration also affect the unskilled labour pool most. The declining strength of unions has a similar effect, as does deregulation of the economy. All these factors have kept the wages of less skilled workers in the U.S. from rising. Trade is only one factor among many at work.[7] As several authors have pointed out, the real problem may not be globalization, but rather a crisis of the post-World War II welfare state brought on by internal changes.

This perspective seems particularly apt for Europe, where high levels of unemployment have persisted right through the 1990s and into this decade. Other writers refuse to blame globalization. If unemployment remains high for structural reasons, it should be addressed through labour-market policies, not foreign economic policies. Thus, those who blame globalization for unemployment should look to the recent experience of the Netherlands, where policies have made labour markets more flexible, increased labour mobility, and helped improve the education of workers.[8]

Moreover, the mechanism by which low-wage countries are said to be causing these disruptions is doubtful. Trade and international investment remains concentrated among the members of the OECD. Economically less-developed countries' exports account for an estimated *total* of only 4 per cent of economically developed countries' production. Moreover, many economically developed countries have trade surpluses with developing countries![9] It is worth remembering, however, that there could be those who are hurt within the industrialized countries—though the factors at work are not necessarily only international in character.

There have always been those who criticized the liberals' intense faith in markets. Charles Dickens is a prime example. His novels portrayed the seamier side of a society whose economy was based on markets: child labour, debtors thrown in prison, people who judged others purely on a monetary basis, the lack of compassion in market transactions, and other anti-social aspects of liberalized economic transactions. These same themes resurface these days in the attacks some groups have made against large corporations. Do corporations care to be good citizens in society? Do they realize the stake they have in a well-functioning society? Do they recognize their interests in the environment, to the same extent as an informed citizen might? It should also be remembered that even Adam Smith saw a continued role for government. He recognized that the market could not provide certain societal needs, such as defense. He never argued that the state should be dismantled completely. He wrote at a time when the state exercised as much control over international economic connections as it could. He never argued that we would all be better off by moving to the opposite extreme.

Some people, including those who largely believe in specific liberal theories and models, voice concerns about the weakening of the state's ability to control economic activities for other purposes. Liberalization of financial flows, for instance, has created more complex problems tracking illicit gains, or stopping tax evasion. Larger volumes of trade make it harder to monitor or control flows of illegal substances, such as drugs, or even of products regulated for health concerns. The international spread of bovine spongiform encephalitis (BSE or "mad cow disease") is a case in point. As Stanley Hoffmann noted, even if liberals could promote the liberalization of international economic activity in general, they would not support it to the extent that these negative consequences are increasing.

> The new transnational economy has not merely, and beneficially, constrained the power of states. It has not only deprived them of much of their capacity to build command economies that ignore the signals given by markets and produce colossal inefficiencies. It has, alas, also deprived them of some of their ability to perform necessary tasks, to carry out basic functions liberalism never intended to remove from them.... Governments find it difficult to restore against such "bad goods" the controls they removed to facilitate the flow of the good ones.[10]

Even if we do not focus on criminal activity, there are those who simply equate the shift to liberal political economic practices as a victory for corporate power versus the state.[11] Why should corporations hold power over social outcomes, rather than the state? Liberals, therefore, support economic globalization, but have come to question how best to balance its supposed economic advantages with other interests. If that balance cannot be maintained, the benefits they currently associate with continued globalization will be endangered by a backlash.

MARKETS—AND THEREFORE GLOBALIZATION—AS A SOURCE OF INSTABILITY: THE KEYNESIAN VIEW

The classical liberals' view of markets was challenged in the late 1800s when leading economies experienced their first serious downturn. Many states, like Germany, turned away from free trade. Its faith in markets shaken, the German government allowed companies to co-operate in cartels to stabilize prices and output. It also began instituting social policies to compensate those hurt by the market, such as disability insurance and old-age pensions. While these actions do not all reflect a backlash to globalization, they do reflect a change in thinking.

The conservatives at the helm of the imperial German government were interested in pursuing these new policies up to a point, because they feared their working class might soon make demands for political reforms. The desire to shield the population from the vagaries of the market became widespread after World War I, as many countries adopted democratic institutions, or expanded the suffrage. With more of the working class voting, government responsibility for stable economic performance and the attainment of minimum goals (such as avoiding high unemployment) increased. Policies of unemployment insurance, social security schemes, and so on became much more widespread in the 1920s. These were expanded further after the collapse of the economies in the 1930s.

Karl Polanyi, among others, noted that markets could never be separated from societies; in fact, not even when we conceive of them as being separate when we theorize about them. Polanyi observed that where markets had been allowed to reign unfettered, they had not always delivered everything promised. Even when markets worked well, they could result in outcomes many did not want. Although liberal policies were widely implemented in the late nineteenth century, as symbolized by the widespread adoption of the gold standard, societies had sooner or later fought back against markets.

Moreover, markets proved to have their own internal potential for instability. The American stock market boomed in the 1920s, but the unregulated nature of the financing of investments left it vulnerable. When the steady rise in stock prices to unreasonable heights ended, investors who were banking on prices continuing to rise suddenly faced debts they couldn't meet—they were thus forced to sell their shares. This caused prices to drop precipitously. The market collapsed. The instabilities in this particular market had repercussions across the rest of the American economy. As firms lost financing, and as paper wealth evaporated, demand for goods was reduced. Firms lost business, orders dropped, and the economy headed into a downward spiral. Charles Kindleberger has offered us an excellent description of just how this downturn built upon itself, as the Great Depression worsened.[12]

It was in this economic environment in the early 1930s, with markets in chaos and unemployment rising, that several governments experimented with interventions in the markets. In Germany, the economic crisis set the stage for the Nazis' seizure of power; Hitler's government then intervened in the economy to stimulate recovery, as well as to reshape society. In Britain, the U.S., and elsewhere, governments discovered that simply by shedding constraints they had imposed upon themselves in monetary affairs, they created new possibilities for helping restore employment. By dropping the gold standard rules, governments could use monetary policy to make lending easier, thereby stimulating the economy.

John Maynard Keynes helped develop a better understanding of these changes in adapting liberal models of the economy. His writings illustrated how government expenditures and conscious manipulations of the money supply could push aggregate demand and consumption to higher levels. His ideas justified an explicit role for government in managing the macroeconomy. Management of the economy via the policy instruments he identified—aiming to attain certain levels of employment, growth, and so on—became the mainstay of government policies in Britain, the U.S., and many other countries from the 1930s on.

Keynesianism came under attack in the 1970s, when governments began to find it increasingly difficult to achieve their aims through the established fiscal and monetary policies. Partly, this was due to mismanagement of the U.S. dollar. Inflationary pressures had been building in the United States in the 1960s, and these led to expectations of further inflation. That made monetary policy less effective as a tool in domestic affairs. Fiscal policy was less useful, if only because government expenditures now regularly accounted for a large percentage of economic activity during the best of times. While Keynes's suggestions had been particularly potent at a time when government expenditures were low, and when central banks had not been given much discretion in policy, by the 1970s both tools had been used so much that their marginal effects were extremely weak.

Globalization is seen as an even stronger threat to the functioning of Keynesian models. Globalization of finance in particular is regarded as such a powerful force that Keynesian principles no longer apply. Competition for the funds the government needs is seen as the main problem. This in turn is driven by the changes in regulations concerning capital flows. Policies controlling the flow of capital across borders were changed over the years, and as they were, the relationship between governments and financial markets changed in some interesting ways.

The changes cut against the effectiveness of the state's economic policies in two ways. First, the government has to be concerned with its policies affecting decisions about capital generated domestically. Making it easier to take capital out of a country meant that government would have to take steps to make it attractive for capital to stay at home. Since governments pursuing Keynesian policies usually placed higher employment levels over other goals, inflation had become quite common. Yet in a competitive environment, if one state emphasizes employment objectives too much, and high inflation results, capital may be withdrawn and invested in a country where inflation is much lower. Though we should keep in mind that by all evidence, in the OECD countries capital flight is hardly a problem.

Second, states must also compete for international investors. As other states opened up their capital markets, allowing capital to be invested abroad, it became possible for these governments to attract investments from foreigners. So on the one hand, governments must be wary to follow policies that ensure that their own investors do not pull up stakes and flee, but this same international environment makes it possible for states to tap into capital saved up in other economies. This may present new opportunities for governments with good credit ratings to borrow from international sources.

In either case, however, pressures have developed for governments to reduce their borrowing from previously high levels. To convince foreign creditors to continue to lend, or even to persuade domestic owners of capital that inflation will not be a problem in the future, governments have been reducing their spending and balancing their books. Much of the consternation expressed about the pressures of globalization on states may be attributed to these conservative measures.

Geoffrey Garrett describes these new pressures from the point of view of the government. As insecurities arise in the face of apparent market integration, groups hurt by trade or international competition will ask the government for support. Governments will be faced with the "political logic of voice versus the economic logic of exit." Labour, in particular, that faces adjustment or retraining costs will make demands with political force behind them; capital, however, now has the option of exiting if the government's responses do not satisfy its needs. There may be costs to reducing government activity, and the benefits of government activity can out-weigh those costs.[13] For instance, Canadians would probably argue that national health care is not only more equitable than an American-style market-driven system, but that it is cheaper for society, too.

It is important to recognize that governments accepted the constraints that came with more open capital markets. Government policy determined the opening up of capital markets. There were some pressures to do so from some of their constituents, but governments do not automatically respond to all such demands.[14] Moreover, governments themselves had also decided to borrow funds and accumulate such large debts. This had been governments' response to pressures for greater expenditures. Now they were living with the accumulated results of their decisions.

Hans-Peter Martin and Harald Schumann view this outcome as an inevitable result from states' decisions to join the international finan-cial system and play by the liberal, open rules. By joining in, govern-ments gain access to global capital, which is an irresistible lure. Once states partake of international loans, they find they must submit to a host of longer-term conditions and influences.[15] Governments find they need to reduce their debts by first reducing current deficits—this requires cutbacks in existing programs. International finance became "the bad guy" in politicians' explanations of these trends.[16]

It is not clear, however, that these pressures impacted countries in quite the same ways. Looking across the OECD countries, one finds a wide vari-ation in the role different governments have played in their own national economy. No clear pattern emerges as to how governments have responded to higher interest charges in international lending. Those who oppose globalization would argue that international finance leads to a reduction in the role of the government everywhere, and thus a weakening of Keynesian policy instruments everywhere, but the evi-dence does not support this conjecture.

There is a logic that runs counter to the Martin/Schumann line of think-ing. International investors want to invest capital where it earns high returns. This may occur in places where the government has high expen-ditures, but where those expenditures are positively correlated with the level of infrastructure developed, or the quality of the workforce (which implies expenditures for public health and education). Government expenditures per se do not contribute to investment—the quality of what is produced through those expenditures is what matters. Keynes's ideas still have relevance, even in a world of global finance. Some would say that the competition between states that many blame for pressuring all governments to conform to low standards in order to entice investment could have the opposite effect. As states compete for economic activity, investment, and human capital, they must do a better job of delivering services for a low cost. Only by doing so will they be able to seize the opportunities presented by globalization, but also shield their citizens from globalization's risks.

GLOBALIZATION AS "CREATIVE DESTRUCTION": A MARXIST VIEW

While Polanyi and later Keynes wrote about the ways liberal faith in markets was misplaced, they both saw ways in which the market's ill effects could be corrected. Keynes sought to save the liberal market economy from being replaced by either the socialist or fascist models developed in the interwar period. These rivals were founded on the belief that liberal practices were inherently flawed. The socialist alternative was based on Karl Marx's criticisms of liberalism.

One might think that Marx would shed few insights on globalization, since Marx himself focused almost entirely on issues found within the domestic political economy. He said very little about international politics in general. In some of his few observations, he wrote about British imperialism in India. These were included in a series of newspaper articles written in the 1850s. In this account, Marx gave us a good idea of how he might view globalization.

Marx vividly described the British economic penetration of India — how development of the rail transport infrastructure was allowing Britain's exports to alter the economy of India. Thanks to technological advances in shipping and production, cotton from sources around the world were shipped cheaply and easily to England. Since Britain was the only country industrialized at the time its textiles were mass-manufactured— woven and dyed and turned into cloth that could then be shipped from England to India.

Marx went on to describe how textile imports into India undercut established patterns of employment. It was no coincidence that Gandhi would decades later take up the hand-turned spinning wheel as a symbol of the Indian independence movement. Manufactured goods imported from Britain threw large numbers of Indian labourers out of work. This in turn was shaking Indian society. It was, in Marx's terms, "creative destruction," since he believed this reshaping of Indian society was necessary for further economic and social developments.

These views are echoed by contemporary Marxist arguments, and seconded by others on the far left of the political spectrum. They see globalization as a destructive force that can sweep away barriers to further political change. As Hirst and Thompson put it, "For the radical left the concept of globalization also provides release from a different kind of political impasse."[7] Globalization reminds us of how pernicious and painful capitalism can be, even in the wake of capitalism's victory in the Cold War. Moreover, to many observers, globalization illustrates the failure of national-level policies to control the economy that has been noted already, even among liberals. To those socialists who had put their faith in reform of capitalism, globalization's onrush makes them question whether or not social democratic policies are more than mere short-term compromises doomed to failure.

On the other hand, globalization illustrates how vibrant capitalism is. Most people would argue that globalization represents the failure of Marxist and other alternative ideologies. These great ideological debates of the past seem to have lost their relevance. To those who remain faithful to Marxism, the triumph of capitalism spells its own end. Immanuel Wallerstein views globalization as the last gasp of capitalism. It is a sign of capitalism's weakness, its need to sap the economic surplus of new, untapped regions of the globe. With the end of the Soviet Union, China's opening up economically, and the widespread adoption of liberal trade practices in the Third World, capitalism will have no further areas to tap into. If capitalism does indeed require new economic sources for sustained growth via exploitation, they would have a point. The basis for their arguments are not widely agreed upon, however.

According to Hoogvelt, globalization represents a "complete, radical break, a *qualitative* change, in the historical development of capitalism."[8] What makes this new version of capitalism different, in her eyes, is the fact that earlier forms developed within the territorial borders of a single state, and were then extended beyond those borders. This version is global from its inception, she argues. If that is the case, the Marxists' criticisms of capitalism's workings still ring true, but they will need to think longer and harder about what sort of alternative formulation could deliver more equitable and just benefits, but also satisfy widespread demands for economic growth. One thing is certain, they see these changes leading to political clashes in the future. They do not expect globalization to continue to proceed unabated.

NOTHING'S REALLY CHANGED: THE REALIST VIEW

One of the oldest and most important strains of thinking in international relations is realism. Realists assume that the state is the key actor in international relations. This is based on the state's claim of sovereignty. Since the treaties ending the Thirty Years' War in the mid-seventeenth century states have claimed to be the ultimate political authority. They respect no higher political authority as legitimate. Realism treats this claim as an assumption to build on when trying to develop theories about international relations. This assumption is one of the defining features of the realist paradigm.[19]

Because each state claims to be sovereign, the resulting politics of the inter-state system are best described as "anarchic." A political system where no constituent member respects an authority over itself is one where we would expect certain problems in dealing with common problems, or developing mechanisms for governing itself. In practice, states do cede authority to other actors, including other states under certain circumstances. Realists recognize these instances, but seek to explain why and when states would do this by framing the situation in terms of sovereignty. Realists therefore have a particular perspective on the issues bound up in globalization.

Realists argue that even if globalization is taking place, it remains a consequence of policy choices. If a state chooses to resist globalization, or even to reverse it, it can do so through its exercise of sovereignty. States should not yet be willing to share sovereign powers with other actors, realists maintain. They may have been more willing to lower the barriers to entry into the national political economy in recent years, because states see gains to be made by doing so. But realists remind us that in the past states have lowered these same barriers only to raise them again. In fact, many would point to the pre-World War I period as the time when globalization truly had reached its zenith.

In those days, there were ample ties between states. For one thing, there were fewer states around than there are today. Several states had used their power in the preceding decades to build up vast empires. Several of these empires engaged in open trade in the late nineteenth century. These major economic and political powers also were linked together by the gold standard. The gold standard linked their financial systems together, and allowed for the relatively free flow of capital across borders. International investment hit extremely high levels, especially in terms of long-run investments. Yet these ties between empires did not stop them from engaging in a world war. In the wake of that world war, some states shut themselves off from the world economy (as the Soviet Union did in the 1920s), while others tried but failed to resurrect the open economic ties from the pre-World War I period. By the 1930s, all the major economies had turned their backs on liberal trade and investment rules.

As will be detailed in later chapters, several authors argue that states retain a great deal of choice in accepting to participate in globalizing processes, or tempering that participation in some respect.[20] Politics still matter. Yet what is the basis for making these decisions? Realists are unable to provide much insight into how domestic interests interact with international opportunities in the state's calculations.[21] They can remind us that the state still matters, but the ways in which domestic interests vary across states, or the ways in which domestic demands constrain states, forces us to go beyond the realist perspective. Because realism cannot tell us much about who wins or loses in these changes, it does not help us understand why or when a backlash to globalization might develop.

GLOBALIZATION AS CO-OPERATION AND INTERDEPENDENCE: INSTITUTIONALISM

One of the most powerful responses to the development of realism was a paradigm that became widely used in international political economy: Institutionalism. Institutionalism shares certain assumptions with realism, but they differ quite strongly on one. Realism assumes that states rank security as their highest goal. All other aims of a state are subordinated to the goal of attaining more power. Institutionalism, on the other hand, assumes that states pursue a mix of goals. Since some of these goals are economic in character, the opportunities for co-operation are viewed quite differently in Institutionalism than in realism.

Realists expect states to be wary about co-operating, since each state would fear what others might possibly gain from any interaction. Institutionalists' assumptions, however, leave it possible for two states to interact and achieve mutual gains. This would be an excellent starting point for understanding the desire to engage in trade. Institutionalists accept the realists' characterization of the international system, but would point out that states are harmed by having poor arrangements for governing the interstate system. To overcome the uncertainties and risks that arise in an anarchic environment, states seek to gain better information about how other states are behaving, and about how states will act in the future. They seek to bind other states in these arrangements that produce positive benefits for all, hence the emphasis on "institutions."

As the gains from interaction increase, states should be expected to develop more numerous and more elaborate institutional arrangements to help them manage their interconnected affairs. Globalizing economic and cultural processes should produce recognizable changes in international affairs. There are a great number of variations within institutionalism, so precise predictions vary, but the style of argument is clear: as the ties between states change, the institutional arrangements will change. Debates are beginning over just how the institutional set-ups will vary.

Institutionalism can help us understand how and why states might come together to manage any problems associated with globalization. It offers us insights into how "global governance" might emerge—ad hoc interstate governing mechanisms could arise when needed. Institutionalism at least proposes that such opportunities exist, and will be seized on under the right conditions.

New Perspectives on Globalization

Many people argue that all the older paradigms have lost their relevance. Andrew Baker, for one, has noted how the traditional perspectives in international political economy miss the very points that make globalization worth talking about.

> Globalization is not a process that involves the "retreat of the state" because the state remains a strategic contested terrain, control of which is pivotal to world order. It is a process involving increased cross-border socio-economic activity, making it enormously difficult to distinguish between global and national—in fact, the global becomes the national and vice-versa. This renders the excessively vertical view of the world found in mainstream international relations theory in the form of traditional levels of analysis and dichotomous external-internal approaches increasingly meaningless.[22]

Several more approaches to political phenomena have been developed more recently. Do these approaches offer us a better lens for comprehending globalization?

GLOBALIZATION AND A GREEN PERSPECTIVE

Eric Helleiner makes a strong case that the traditional paradigms fail to provide powerful descriptions or insights for grasping the impact of globalization. Helleiner is concerned because they therefore also fail to provide people with the right tools for critiquing globalization. Being unable to critique globalization, people are unlikely to develop appropriate strategies for countering globalizing trends. Helleiner points to an alternative view of the world: a "green" perspective, which he would argue globalization spawned. Green political thinking is a response to globalization—and its characteristics can be seen as a reflection of globalization's political and economic dimensions.

> [T]he greens' analysis addresses the central feature of this phenomenon—the expansion of the scale of social life—in a much more direct way than the other schools. And their concerns about it seem to tap into a widespread sense of unease about democratic accountability, environmental degradation, and social upheavals and alienation in the new globalized economy. Furthermore, their promotion of "global thinking" also resonates well in an age when there is a growing sense of worldwide interconnectedness and global diversity as well as increasingly widespread post-modern scepticism of universalistic political projects. Similarly, the greens' advocacy of localism attracts attention as globalization encourages both a search for local identities and a sense that the nation-state is no longer the most capable or even most appropriate agent of social change and protection. For all these reasons, the rise of the greens is unlikely to be a transient phenomenon and IPE scholars would do well to recognize their contribution to the widening of debate in the field at the end of the twentieth century.[23]

The greens' analysis of recent trends rests on the tension between "the local" and "the global." It does not emphasize traditional boundaries such as that between the nation-state and the international. Instead it speaks of loss of control over local decisions.

As the scale of economic and political affairs increases, this loss of control is felt more keenly. The greens offer a simple tactic in the face of these trends: "think globally, act locally." By this they mean support local producers (local employment), small business, and so on. This strategy is meant to pit the local against the global, but there is also the sense that one must think about the global implications of "local" acts. At first glance, the economic logic would be easily challenged by liberals; buying locally when cheaper alternatives exist elsewhere appears foolish. Yet greens would argue that market failures result from these distant transactions. Distance blinds one to the side-effects produced by these transactions, such as abuse of labour or destruction of the environment. Distrusting both big business and government, greens want to see things with their own eyes. When told by liberals they could be saving money by engaging more extensively with the global economy, they would probably respond that distant workers or environments are worth something to them as well.

The green perspective is interesting to us precisely because it is in many ways a reaction to globalizing processes. By understanding the greens' complaints and strategies, we may have a clearer understanding of how people are being affected by globalization. As Helleiner claims, we may be seeing much more developed from this perspective in the future. As a paradigm stressing normative goals, however, the green perspective is weaker on developing arguments or theories addressing empirical questions of the sort driving our interest in globalization: will globalizing processes continue, or will these trends be slowed or even reversed? Greens have their own preferred answer, but do they have the tools for answering that question? In their view, much depends on how people think about their own role in the global political economy.

THE CONSEQUENCES OF GLOBALIZATION FOR DEMOCRACY

One of the chief concerns of greens is that the scale of political decision-making has grown to such a vast level that democratic impulses are lost. More decisions are being made through inter-governmental organizations, such as the WTO or EU. Distance is created between those making policy covering the international economy and those who are truly accountable to the voters. Greens are not alone in voicing these concerns. Within Europe, people from different perspectives speak of a "democratic deficit" within the European Union's arrangements.

Originally, people who studied economic interdependence viewed it as a vehicle for several normatively preferred outcomes. Economic interdependence would tie the fortunes and destinies of countries together, therefore making war too costly to undertake. The need to co-ordinate economic policies would lead to the development of a technocratic elite—an elite holding only weak allegiances to states. Scientific management would dominate the narrow interests of particular states. Mutual interests would win out. Yet over time, the grounding of such thinking, and the linkages back down to domestic interests, have been questioned. These have brought about some interesting changes in thinking, though I would argue that we have yet to consider the full implications.

One of the more interesting twists within the perspective that explores these tensions can be found in the recent work of Helen Milner and Peter Rosendorff.[24] Milner and Rosendorff studied the impact of interdependence on national decisions to integrate economies more tightly. What they suggest is that democracies may have a slightly harder time making binding arrangements than those states where decision-making is vested in the executive branch.

This makes perfect sense. In fact, it coincides with much thinking about the key piece of legislation in American history that turned the U.S. away from closure and more towards an open stance with the international economy in the 1930s: the Reciprocal Trade Agreements Act (or RTAA). On the one hand, the RTAA built upon a long tradition in American trade policy by focusing on the principle of reciprocity. On the other hand, the RTAA represents a reversal of the American trade policy of its day. It was passed in 1934, just four years after the notorious Smoot-Hawley Tariff. The relationship between Smoot-Hawley and the RTAA is important.

Smoot-Hawley raised American tariffs dramatically. It was a response to the economic downturn of the late 1920s. This tariff is often offered as the classic example of a legislative "log-roll"—when every group lobbies for its own narrow interests, but the legislators roll all these demands together. The legislation passes because each legislator agrees to accept the demands of others in exchange for their support for his/her own narrow demands.

The RTAA represented Congress's recognition that Smoot-Hawley had had negative consequences for the United States. Moreover, it may also have been a recognition that the legislature would tend to produce higher tariffs; thus the RTAA is not only about reciprocity in trade agreements, it also passes the responsibility for tariffs to the President. As the only elected official in the United States voted on by the entire country, the President appreciates the needs and interests of the nation as a whole better than other elected officials. Of course, the sweeping change in the number of Democrats after the 1932 election also skewed the representation of interests in Congress towards free trade.[25]

Increased interdependence is related in this case to the concentration of decision-making in fewer and fewer individuals. This is not an isolated example, however. Indeed, the whole trend of American economic leadership in the international political economy after World War II is associated with "the imperial presidency." The executive branch has accumulated more and more decision-making power, beyond its original constitutional powers. Rather than sign treaties, which would then require approval by the Senate, the U.S. has conducted a large number of "executive agreements." Much the same can be observed in Europe of the way economic interdependence has developed there. The Common Market, which evolved into the European Economic Community, and now the European Union, rests on a series of agreements that bind together states. When these have been considered in referenda in some member states, the results tend to show a lack of enthusiasm in the public in several states.

One inference we can derive from these cases is that there seems to be some tension between democracy and high levels of interdependence. As interdependence increases, agreements between states (or co-ordinated policy-making to ensure that economic interdependence continues) has to be conducted by executives shielded from the tempests of short-run democratic politics. At the same time, research also highlights how democratic states are more likely to pursue the gains from trade than are non-democratic states. Democratic states are also more likely to engage in binding agreements to liberalize trade. Once they make such agreements they are more likely to adhere to them. We are left then with the idea that globalizing processes will likely continue, even though opposition to them also will surface. The political contests will pit leaders with broad national concerns against the narrow interests of those hurt more directly by globalization, in this framework. It is the political parallel to the Liberal or even Keynesian approaches already discussed.

GLOBALIZATION AS A NEW SOCIAL CONTEXT: CONSTRUCTIVISM

The advent of a fully theorized new paradigm has been one of the more exciting developments in recent years in the study of international affairs. Social constructivism, as it has been called, emphasizes the need to consider how social relations construct the identity of relevant actors. Whereas most paradigms begin with assumptions about who the relevant actors are, and then make assumptions about what these actors are interested in, before examining any empirical examples, social constructivism takes a very different path.

Using this approach, we would examine the actor's social context. Actors' identities are generated by the social situation. If we were to consider an individual, for instance, we might find that an actor's identity changes as the individual moves from one context to another. During a meeting with colleagues, a woman may think of herself and her goals in one way, yet find herself thinking about her desires in very different terms when spending the evening out with friends. This sort of change in identity and aims holds for states, too. This can prove valuable for understanding how states developed their aims, as well as providing some insight into how such aspirations might change over time.

Alexander Wendt might argue, therefore, that the Westphalian system, which rests so much on the notion of state sovereignty, was generated and maintained by the states themselves. The interstate political system developed into a "self-help" arrangement, with no higher political authority, because that is how states thought about their relations with each other. It didn't have to turn out that way—but since states thought about their relations in those terms, developed their goals based on these beliefs, and behaved accordingly, they wound up with that sort of arrangement. If states begin to think about their relations in different terms—such as interdependence and shared destinies—they will begin to think and behave differently.

The changes we describe with the concept "globalization" can be seen in these terms, along the lines that the greens advocate. Actors' identities are changing, as the political economic context they find themselves in is becoming more global. If people communicate over international borders on a regular basis, or do business internationally every day, their terms of reference change. The greens focus on individuals, however, while constructivism is open about which actors are most relevant. Perhaps the most obvious change constructivists discuss concerns the ways states behave. The changes have been gradual, but they are still observable. At the beginning of the twentieth century, states were primarily responsible for maintaining a nation or people's external relations, and creating a stable internal order. Management of the economy was important for achieving other ends. Naturally, inspiring economic growth was useful for keeping people content, and for generating the economic base for developing international power. But governments rarely made any explicit promises concerning the country's economic performance, such as employment levels or inflation rates. Such promises are commonplace nowadays. The governments of many states would be judged by their ability to fulfill economic needs rather than achieve complete sovereignty over their own territory. States think about themselves as having different responsibilities these days.

As the balance between goals shifts from a tilt towards military security to one emphasizing economic achievement, states have begun behaving differently. They are willing to make the trade-off between sovereignty and economic achievement that several writers have described. Social constructivism may give us a very good set of tools for describing these changes. What is missing, however, is a better understanding of why these changes have taken place. Why did some states move in this direction first? Why have others followed? Why have others chosen not to follow this trend? Unfortunately, social constructivism can point to some processes of competition and emulation that occur, but if we are to do more than describe current trends the conditions for such changes need to be further elaborated.

Conclusions

Stanley Hoffmann recently observed that while the economic policies associated with globalization represent victories for the liberal viewpoint, the consequences of unleashing market forces can undercut other values or policies associated with liberalism.

> The other effect has been a frequent backlash against the constraints imposed by interdependence in general, a reaction to the sense that the fate of individuals even in liberal polities is no longer under their control or that of their representatives. It is hard to target the force that is most responsible for this loss—the transnational economy—and too late to do more than delay or restrain a bit the removal of barriers to the free circulation of capital, goods, and services that allows this economy to grow in all directions. Thus, the reaction often strikes instead at efforts at interstate cooperation (such as the European Union) and takes various forms of xenophobia, as in attacks on migrant workers and restrictions on asylum. These are defeats for liberal values.[26]

We might well conclude, then, that while liberalism has provided much of the guidance for the initiating globalization, and even helps us understand or describe some of the economic aspects of globalizing processes, it does not provide us with a full picture. Keynesians, or more modern liberals, are concerned with the ways in which the balance between market and state has swung too far in favour of the former. Greens share these concerns but also voice sharper criticisms of globalizing processes, be they economic, cultural, or political. Realists seem to offer little insight, other than to add to the descriptions of how things are changing. Constructivists do much better at describing both the previous periods and the current one within a single framework. They seem less able to explain why things have changed, however. In short, each perspective can be useful for addressing some of our concerns. None can address or answer all our interests in the subject. As we look in the next chapter at why globalization may have been promoted in the past, or may be opposed today, we can refer to some of these paradigms for insight into how globalization can engender particular political models.

NOTES

1 It is possible that our models or theories could help us get a better understanding of what has occurred in the past, and provide us excellent predictions, but still leave us unable to do anything to alter our future.

2 Alan Scott, "Globalization: social process or political rhetoric?," in Scott, ed., *The Limits of Globalization: Cases and Arguments* (London: Routledge, 1997), 1-3.

3 Paul Hirst and Grahame Thompson, *Globalization in Question: The International Economy and the Possibilities of Governance*, 2nd ed. (Cambridge: Polity Press, 1999), 262.

4 Hans-Peter Martin and Harald Schumann, *The Global Trap: Globalization and the Assault on Prosperity and Democracy*, trans. Patrick Camiller (Montreal: Black Rose Books, 1998), 112.

5 Paul Krugman, *Pop Internationalism* (Cambridge, MA: MIT Press, 1996), 56.

6 Martin and Schumann, *The Global Trap*, 110-14.

7 Daniel Cohen, *The Wealth of the World and the Poverty of Nations* (Cambridge, MA: MIT Press, 1998), 48-49.

8 Karl Socher, "Globalization and International Monetary and Capital Markets," in John-ren Chen, ed., *Economic Effects of Globalization* (Aldershot, UK: Ashgate, 1998), 40.

9 Ibid., 40-41.

10 Stanley Hoffmann, "The Crisis of Liberal Internationalism," *Foreign Policy* 98 (Spring 1995): 175.

11 Philip McMichael, "The New Colonialism: Global Regulation and the Restructuring of the Interstate System," in David A. Smith and Jozsef Böröcz, eds. *A New World Order?* (Westport, CT: Praeger, 1995), 39.

12 Charles Kindleberger, *The World in Depression* (Berkeley: University of California Press, 1971).

13 Geoffrey Garrett, "Global Markets and National Politics: Collision Course or Virtuous Circle?," *International Organization* 52, 4, (Autumn 1998): 790-91.

14 Eric Helleiner, *States and The Reemergence of Global Finance* (Ithaca, NY: Cornell University Press, 1994).

15 Martin and Schumann, *The Global Trap*, 65.

16 Of course, in true Keynesian views, the government was supposed to spend on the margin—stabilizing markets. When demand fell too low (as in the 1930s) the government was supposed to spend additional amounts; when demand was too high (as in the 1960s) the government was supposed to spend less. Or alternatively, it was supposed to assist in bad times, but exit (or even save money) in good times.

17 Hirst and Thompson, *Globalization in Question*, 262.

18 Ankie Hoogvelt, *Globalization and the Postcolonial World* (Baltimore: Johns Hopkins University Press, 1997), xii.

19 Mark R. Brawley, *Turning Points* (Peterborough, ON: Broadview Press, 1998), chs. 1-2.

20 For example, the research of Eric Helleiner, or of John Goodman and Louis Pauly, on the breakdown of the Bretton Woods regime—though these three are not coming from realist perspectives per se. Stephen Krasner's *Sovereignty* is the best example of a realist work.

21 For instance, consider how Richard Rosecrance combines these different mechanisms at work in *The Rise of the Virtual State*.

22 Andrew Baker, "Globalization and the British 'Residual State'," in Richard Stubbs and Geoffrey R.D. Underhill, eds., *Political Economy and the Changing Global Order*, 2nd ed. (Toronto: Oxford University Press, 2000), 366-67.

23 Eric Helleiner, "New Voices in the Globalization Debate: Green Perspectives on the World Economy," in Stubbs and Underhill, eds., *Political Economy and the Changing Global Order*, 67.

24 Helen Milner and Peter Rosendorff, *Interests, Institutions and Information* (Princeton, NJ: Princeton University Press, 1997).

25 Michael Hiscox, "The Magic Bullet? The RTAA, Institutional Reform and Trade Liberalization," *International Organization* 53, 4, (Autumn 1999): 669-98.

26 Hoffmann, "The Crisis of Liberal Internationalism," 176.

3 | What People Fear—or Anticipate—about Globalization

So far, we have reviewed different definitions of globalizing processes, and different theoretical lenses for interpreting those changes. How do these theories tie more directly to the possible political stories that could unfold? One common theme begins with the unleashing of market forces, which make national boundaries less meaningful. The consequences most people fear—and which many people expect to happen—involve the weakening of national policies in the face of these economic changes. That is not the only possible political outcome from these same processes, however. Some eventual influences could even have positive ramifications. Therefore it is worth examining more closely what might be occurring in globalization to create opposition, or to build political support behind these policies.

Is Globalization Inevitable? Is the Race to the Bottom Unavoidable?

One of the fears often expressed about globalization is that it generates a "race to the bottom." This was a fear expressed by greens, by Marxists, and by others more generally fearful of market power becoming unbalanced. These people think that economic competition in globalization will undermine various existing regulatory schemes. States will lose their ability to lessen the negative impact of markets, or to provide various services and functions as their ability to generate tax revenues is undercut by competition. In the globalized economy, the states that win will be those that impose the lowest tax rates, and hinder business least. No state will be able to escape such pressures, many fear.

Several of the discussions of definitions from political scientists cited in the first chapter pointed out that little in "globalization" could be described as inevitable. Governments retain choices in the policies they implement. Technologies can only play a role in changing the political economy if governments allow them to. Government policies allow individuals to adopt new technologies to exploit opportunities to undertake international exchanges. The creation of a new form of communication does little good to advance globalization if a government refuses to allow its citizens to adopt that technology.

The most extreme historical example would be Japan's closure from the world in the late sixteenth century. When the first European traders reached Japan, they brought with them ideas and tools that the Japanese rulers perceived as threats. Japan's rulers therefore decided to prohibit contact with the outside world. This policy remained in place for centuries until the country was forced to open up after contact with Western military forces in the mid-nineteenth century. Japan lagged behind other countries in all facets of technology—but especially in the military and economic realms. Other countries were already industrializing, and harnessing gunpowder and steam engines. The country had cut itself off from outside influences successfully, allowing its rulers to remain in control, but retarding the country's economic development.

It is important to recognize that this is not an isolated example. China, too, sought to limit the introduction of Western technology at roughly the same time as Japan did. There are current examples of states that have chosen to limit or curtail the impact of certain forms of technology. North Korea is not about to let its citizens get a better understanding of the outside world, or suddenly let them begin communicating with others freely. In more limited fashion, there are governments that regulate the content of the Internet in order to promote other goals – but may in fact hinder the development of their businesses in adopting this technology. Quebec has regulations governing the use of French on Web pages displayed by businesses based there, though they can only be enforced on servers based in the province. While the goal is to promote the language component of Quebec culture, such legislation shapes the role these businesses will have in a global economy.

States get our attention because they claim to exercise sovereignty. In other words, states maintain that they alone are the highest legitimate political authority. The relationship between sovereignty and globalization is complicated. States have not rescinded their claims to sovereignty, yet their own decisions seem to place limits on how they may be able to exercise such claims. It is important therefore to separate the claim from the ability to act upon that claim. States may decide to cede sovereignty in certain areas, but such adjustments are only through their approval. This was most strikingly illustrated on 11 September 2001. As it became clear that the first plane crash into the World Trade Center was no accident, American authorities moved to shut down that country's borders. They could do so—if at tremendous economic cost—but clearly the authorities could exercise that option.

The processes at work in globalization erode the barriers between states, but we should remember that these barriers were *constructed* by the states themselves in the first place.[1] Many of these barriers were erected only in the twentieth century, and thus do not have such deep historical roots. Ironically, globalizing processes have been thought of in the past as having positive repercussions. Since the turn of the century, there have been proponents of a global society; in such a society, where states no longer claim priority in defining individuals' political allegiances or identities, wars might well become unthinkable. In many ways, in fact, people view the progress made by the countries of Western Europe in promoting economic and monetary union as steps towards constructing a political arrangement that enables people from different countries to work and live together in peace.

Why have many groups, especially those on the left of the political spectrum (such as adherents of the Marxist or green approaches discussed in the previous chapter), more recently decried the trends of increasing globalization? The answer has two parts. On the one hand, many groups on the left now see the state not as a dangerous actor one should be reluctant to trust, but rather as a defender of society's true interests. Whereas states may claim our political loyalty and pit us against other the citizens of other states in various ways, many on the left see the state as the only power capable of cushioning the impact of market forces.

The state is viewed in these terms as an important provider of public goods. Remember that public goods will not be provided sufficiently by markets operating in or near perfect competition. Where the market fails, the state can step in to promote outcomes more beneficial for society as a whole. Importantly, groups oriented towards environmental concerns, issues of social equity, protection for labor, etc., see the state as the only actor capable of deflecting market forces. Barriers between states become important, in the eyes of such groups, because they allow individual states to pursue different paths for protecting local interests.

61

Groups with these concerns naturally fear that eliminating barriers between states will unleash market forces that put pressure on regulations. That is the first concern expressed among fears of a "race to the bottom." If states compete for international investments, or seek to enhance the competitiveness of their citizens in trade, or in other international economic interactions, they might be tempted to reduce some of their regulating of the economy, or at least lower their taxes. Lower taxes reduce the state's revenues, which eventually will limit its capabilities to provide public goods. The whole argument rests on the belief that the market rewards those states with the fewest regulations. In the next chapter we will consider whether the evidence bears out this last assertion.

The logic of this argument can be challenged. Investment would never concentrate on the country with the weakest regulatory powers – investors need to know their own property rights are secure. International investment has always focused on the most economically advanced countries, where regulations tended to be broader and more enforced. Investors are not lined up to place capital in countries such as Russia or Rwanda, where environmental and safety standards are significantly lower and laxly enforced. Instead, investors balance the returns on their investment versus the risks. Returns are based on a variety of factors, and often the services provided by the state factor into the equation in a positive way.

Investors might view Canada's national healthcare program in the same light as Canadians, for instance, as a mechanism for giving complete, fair coverage at a low cost. This should make Canada an attractive place to do business, not hinder it, so long as the system keeps health costs down. Likewise, NAFTA has not led to the "giant sucking sound" Ross Perot predicted. Investment did not flee the United States for Mexico as he and many others expected. Instead, in the years since NAFTA was signed, the U.S has experienced record low levels of unemployment—not record highs. Studies indicate that labour costs are only one of a number of costs investors consider when deciding where to locate their businesses. Infrastructure development (in terms of roads, airports, rail facilities, etc.), taxes, local suppliers of inputs, energy costs, and many other factors also come into play.

Geoffrey Garrett has argued that states do compete for investment by multinational firms, but businesses do not prefer low levels of regulation before everything else. Businesses try to gauge whether the services provided by the state are roughly equivalent to the sorts of taxes charged. States that charge higher taxes are expected to provide better services—if they do not, they will not do well in this competition. For example, the value of Canada's health care system is not viewed simply in terms of how much

62

it costs; it is judged by its quality in comparison to its costs to taxpayers. Businesses may well prefer to invest where a state charges high taxes, so long as the state uses these funds to maintain and develop infrastructure, to invest in a skilled workforce via the education system, to protect the local environment (a key to drawing in talented workforce these days), and provide other collective goods.

Garrett's figures bear this argument out. Not only does he reject the notion that there has been a race to the bottom among the most economically advanced states, he even rejects the notion that there has been a convergence around a similar level of government activity. His attention is focused on these countries—the members of the OECD—because they have been feeling the pressures of competition in trade more strongly and for a longer time than any other countries. They are also both the sources and recipients of the greatest flows of international capital.[2] The statistics are clear: at least among the OECD countries, levels of government spending are not converging. They are more diverse in recent years than before. Tax rates on capital remain quite varied as well.[3] This evidence will support the views of the Keynesians, in that they believe the government can still tax the benefits from globalization, and compensate those whose interests are damaged. It is hard to believe in "the race to the bottom" in its simplest form, but we shall explore this argument in more detail later.

Could Globalization be a Positive Force?

A much more positive outcome is imagined by Liberals of both the Classical and Keynesian stripes. Economists and historians often associate a rise in trade with an increase in wealth. Erich Weede's statistical analysis suggests that as countries engage in trade, their average wealth, as well as the distribution of wealth within society, changes. As wealth becomes more widespread a middle class develops. This becomes a political force promoting the development of democracy. Globalization could become a powerful force pushing the spread of democracy, rather than a force undercutting it, as so many left-wing activists currently fear.

Similarly, there are those who see a relationship between trade and specific developments within democratic states. Economic competition can actually lead to some changes in political economic practices that have positive spillovers. To understand this story, we must begin by defining *rents*. Economists use this term to mean *economic gain from non-productive activity*. For example, a monopolistic producer is able to charge a higher price for its products. The extra profit is generated not by the provision of a better good, or more of it, but simply by the producer's exclusive access to the market. Such transitions to monopolistic positions in the market often are achieved through political favours. A firm gets a license to produce something, with legislation prohibiting others from competing. The government raises tariff or non-tariff barriers to prevent foreign producers from entering the market.

Firms lobby the government to pass such rules so that they can enjoy these rents. Long have economists studied some of the perverse results that can occur. In trying to capture rents through government sanctions, firms are willing to invest in lobbying—an expenditure that will not make society as a whole more productive, or wealthier. Rent-seeking activity redistributes a society's existing wealth, rather than adding to it. In fact, once a monopoly position is attained, the redistribution of wealth can have negative consequences for many in a society, since the transfers take away their money and give it to someone else.

If the monopolistic firms are selling inputs others use in producing their own goods, then the negative consequences have an additional, indirect effect. Not only do the other firms pay more for their consumption of these goods than they would in a competitive environment, but now their costs and hence the price of their own output is raised. Here is where the increased international competition generated by globalization factors in. For instance, in an economically developing country where the government decided several years ago that to foster the development of its own industry it not only loaned cheap money to a new national steel firm, but it also gave this firm the sole right to sell steel, and raised tariff barriers against imports of steel. Imagine that you produce automobiles in this country. You must now buy your steel for making cars from this one producer—despite the fact that this producer will charge you a much higher price than you had to pay before.

Now bring in globalizing trends. There are foreign markets open to you, if you can produce your cars at a competitive price. Yet, so long as you have to pay an extremely high price for an essential input such as steel, you probably will be forced to charge a high price for your own output. Moreover, if other states can force your tariffs on automobiles to very low levels, they will want to sell their cars in your market. Will you be able to stem this inflow of cheaper goods?

Picture this sort of story unfolding for all the other consumers of raw steel. Add to this the dynamic of all the other sectors of an economy that might be benefiting from government-sanctioned rents. Economic globalization will spark sharp conflicts between those who benefit from government-sanctioned rents and those who must face international competition. One possible result is that the firms confronting foreign competition will try to eliminate the rents themselves. That alone may be good for societies, since it will push them towards more productive (and probably more equitable) policies.

The opponents of rents may push for a more permanent fix to their problems however. Rent-seeking leads to more rents under particular political settings. In some institutional arrangements, it is easier for a small group to get the government to give it privileges. Political scientists have theorized that democracies are less prone to give out rents than non-democracies.[4] Even among democracies, there are probably observable differences, though work on this front remains more theoretical than empirical. Theorists expect that in democracies with single-member constituencies a narrow group may position itself to dominate policy. Moreover, in one with many constituencies, many narrow interests may come together to "logroll."

Hypothetically, in democracies that depend heavily on trade, people will not tolerate persistent rents. They instead adopt political institutions that are difficult for narrow interests to capture. The most heavily trade-dependent industrialized democracies adopted proportional representation systems with fewer constituencies than those industrialized democracies less dependent on trade.[5] These results hold over time, though they are not completely useful for understanding the institutional choices of democracies yet to industrialize.[6]

Miriam Golden has studied the impact of rising levels of trade on the political institutions of Italy.[7] Italy modified its political institutions in the mid-1990s. The overall goal was to shake up the system—the proportional representation rules that had been in place produced a steady stream of similar governments. In the Cold War, this arrangement had effectively blocked the Communists from joining in governments, but it had allowed embedded corruption as well. Rents, in the form of government over-paying for contract-work or for employees who didn't really show up at work, or in the form of donations to political parties, grew in size over the years.

Golden's research shows that areas highly dependent on international trade showed the greatest enthusiasm for overturning the political institutions that fostered these rents. Particularly in northern Italy, where more and more businesses were integrated into the international economy, people resented the transfers of wealth associated with rents. It made it difficult for firms to compete internationally. Golden's work is interesting because it highlights how trade interests mattered in both the north and south of the country, unlike simpler less insightful analyses that portray the two parts of the country as opponents.

Golden's paper on this subject concludes that the economic pressures created by globalization and competition have important political consequences. She highlights decreasing tolerance for politically sanctioned rents.

> Globalization is typically depicted as harmful to ordinary people because of its economic impact on wages and jobs. Its political impact has been largely overlooked. The processes linking the world's national economies more closely together may give those interests that are most strongly connected to internationally-exposed parts of the economy more in common, and those commonalities may include an interest in making political institutions more transparent, more accountable and more authoritative. Globally-oriented capitalists may come to be counted among the world's strongest proponents of democratic institutions.[8]

We should keep her conclusions in mind as we examine other points of view. They illustrate how the liberal and Keynesian viewpoints can lead us to expect positive improvements from globalization beyond mere material gain; and they illustrate the ties between the spread of democracy and the continuation of globalizing trends.

Concerns for International Politics: Globalization, Peace, and War

Among those who study international relations, a number of different hypotheses have emerged about the consequences of globalization. As we have found among the attempts to glean inferences about the consequences for domestic politics, there is little agreement on what one should expect, even though people in international relations are building upon a longer tradition of study of interdependence in the international political economy. As noted in the discussion of the Institutionalist perspective, many of the old debates about interdependence have resurfaced in slightly different form in current discussions of globalization.

One of the most important expectations from greater international economic integration has been that such ties would deter states from engaging in war with their economic partners. Norman Angell made this claim both before and after World War I. Cordell Hull reiterated it in vain during the Great Depression, just before World War II. The fact that countries with many economic ties still went to war with each other in the first half of the twentieth century caused many to reject such arguments, though both Angell and Hull would have said economic ties had not been allowed to reach high levels even then. With greater economic integration the gains from war seem to be lessened in two respects.

First, as trade and investment increase, the benefits generated from economic intercourse are raised. If we frame the choice to go to war in economic terms, then we would want to consider the costs and benefits associated with each alternative.[9] Higher trade and international investment increases the potential gains from peace.

Three factors affect the potential economic benefits from waging war. To get economic benefits from using military power, a state must be able to seize the territory and other assets of its opponents. It must be able to do so at small cost and be able to control these assets at small cost. Finally, it must be able to extract the economic benefits associated with these assets at small cost to itself. If any of these three forms of costs are increased, then the economic returns associated with warfare and conquest are reduced.

Richard Rosecrance has argued that technological advances in the second half of the twentieth century have tilted the balance sheet in favour of using trade and international economic ties rather than war. As technology makes it easier and more profitable to transport goods and services over borders, states seek to deliver benefits to their citizens via globalization. Technological advances in weaponry make war less and less attractive. Nuclear weapons raise the costs of conquest to unreasonable heights. Even advances in small arms make a difference. Precision-guided munitions, in the form of anti-aircraft and anti-tank missiles, make it possible for small groups of poorly trained infantrymen to take on high-tech weapons systems. Such changes make it difficult for even the greatest military powers of our day to seize and hold territory where the local population resists. The U.S. learned that lesson in Vietnam, the Soviet Union in Afghanistan. Joining the world economy simply makes much more sense than trying to build an empire through the exercise of force.[10]

More recently, analyses of interdependence have pointed in more than one direction. As Daniel Geller and David Singer remarked, logical arguments can be put forth for either the position that globalizing forces enhance peace, or that they increase the possibility for conflict. [11] On the one hand, as contacts between states become deeper and more numerous, this may give them more reasons to engage in disputes. On the other hand, their ties may increase the costs of going to war. Since logical arguments can be made for both positions, only empirical investigations can highlight the possible implications of either one, or help us untangle the interactions of the two.

Geller and Singer locate other possible implications of globalization. They identify the increasing importance of non-state actors in international affairs, such as international organizations or NGOs. This echoes the arguments of the constructivists we reviewed in the previous chapter. International organizations are often servants of states, but they can have a powerful impact on the choices states make. For instance, Martha Finnemore has studied how these organizations can influence the way states determine their own responsibilities. [12] NGOs on the other hand are not seen as the servants of states at all. Groups such as Greenpeace or Amnesty International can be aggressive critics of states —and they, too, can help to shape states' determinations as to what they ought or ought not to be doing. The recent success in limiting the world's production and use of landmines is one example of the impact of NGOs. These different interactions may increase problems for states, as well as offering different ways for solving some states' problems. International organizations can be a tool for getting states to co-operate to achieve their desired ends, or they can be an instrument for engaging in disputes.

NGOs themselves have increasingly turned their attention to international organizations, but these days for the most part they do not view them in a very positive light. The reasons for the different interpretations by Institutionalists and NGOs are interesting. Environmental and labour organizations criticize the WTO and IMF regularly. Protests outside international trade negotiations are commonplace. NGOs mounted a successful Internet campaign to discredit the proposed Multilateral Agreement on Investments (MAI). Why have they come to see these bodies as enemies?

Part of the answer lies in political accountability. NGOs think the WTO or IMF is not accountable to anyone—though this is not true, as the Institutionalists would be the first to point out. These international bodies are accountable to their member governments. It was the member states that created these organizations to perform specific functions. Individual citizens can only indirectly express themselves when it comes to these organizations, by making their demands felt through their national governments. The NGOs themselves are often inconsistent on these issues since many are quite willing to trust other international bodies, such as the UN, run on exactly the same principles.

One might wonder why these same groups do not choose to adapt these organizations for their own ends. That presumably is their ultimate political goal in confronting these bodies. There are those scholars who fear this possible outcome, however.[13] Using the WTO to enforce global environmental regulations makes some sense, but going down such a path also would make it possible for groups to pursue other policies in the guise of environmental interests. Some of the greatest remaining barriers to trade are environmental and safety rules (what we refer to as non-tariff barriers, or NTBs). States may deploy such regulations as a way to block another country's goods from entering its markets. It may be legitimate to worry about the safety of meat imported from a country where a particular disease is present, so such barriers may be called for. Yet we find such rules being abused quite often, as when the Japanese officials claimed American rice should not be allowed into their country on the slim pretext that its people could not digest foreign rice.

In sum, we have NGOs and others voicing loud criticisms of the international organizations that help states develop and maintain the rules governing the international economy. These groups do not share a clear vision of what should replace these organizations; they are not even very clear about whether they want to end these organizations or merely instigate major reforms. Reforming them would open up the possibility of using these international organizations to enforce rising regulatory standards, but at the cost of undercutting international trade and investment. Many groups on the left might see that as a welcome trade-off, but political leaders disagree. They want to continue to deliver economic benefits to their constituents, and have made that a priority for these organizations. Separate treaties and institutions still could be built to deal with issues concerning regulatory standards for the environment or labour practices, however.

The institutionalist perspective tells us that globalization will likely spawn more international organizations and agencies, as national governments seek to manage their relations more effectively. In order to reduce uncertainty, exchange information, and come together to discuss the best way to exploit their mutual interests, states have an incentive to strengthen and develop these mechanisms. Yet constructivists point out how these organizations can also become powerful vehicles for change; groups opposing globalization have placed their focus on these organizations rather than national governments because they see them as more pliable, or as less legitimate and therefore more vulnerable. Whether one view is more accurate is hard to say, but the obvious conclusion is that these international institutions will be the focus for further political battles.

Might Globalization Lead to Acceptance in Some Places, but Backlash Elsewhere?

Because globalization may have different effects on different countries, some authors expect the world to bifurcate. One group of rich, powerful, industrialized states can stand up to the pressures of globalization. In these cases, governments exercise their authority without any real challenge, economic infrastructures are already developed, as are economies. As democracies, their publics demand not only that they tap into the benefits of globalization, but that anyone hurt by these changes be adequately compensated. These states can also defend themselves well, thanks to their employment of advanced technologies. They will compete in economic terms only, and eschew the use of force.

The other group of states will be less capable of dealing with the negative impact of globalization. They are already behind economically, and will not be in a very good position to exploit the benefits attainable from economic globalization. The negative aspects—lower taxes, competition for international investment, etc.—will weaken governments that already have only a tenuous existence. These states may collapse, as we have seen happen in Somalia and elsewhere in Africa. They may still compete in terms of military power as, for example, many states have joined in Congo's wars in the last decade, each hoping to make up for some of its difficulties at home.

Other authors expect instability, and therefore conflict, to increase everywhere as states are confronted with a series of problems associated with globalization. These people fear that, if the "race to the bottom" hypothesis proves to be true, then states will lose their effectiveness. As states become less effective in delivering their services, different forms of social conflict could arise. Susan Woodward's description of the breakup of Yugoslavia follows this exact line. International economic pressures led to devolution of political power to more local levels—but also pitted different levels of political authority against each other.[14]

Privatization of the economy, combined with these economic pressures from the international economy reconfigured political power in unexpected ways. Political conflict followed, as people turned to those authorities able

70

to deliver services and benefits, and turned their backs on other institutions. Politicians in this competition used ethnic differences and history to mobilize their support. The shakeup led to bloody conflicts that drew in the international community. If globalization will create similar instabilities in other countries, then similar types of internal conflict might ensue, leading in turn to conflict between states.

Although we might expect globalization to have this sort of impact, it is possible that it could also drive some states to co-operate more effectively. If globalization exerts similar pressures across all states, then these states might realize they face some common problems. That realization could be the first step in bringing states together to respond to the challenges of globalization. If all states find they are getting weaker in the face of globalizing trends, their incentives to work together might increase. Despite this possibility, most scholars who have studied globalization tend to expect it to pit states against each other, not encourage them to co-operate. Once again, this has to do with expectations that globalization will affect countries unevenly. When we zero in on the political consequences of globalization, the differential impact of globalizing trends is one of the main sources of peoples' fears for the future. Either way, one of the most important issues that still needs to be addressed concerns the conditions for successful international co-operation.

International inequality is one example where the globalization may be making it difficult for states to co-operate. Trade liberalization, even into areas previously restricted, such as agriculture and services, appears to be creating new winners and losers among nation-states. Here again is the picture of a bifurcating world. The volume and value of trade continues to rise yet the benefits don't seem to be distributed evenly. In the words of Daniel Cohen, "poor countries are becoming richer and rich countries seem to be becoming poorer, inescapably giving credence to theories according to which the first phenomenon is responsible for the second," though Cohen himself argues against such thinking.[15]

Cohen's chief theme is that people in industrialized countries are frightened by what they see occurring throughout the world. Countries in East Asia have successfully industrialized—primarily by exporting manufactured goods to the markets of the industrialized countries. Other less-developed countries are following suit. If these also industrialize, and export the bulk of their production to the markets of North America and Europe, how can industries established within those markets survive? Doesn't the industrialization of one country cause the deindustrialization of another? Isn't that the consequence for the U.S., Canada, and the members of the European Union?[16]

Economics tells us that this is not the only way to interpret the evidence. People in the economically advanced countries could be shifting from employment in the industrial sector to the service sector. Rising standards of living in the world could mean an increase in the overall demand for industrial goods. The only way to discern which story is the most persuasive is to consider all the evidence.

Conclusions: Why the Fears Outweigh the Anticipation

On balance, there are many more fears expressed about globalization than there are thoughts about possible benefits. Much of what motivates the fears, however, comes from impressions of what is possibly going on now. The evidence has not always been closely examined. Fear feeds on the unknown. The stakes are potentially high, which makes people even more worried. Until we figure out which processes are driving particular outcomes, it would be difficult to select the proper policy responses to guide us into the future. Moreover, some arguments suggest that there may be some positive consequences to globalization, such as the further spread of democracy, as well as its strengthening in places where democracy has already been established. Globalization may also encourage opposition to rents, which on the whole could bring greater equity and economic efficiency to many societies.

We need to look more closely not only at the possible forces at work, but also at the probabilities of the various outcomes described above actually coming true. That would allow us to make more informed analyses of which policy recommendations might be most appropriate for bringing about a future we all can live with.

NOTES

1 See Geoffrey Garrett, "Global Markets and National Politics: Collision Course or Virtuous Circle?," *International Organization* 52, 4 (Autumn 1998): 787-88.

2 Prior to World War II, international investments went to a mix of states, some economically developed, some not.

3 See Garrett, "Global Markets and National Politics: Collision Course or Virtuous Circle?," 815.

4 See Mark R. Brawley, "Regime-Types, Markets, and War: The Importance of Pervasive Rents in Foreign Policy," *Comparative Political Studies* 26, 2 (July 1993): 178-97.

5 Ronald Rogowski, "Trade and the variety of democratic institutions," *International Organization* 41, 2 (Spring 1987): 203-23.

6 Mark R. Brawley, "Re-examining the Influence of Trade on the Variety of Democratic Institutions," forthcoming.

7 Miriam Golden, "International Sources of the Collapse of Rent-Seeking Regimes: Hypotheses Drawn from the Italian Case," paper presented at the Joint Sessions of the European Consortium for Political Research, Grenoble, France, 6-11 April 2001.

8 Ibid., 24.

9 This sort of exercise is done by Richard Rosecrance in *The Rise of the Trading State* (New York: Basic Books, 1987).

10 This lesson has not been learned by a number of state leaders, however. The recent leaders of Serbia, Iraq, and elsewhere seem to place their personal enrichment over broader societal interests, and therefore accept the distribution of costs and benefits associated with conquest.

11 See Daniel Geller and J. David Singer, *Nations at War* (New York: Cambridge University Press, 1998), 24-25.

12 Martha Finnemore, *National Interests in International Society* (Ithaca, NY: Cornell University Press, 1996).

13 Kym Anderson, "Environmental and Labor Standards: What Role for the WTO?," in Anne Krueger, ed., *The WTO as an International Organization* (Chicago: University of Chicago Press, 1998), 231-55.

14 Susan L. Woodward, *Balkan Tragedy: Chaos and Dissolution after the Cold War* (Washington: The Brookings Institution, 1995).

15 Daniel Cohen, *The Wealth of the World and the Poverty of Nations* (Cambridge, MA: MIT Press, 1998), 1.

16 Ibid., 40.

4 | Is Globalization Occurring? Assessing the Evidence

One of the most contentious aspects of the academic debates swirling around the concept of globalization concerns a simple question.[1] Is globalization occurring? To what degree? The evidence one considers depends entirely on how one defines globalization. Given that we might emphasize different processes, we might well find a complex answer to this question. Is globalization occurring fairly evenly, or is it proceeding at a much more rapid pace in some regions of the world compared to others? Does it matter how widespread the changes are? Only by addressing some of these issues will we be prepared to examine whether globalizing processes are likely to gain momentum, or whether these trends will provoke a backlash. If there is little evidence that globalization is occurring, why should we expect to see any political consequences?

Since most of our definitions of globalization include some notion that improvements in technology have made it easier for people to interact across borders, there are several potential measures for us to employ. If we follow the general path of change described by most writers, increased levels of international communication should be occurring, followed by a whole series of possible economic changes. Globalization entails higher levels of trade, cross-border movement of the factors of production, more foreign direct investment, greater movements of liquid capital across borders, and further specific changes. Each step in these sorts of changes should be fairly easy to measure and track—though the data may not all point in the same direction.

Though we might be able to track changes in the level of communication across borders, or even to measure most of the economic processes at work, it is harder to capture meaningful indicators of the cultural changes that might be occurring. More specifically, for those

75

FIGURE 4.1 | GLOBALIZING PROCESSES

Technological Change

causes

Increases in Communication

which in turn causes

Expanding Trade and Expanding International Investment

causing

Various Possible Political Consequences
(*Changing Identities, Pressures to Reduce Rents,*
"Race to the Bottom," and so forth)

who expect to see alterations in how people think about themselves, or how their political identities are shaped, there are greater difficulties in coming up with measures that can command a wide acceptance. In speaking about globalization and the politics of identity, or changes in patterns of communication, we can probably find some crude measures, but these may not be as clear as those covering the economic processes of globalization.

After discussing some of the general perceptions that support our impression that globalization is taking place, we turn to some specific economic indicators as well as other, perhaps less precise indicators of other globalizing processes. We can then start to explore some of the potential political consequences that would flow from these changes in the subsequent chapters. First, however, we should examine the evidence that lends credence to the claims that our world is changing in some important ways. What makes us think globalization is occurring?

Impressionistic Evidence of Globalization

Most of the evidence offered in existing studies of globalization is impressionistic. A journalist wakes up one morning and realizes that the robe she has just pulled on was made in Guatemala. She investigates other items near her; the sheets on her bed come from Hong Kong, and the pillow from Canada. Struck by the realization that products as common as these are being delivered to her from all over the world, the journalist decides to do a story with this theme. She gets up, starts her coffee-maker designed in Sweden but manufactured in Germany, with beans grown in Brazil, pours it into a mug made in Mexico, sits down at her computer (made mostly in Thailand, but assembled in Taiwan), and begins to write.

A story like this is easy to repeat in different forms. Yet what does this tell us in the end? How scientific are the results? We all recognize how high the percentage of foreign material goods around us is, and for Americans certainly higher than it used to be. On the other hand, some of the key questions we are asking ourselves cannot be answered by these impressionistic descriptions of the goods we consume.

The origins of some things are difficult to ascertain. Where did that lettuce in the refrigerator come from? How about the tennis shoes in the closet? If those shoes are a well-known brand, does the brand name mean anything? Perhaps they are shoes from an American-owned company, but produced somewhere else—how should we think of that good's national origin? What about the car across the street? It may have a European label (reflecting where it was engineered), and even have parts from the U.S. and Germany in it, but be assembled in Mexico. While you might not be surprised to find a car put together that way, you could be surprised to discover your winter coat has a similarly complicated multinational history.

Then there are the more amorphous products we consume, which also have more difficult origins to trace. How about that song you just heard on the radio—was it recorded in the U.S. or Canada? Is there any way you could tell? Or what about a movie or ad you watched on TV last night? These questions lead us to another: Does it matter to you that these products could be of foreign origin?

While Americans may often answer in the negative ("No, it doesn't matter"), the same sentiments may not be held elsewhere. The content of music, films, videos, books, magazines, and other cultural products is a real concern for those who feel the distinctiveness of their local culture is being eroded by the inroads of foreign cultural goods. This issue surfaces regularly not only in France and Canada, but in many other countries. Rapid improvements in technology mean cultural products are more easily shipped or transmitted ever greater distances. Canadians have been concerned about American television programming for several decades now, simply because so much of Canada's population resides within a short distance of the U.S. border. American broadcasts could always reach large Canadian audiences. Now, with satellite TV and Webcasts, these same issues are surfacing elsewhere as American programming reaches greater numbers of people around the world.

Americans may not be so concerned about these cultural issues, because they are the most prolific producers of cultural products. They seem to have little to fear from foreign products in these areas, because their own producers compete so well in these areas. Still, there have been fears expressed at times, as when foreign investors have purchased large American movie studios, or bought up television and newspaper networks. In a democracy, journalism is often considered "the fifth estate" for it plays an important political and social role, including serving as a watchdog on the government. Concerns about how journalists operate are a legitimate political issue, in that sense. Of course, on the other extreme, states that aspired to total control over their societies can hardly accept the widespread penetration of their societies by media from elsewhere, whether it is coming in by the phone, Internet, fax, satellite TV, or the old-fashioned way, mail.[2]

How often do these issues about cultural goods gain in political salience? There are some problems attempting to measure this because we have designated political results as the outcome we wish to explain. But, politicians may develop the rhetoric of cultural defense as part of a particular strategy, regardless of whether globalizing processes have a basis in reality. The same could be said of disputes over trade or foreign investments. Simply because an issue emerges as the basis for political conflict does not mean that the underlying cultural patterns have changed. Instead, it could simply be that people's perceptions of the issue have changed. Since it is clear that globalization has become a hot topic in recent years, we can assume that people's impressions have changed. Impressionistic evidence does abound.

On another front, we might note that many of the definitions provided in the previous chapter emphasized the challenges economic and technological changes pose to state control. Some authors note that globalization contributes to a decline in the popular belief that governments can govern effectively.[3] Politicians wishing to disavow their responsibilities, or at least wishing to discredit certain policy options, use arguments about globalization to support their positions. We therefore need to try to separate out those indicators we can use with some reliability from those which are overly subjective.

Beyond Impressions: Other Qualitative Evidence

Globalization should leave us some indications of its progress that are fairly easy to observe. Moreover, we should be able to find some measures of processes that are largely qualitative in nature, yet are still quantifiable. This would make comparisons across time or across countries easier to execute, and more effective. It would certainly help us decipher when all sides could agree something different is going on, rather than relying on one person, or one group's perceptions or positions. Also, the indicators may provide us some insight into what is happening at the global level itself.

One sign of the growing number of countries open to trade is the number of international agreements aiming to reduce the trade barriers currently in effect. The transformation of GATT into the WTO itself is one such sign. The increasing membership of the WTO is another. Alongside these changes is the growing number of regional agreements aimed at liberalizing trade. The World Bank regularly reports trade data on more than 30 regional organizations these days.[4] By all accounts on this front, the current period is more open than previous decades.

Travellers may also notice how easy it is to cross many borders. This is especially noticeable in the countries of Western Europe. The members of the European Union have dispensed with their border posts. Any traveller with experience of international travel from some 25 years ago would immediately note how much easier it is to cross these borders. But it is also easier to cross other European borders than it used to be, and even those who travelled extensively in the early 1990s would notice the difference today. The end of the Cold War has made it possible to travel much more freely throughout Eastern Europe and Central Asia. Travel in North America has always been fairly open, and this continues to be true. For some sort of numerical measure, we could count the countries an American can enter without a visa. This number has clearly grown in the last 10 years. These patterns may already be reversing, however, in the wake of the terrorist attacks on 11 September 2001.

Likewise, it has become easier for individuals to transfer funds across borders. Two decades ago, travellers had to carry either large amounts of cash, with all the risks involved, or use travellers' cheques. Only a couple of brands of travellers' cheques were widely accepted. Nowadays, automated teller machines (ATMs) make it possible to withdraw money from one's home account in one country in a variety of locations around the globe. Since such machines were relatively rare 20 years ago, any number showing international transactions would have to be a great increase from earlier periods.

These examples could provide some numerical evidence, but the numbers would not carry as much meaning as we might like (nor would they stay accurate for very long). These do provide us with impressions of change over time. But the concepts behind the numerical values are not entirely clear. To get a real grasp on the quantitative evidence, we need to return to our theoretical models, in order to examine more specific indicators to measure globalization. These may overly emphasize the economic aspects of globalization, but since the economic component is central to most of the processes having important political consequences, it is an important place to focus our attention.

The Numbers: The Economic Evidence

Economic flows across borders are among the most quantifiable aspects of globalization. Governments provide many of these statistics, and they have an incentive to track them as most provide a basis for taxation. Traditionally governments have tried to exercise their sovereignty, though not always with success. It is generally agreed that there are three economic facets to globalization: trade, the multinationalization of production, and the internationalization of financial markets.[5] Moreover, most economists would agree that to capture the essence of what is different about today's global economy, it is necessary to examine all these dimensions together.[6] What do government statistics show about flows in these areas?

ARE FINANCIAL FLOWS INCREASING?

Are financial flows more international now than in the past? Have international flows of capital increased in volume and speed in recent years? As many authors note, the most commonly held view of globalization is that international financial flows have accelerated and grown in volume in recent years. When we turn to the political consequences of globalization, international capital markets are often cast as the villain, since they are portrayed as imposing powerful constraints on government policy.[7] To what extent, then, is globalization of finance occurring?

As the numbers below indicate, the answer is a strong affirmative. An undeniable trend in the most basic indicators points to lower barriers between national financial systems in the last 20 years. Global foreign exchange trading was negligible in the early 1950s. In those days, foreign exchange purchases were primarily to finance trade in goods and services. By the early 1990s, it had reached a startling $1 trillion per day—some 40 times the value of daily trade flows.[8] Money was being traded as a good itself. By this time, the gross value of international capital flows was $600 billion, or twice the size of aggregate global current account imbalances.

The amount of cash moving over borders each day is not the only important measure of financial activity, but the first in a string we must take. What are the economic consequences of these greater financial flows across borders? Here there is much less agreement, since the answer will depend on one's assumptions and models. Popular impressions are that international finance plays a largely disruptive role. It punishes those firms or countries where workers earn higher wages, and flees from those countries where governments are generous in their social policies.

Plenty of economists are skeptical of the arguments that international investments are now proceeding at such a high rate that they detract from investment and jobs in the economically advanced countries. Is capital flowing so strongly from these countries in order to find cheap labour and less stringent legal strictures in less advanced countries as to jeopardize their own stability? Paul Krugman notes that the highest levels of international investments in the early 1990s were reached in 1993 when $100 billion was invested by the most industrialized countries in the economically developing countries of the South. Yet this was a drop in the bucket in terms of overall investment. The combined GNP of the U.S., Canada, Japan, and Western Europe was approximately $18 trillion. Combined investment in these areas was $3.5 trillion. Existing capital stocks in the industrialized countries totaled some $60 trillion. How could these capital flows to the South, accounting for only 3 per cent of these countries' annual investments, be expected to have much affect? An additional $100 billion invested in the Northern economies would only add to its existing capital stocks in a meager way—less than .2 per cent. If people in the economically advanced countries want to look for a diversion of capital away from investment in national economic resources, they should compare the size of the capital flows to economically developing countries with the size of their own governments' deficits.[9]

Economists have developed several tests or measures to get a feel for how much capital is invested internationally, and whether these levels are changing. The most surprising thing these tests tend to show is what a small amount of total investments are in fact international. The Feldstein-Horioka test was first developed and executed in 1980 by Martin Feldstein and Charles Horioka.[10] The test simply measures the percentage of assets investors hold abroad. The findings in 1980 illustrated a very strong "home bias" in investments. Overwhelming, citizens held investments within their own borders, though later applications of the test do tend to show a slight decrease in this bias over time.[11]

When we consider the equity capital held by individuals, it is usually concentrated in domestic firms. For instance, in the late 1980s, Americans held 98 per cent of their equity investments in American companies. As Bill Watson warns, "Lest that be ascribed to American know-nothing-ness or xenophobia, in Sweden the equivalent number was 100%; in Italy, 91%; in Japan, 86.7%; in the United Kingdom, 78.5%; and in Germany, 75.4%."[12]

Using similar analyses we can disaggregate some of these findings, to see if informational barriers might be responsible for the results. We might expect individual investors, who lack the adequate resources to research and interpret information about foreign investment opportunities, therefore to be shy about investing abroad. These same attributes would not be an accurate characterization of institutional investors. Institutional investors are some of the biggest players in financial markets. Institutional investors' holdings of foreign securities are surprisingly small, however. Table 4.1 illustrates the low percentages of their holdings composed of foreign assets. (We might note, however, that sometimes there are legal limits to the amount such investors can invest abroad—though investors do not seem to be straining to reach these limits. A case in point might be the figures on personal retirement accounts in Canada, where the legal limit in 2001 was 30 per cent).

If we examine another category of knowledgeable investors, who should be at the forefront of financial globalization, there are again surprisingly small levels of international holdings. In this case, the figures are for assets and liabilities of commercial banks. We often think of banks as being extremely involved in international investment, but these figures paint a different picture.

Perhaps the most interesting aspect of these figures is the disparity between the numbers from various states. Some countries' banking sectors are strongly involved in international business: Britain, the

TABLE 4.1	FOREIGN SECURITIES IN INSTITUTIONAL INVESTORS' HOLDINGS, 1993 (%)
U.S. private pension funds	7.1
U.S. mutual funds	8.0
Japanese postal life insurance	12.3
Japanese private insurance companies	22.3
Canadian life insurance companies	3.1
Canadian pension funds	10.6
Italian insurance companies	12.2
Australian life insurance companies	18.8
Austrian insurance companies	9.9
Austrian investment funds	25.1
Dutch insurance companies	26.0
Dutch private pension funds	36.9
Dutch public pension funds	20.2

SOURCE: M. Edey and K. Huiding, *An Assessment of Financial Reform in OECD Countries*, OECD Economics Department, *Working Paper #154* (Paris: OECD, 1995).

Netherlands, and France stand out. Those of others, such as Japan and the United States, are much less involved in international business. The impact on these countries of their outward investments are likewise going to be quite different.

So far we have been examining only percentages of investment at home and abroad. The eye-catching figures these days concern the amount of money crossing borders. As mentioned earlier, the sheer volume that goes over a border in a single day was an eye-popping $620 billion in 1989. That rate has grown 30 per cent per year in the early 1990s, so that by 1995 the daily turnover was amounting to $1.3 trillion.[13] Foreign bond loans also grew at a dramatic pace. In the late 1950s, these stood at perhaps $1 billion. By the early 1980s, the total reached $1.3 trillion.

TABLE 4.2	FOREIGN ASSETS AND LIABILITIES AS % OF COMMERCIAL BANK HOLDINGS, 1996	
	Assets	*Liabilities*
France	30.9	30.2
Germany	16.0	12.9
Japan	13.8	10.6
Netherlands	33.2	34.1
United Kingdom	47.0	48.8
United States	2.6	8.2

SOURCE: IMF *International Financial Statistics Yearbook 1997*, Table 7.11, as cited in Paul Hirst and Grahame Thompson, *Globalization in Question: The International Economy and the Possibilities of Governance*, 2nd ed. (Cambridge: Polity Press, 1999), 46.

The potential for such large volumes of exchange transactions to cause disruptions, more than any actual damage having occurred, prompts people's fears. There is undoubtedly an "increasing interpenetration of national monetary spaces," to use Benjamin Cohen's terminology.[14] And, as he argues, this creates market forces that affect how currencies are managed, which in turn has an impact on other facets of economic policy. These indirect effects are quite difficult to measure. One area where people see damage occurring, however, is in exchange rate volatility.

The rapid increase in the volume of financial flows is both a product and a cause of exchange rate volatility. Since floating exchange rates were widely adopted in the 1970s, profits could be made through short-term arbitrage. However, as money was switched from one currency to another, it can also drive exchange rate changes—thus the increased volume is both cause and effect, in most peoples' eyes. Exchange rate volatility is not as much of a problem for the most economically advanced countries, or for those countries that do not rely on international trade. Even those that do rely on trade may be less sensitive to these changes, if their products are not particularly price sensitive. Most economically developing countries, however, have struggled in the last 10 years to limit the volatility of their currency's value.[15]

Yet, what is the impact of such transactions on the rest of the economy? The exchange rate may be affected, but since arbitrage usually involves transactions both into and out of currencies, the net effect over the long-term—or in this case even over the medium-term—may be negligible. If these transactions do not increase the long-term stock of capital or productive capacity of states, how important are they? Few people seem to think that exchange rate volatility has somehow limited trade or investment. The potential for international financial crises may be on the rise, however, particularly when exchange rate volatility is combined with poor regulation of the financial system within countries, as in East Asia in the late 1990s.

CAPITAL FLOWS AS A CONSTRAINT ON OTHER POLICIES

Has liberalization of capital markets constrained states in the policies they might adopt? Capital markets are often blamed for policy convergence and the "race to the bottom" in both regulation and state services—the argument put forward by those on the left of the political spectrum. The mechanisms linking such phenomena are not always very clear, however.[16] A closer inspection of the decision-making mechanisms that tie these results together tends not to support such claims. Instead, the evidence will indicate that governments still have choices—something closer to the thinking of the modern Keynesians. Globalization matters because although governments may still adopt whatever policies they wish, globalizing processes have altered the costs associated with those choices. Globalization of finance may be re-configuring the costs and benefits of some policies, but it has not eliminated choices. Variation in state activity should be observable, in contrast to the convergence expected by Marxists and others.

One pivotal mechanism is "capital flight." Liberalization of international capital markets provides the owners of capital the option of exiting a country as a reaction to the adoption of a new policy. If they don't withdraw their capital, they may simply charge a higher price for its use in the country after the new policy is implemented. But, the range of policies that capital markets react to is surprising small.[17] Layna Mosley used both statistical examinations and interviews with investment advisers to identify which policies trigger changes in interest rates or capital flight.

International liberalization has had some curious side effects, she discovered. Since it is costly to gather information from a variety of sources in standardized (i.e., comparable) form, and then analyze it, it turns out that an increase in the number of countries that investors deal with has led to a reduction in the number of economic indicators tracked.[18]

(Information is a function of the number of countries considered and the number of statistics tracked; therefore an increase in the former leads to a reduction in the latter, in practice.) According to Mosley's research on the economically advanced countries, most investors appear to pay little attention to fiscal policy. When they do pay close attention to it, they do not break it down into its various components, or examine details of fiscal policy. Mosley concludes that one of the mechanisms often fingered by the opponents of globalization—the pressures generated by liberalized international capital markets causing governments to reduce their fiscal outlays, and therefore putting downward pressure on Keynesian practices— is unlikely to be as strong as supposed.[19]

At the same time, there seems to be a much wider consensus that capital controls have become obsolete. Capital controls were once quite widespread. In the years after World War II, just about every country used them, including the economically advanced nation-states. The tide turned in the late 1970s, when the United States and Britain removed their most significant restrictions on capital flows. Capital controls among the OECD members had already eroded significantly. The move by the U.S. and Britain then drove other industrialized countries to follow suit in the 1980s.[20] After that, most other countries removed their capital controls in the 1990s. It appeared to many observers that states held little choice in the matter, since almost all adopted the same rules.

Economist Sebastian Edwards has challenged this orthodoxy. He has examined several examples where in recent years economically developing countries have employed capital controls. Malaysia, in the wake of the East Asian financial crisis, adopted controls on capital outflows in 1998. It was widely expected that these would discourage future capital inflows. However, since Malaysia experienced fewer disruptions than its neighbours in this financial crisis, the gains may outweigh the losses.

Edwards focuses more intently on Chile's experience.[21] Chile employed controls on capital inflows between 1991 and 1998. Chile used taxes and deposit requirements to discourage the short-term inflows we associate with currency arbitrage. These flows can be large and destabilizing, so such a policy may make sense. The negative side effect can be to discourage foreigners from engaging in long-term investments, however. Edwards finds that the effectiveness of these controls has been exaggerated, but they may have helped lengthen the average term of foreign investments. Moreover, they may have provided some insulation from the smaller volatility typical on a day-to-day basis. The controls Chile used could not really cushion it from the impact of the East Asian financial meltdown, however. And there may have been some unanticipated costs, since the controls added to the cost of capital, which may have hurt smaller domestic businesses. That may have been an acceptable cost for gaining greater macroeconomic stability.

Let us turn to consider patterns of long-term investments, by themselves. Then we can consider some other economic indicators of globalization, before trying to trace the consequences of these different elements of international capital markets together.

HAVE FOREIGN DIRECT INVESTMENTS INCREASED DRAMATICALLY?

By definition, foreign direct investment (FDI) involves the direct ownership by foreigners of productive assets in another country. The general impression one gets in the literature on globalization is that FDI has also increased substantially over the last decade or two. Yet do figures support this? It is well established, as well, that FDI first grew in importance in the years after World War II. Has this growth accelerated recently? Has FDI concentrated in particular areas? Has it changed in terms of where it goes, or where it comes from? Can it be blamed for job losses in the economically advanced countries, as some on the left claim? Does it have positive effects on the host countries, as liberals assert?

There now exist more than 46,000 parent multinational companies (MNCs), with up to 280,000 subsidiaries or affiliates in other countries. These numbers are an impressive growth over previous decades. Multinational firms control a stock of foreign direct investment worth an estimated $3.2 trillion in 1996. Their combined annual sales have been estimated at $7 trillion.[22] Moreover, they often control important sectors of the economy. MNCs are especially active in the production of complex products (such as aircraft) and high-end consumer items (such as computers or automobiles).

Foreign direct investment is also much more concentrated among the economically advanced countries.[23] In other words, FDI is overwhelmingly comprised of investments originating in one economically advanced country and placed in another economically advanced country. Only some 8 per cent of FDI originates in less economically developed countries.[24] While this is a higher amount than previously, it shows how much FDI remains a flow between the economically advanced countries.

When we look at the receiving end of FDI, the figures also are concentrated. Many people are surprised to find out that international investment is primarily from economically advanced countries and most of it is placed within other economically advanced countries. Economists who specialize in this area often express concerns that in the future international investors are more likely to ignore the poorest countries— not swamp them with capital from the outside.

Another economic trend that has captured public attention is the increase in multi-national production. Many goods have their roots spread across a number of countries When we are interested in the multinationalization of production, we want to address FDI. Often we hear arguments about production being moved overseas, as firms pursue low-wage workers, or seek to evade taxes. This is an essential element of the picture drawn by Marxists and others when they argue that capital is escaping the control of national governments, or is in a position to bargain down legal restrictions on its activities.

Yet we should also recognize that FDI's impact on the economically developed countries will be much weaker than its impact on less economically developed countries. Though FDI was concentrated on the developed countries, this inward flow of capital equalled only 9.1 per cent of these countries' GDPs. For Eastern and Central Europe, the level was even lower (4.9 per cent), but in the less economically developed countries, it was 15.4 per cent.[25] It can hardly be claimed, then, that foreign direct investment is radically altering the way the developed countries do business internally. The amount of investment is simply too small to be driving changes in their practices.

Another economic aspect of MNCs' activities is that it influences the nature of trade in a number of ways that are not always obvious. First, MNC activity is often thought of as a substitute for trade. Instead of producing goods at home and exporting them to foreign markets, MNCs invest abroad, shifting production to the markets they had once exported to. This is why FDI is related to issues of employment and job insecurity. Those who view capital as "footloose" see FDI as a cause for damage to the domestic economy of the home country directly, but also see indirect damage through an impact on the home country's balance of trade.

Second, when MNCs engage in trade, it is really a transfer of products or goods between subsidiaries. Their trade therefore shapes the content and value of trade. Integrated multinational production means transferring intermediate goods (i.e., inputs for other products) across national boundaries. As much as 80 per cent of American trade, for instance, is probably handled by MNCs, with half of that being between branches of the same MNC.[26] When two subsidiaries of an MNC engage in international trade, the goods are not really being traded on a market. The valuation of the good is set by the firm's headquarters, not by supply and demand. Instead, issues such as tax differences or stock valuation drive the headquarters' calculations.

As noted above, many worry that MNCs escape regulation. Some see this as actors escaping democratic accountability.[27] Several recent studies, however, suggest that MNCs remain largely rooted to one or two countries. If one examines where an MNC's headquarters activities are located, or where its research and development takes place, the answer is almost always in a single country; very rarely are such activities dispersed across several countries.[28] It may make more sense, therefore, to regulate MNCs' global activities from their home countries.

Moreover, many firms wish to retain a national flavour. It may be part of their corporate identity, which ties American cultural attributes to their products' images, such as Coca-Cola, Marlboro cigarettes, or Levis. Or, there could be more strategic calculations going on. Access to the largest pool of American dollars—which remains the most important medium of international exchange—is still critical for many firms. U.S. government agencies such as the FDA or the FAA set technical standards that are then employed elsewhere, so being a firm thought of as primarily "American" may give the firm a privileged position in shaping those standards. U.S. power may also help protect the firm's international property. If the firm can appeal to the U.S. government, or even to U.S. courts, it has a powerful tool for protecting its assets abroad. Finally, U.S. government expenditures, particularly in the area of defence procurement, subsidizes research and development.[29]

On the other end of the equation, governments can use the MNCs' desire to maintain a national identity against them. A company that desires to have an American or a Canadian identity could hardly hope to move its key decision-making functions to another country. If the high-end operations remain in a single country, that gives the government of that country leverage in regulation. As Hirst and Thompson conclude, "the extent of internationalization and its potential detrimental consequences for the regulation of MNC activity and for national economies is severely exaggerated."[30]

There are two points to conclude from these pieces of evidence. MNCs have grown in number and their impact on trade patterns and the location of employment has undoubtedly increased. Second, MNCs are not entirely "footloose and fancy-free." They can move operations to various locations, yet by and large each corporation has strong roots in one or two particular countries—and these ties may be harder to break. Regulation is still quite possible, even if many states are currently declining to take up the challenge. This leaves open the possibility that MNCs may be more effectively regulated in the future.

HAVE TRADE FLOWS RISEN IN RECENT YEARS?

As in the impressionistic story told above, one of the most visible signs of globalization is the greater number of goods we use every day that come from other countries. Among the industrialized countries of the west, trade has been liberalized for even longer than has international finance. Economists have been studying the impact of trade on jobs and welfare for much longer than they have studied the impact of investment or communication. What globalizing processes are at work in trade? What does the evidence indicate? Have things changed in the last decade or two?

In the U.S., any discussion of globalization triggers fear that the American economy is growing weaker. Despite record high levels of employment, a soaring stock market, a strong currency, and many other positive economic indicators, the American public is puzzled by the country's continued trade deficit. If American firms are leaders in technology, and American workers are highly skilled, why can't they sell more goods than they buy internationally? Something isn't right, most Americans feel. The answer many accept is that American wages are too high compared to elsewhere. They therefore conclude that trade causes American jobs to be lost.

Paul Krugman has also challenged this reading of economic statistics. The burgeoning trade deficit in the U.S. can be accounted for by other means. As he puts it, it is a basic accounting fact that savings minus investment will equal the imbalance between exports and imports. In other words, America's failure to save accounts for its ability to import so much more than it should.[31] Krugman would also add that the focus on job-creation or job-loss generated by trade is incorrect. Trade has an impact, certainly, but it is only one factor among many.[32] This is a theme to which we will return. To judge whether globalization is really having the impact alleged, we need to consider possible alternative explanations for the patterns of evidence we can identify.

Some feel Krugman may be on the wrong track. Ethan Kapstein, for one, contests whether Krugman's intuition regarding the impact of imports from less economically developed countries is convincing. Though small, the amount of imports of low-wage countries could create ripples in the economy through multiplier effects. For a comparison, Kapstein points to how small oil imports appear, yet oil-price hikes have strong effects on the rest of the economy.[33]

Every year since World War II, trade has risen at a *faster* rate than overall economic output. According to WTO statistics, world merchandise output between 1950 and 1994 has multiplied 5.5 times, while trade has increased 14 times. Total real output has grown at 3.8 per cent on average, while total real exports have grown at 5.8 per cent on average. The numbers can be broken down further, by OECD and less economically developed countries. For OECD countries, real output grew by 3.5 per cent on average, while trade grew by 5.3 per cent. For less economically developed countries, the same percentages are 4.9 per cent and 6.9 per cent.[34]

Of course, it is important to remember that this trade is primarily concentrated among the economically advanced countries. Despite confusion about the relationship between trade and interdependence, it may be that trade has increased in volume but interdependence hasn't changed all that much. Most American or Canadian imports are not composed of items that have to be purchased from another country. These countries' imports include clothing, cars, shoes, and food brought in to compete against locally produced items.

In the nineteenth century or earlier, most trade was an actual exchange of very different goods. The less economically developed countries exported raw materials, and imported finished goods they could not actually produce. The industrialized countries imported raw materials they had in only short supply, and exported the goods only they could produce. This picture may be an accurate depiction of trade a century ago (as we shall see in Chapter 8), but it is no longer an appropriate depiction of today's trade.

Partly, this reflects advances in productivity generated by technologies that require fewer raw materials to produce the same amount goods, for example, the switch from copper wires to optic fibres. Optic fibres require fewer raw materials, but can carry much more information.[35] Since economically developing countries have historically relied on raw materials exports (or the export of lightly processed raw materials), their role in trade has actually declined over recent decades.

Second, as the economically advanced countries have gotten richer, the role of preferences and tastes seems to come into play to a greater extent. Most simple economic models of trade make assumptions that eliminate the impact of preferences. But people are often willing to purchase a good made somewhere else simply because they like the look or style of the product. Automobiles are made in all the industrially advanced countries, and exported to the others. This sort of intra-good trade cannot be explained through simple models of trade. Yet it comprises the bulk of trade among the most economically advanced countries, and that trade in turn dwarfs the volume of trade between the economically less-developed countries and the developed countries.

Trade levels originally rose in the 1960s and 1970s, in the wake of liberalizing agreements concluded in GATT. Other states joined GATT and its successor, the WTO. Hence, more countries are participating in liberalized trade than before. More countries are feeling the impact of trade. That impression seems to be the most important change in recent years. Yet the true impact of this development is harder to gauge than one might expect.

One of the generally feared steps in the processes leading to the "race to the bottom" is that higher levels of trade generate disruptive side-effects. The most common version of this thesis focuses on the impact of the pursuit of international competitiveness on state policies. The fear is that as governments try to enhance the competitiveness of their constituents, they will reduce the role of the state. This is one potential link between globalization and the decline of the Keynesian welfare state, as the Marxists expect. Dani Rodrik, among others, points out that such fears seem ungrounded from the perspective of the new century. If you look at the experience of the OECD members over the last 30 years or more, exposure to trade and greater government role in the economy are positively correlated.[36] As one grows, so does the other—or, as Rodrik puts it, "the social welfare state has been the flip side of the open economy." This confirms the images laid out by the Keynesian liberals: increases in trade generate greater economic benefits, allowing states to tax and to compensate those hurt by trade.

At the same time, Rodrik agrees that the fears expressed by opponents of globalization have merit. Free trade among countries with different domestic practices can lead to the erosion of these differences. The question is really how such changes might take place—through deliberate policy harmonization, or convergence driven less consciously by markets.[37] There will be changes in domestic practices, but it doesn't have to be in one direction only. Moreover, Rodrik's own statistical evidence is general in character. He illustrates that those countries most engaged in trade (the economically advanced countries) also have well-established social services. There is little in his work that shows that the specific groups hurt by trade are being compensated proportionately, but later work by Brian

Burgoon and others indicates some support for the political mechanisms Rodrik lays out.[38]

There are reasons to think the changes that may come about would increase government supports and intervention rather than reduce it. First, it may be that the states compensating those whose interests are damaged by trade will come out ahead competitively in the long run. If compensation brings greater political and economic stability, including less labour unrest, then there might be ways in which compensation leads to competitiveness. Likewise, programs such as national health care might help keep the overall growth in medical expenditures down. If this is the case (the evidence is mixed, though), there might be important long-term competitive advantages for businesses that operate in countries with national health care programs.

Second, it may be that the pressure for competitiveness leads to the creation of political institutions and practices that help reduce rents. We have already seen that economic competition can be the impetus behind positive political economic changes. Such changes help increase the efficiency (and some might even say the fairness) of domestic political economy. Ronald Rogowski argued that democracies that rely heavily on trade are more likely to adopt institutions that shield policy-makers from pressures for economic rents.[39] When government institutions allow narrow interest groups great influence in shaping policy, the government tends to adopt policies that sanction the capturing of rents—broader societal interests are not heard. This redistribution of income leads to distortions in the economy and additional costs to others—exactly the sort of thing that makes those who are *not* capturing rents less competitive internationally. Rogowski argued that democracies reliant on trade would construct political institutions that deflected these narrow interest groups' demands. They would be expected to employ parliamentary systems (rather than presidential), proportional representation (rather than single-member districts), and establish large constituencies (rather than small). Each of these practices forces elected officials to answer to a larger number of constituents. As mentioned before, this has led some scholars to anticipate globalization's impact. Higher levels of trade could generate political dynamics with positive side effects. But are such dynamics actually unfolding?

Frances McCall Rosenbluth and Miriam Golden have made precisely such arguments about two separate countries. Rosenbluth has pointed out how deeper integration of Japan's smaller businesses into international markets in the 1990s has made them less tolerant of those who received rents via government policy.[40] The special treatment some sectors received meant higher costs for others—either because the price of inputs was artificially lifted, or because the state collected taxes and redistributed funds to the privileged sectors. Small businesses, needing to compete in international markets, could no longer afford to support these policies. A similar story is told by Golden about Italy in the 1990s.[41]

Rogowski originally had examined evidence limited to the OECD countries in the 1970s. Evaluations of more recent evidence suggest that his findings continue to hold for the OECD countries he had looked at earlier. Extending the analysis to the 15 democracies that have emerged from the former Soviet bloc, there is a high correlation between trade dependence and the use of proportional representation. A second statistic is the relationship between the number of legislative constituencies and trade dependence.[42] Again, for the democracies that have emerged from the former Soviet Union and its allies, the relationship is positive (as Rogowski would have predicted). The same findings do not hold across all democracies, however. Among the less economically developed democracies, no clear relationship seems to emerge from trade dependence and the variety of democratic institutions.

As these discussions show, increased trade can have several different impacts. It can increase pressures for democratization. It can also increase inequality of wealth, as it more sharply divides winners and losers in the economy. It can generate greater returns for society as a whole, making it possible for the state to increase revenues through taxation—possibly enabling the state to redress economic inequality. Alone, we cannot say much about the impact of rising trade, though we can recognize how trade has indeed increased in volume in recent years. To be assured of the political consequences of these changes, we need to understand how any political pressures may be filtered through various political settings. This theme will be developed in more detail in later chapters. First, we need to examine one more set of transnational flows that could play an important role in how globalization proceeds.

CHANGES IN FLOWS OF LABOUR

There is one area where globalization does not appear to be proceeding: the movement of labour over borders. Almost everywhere, the trend has been in the opposite direction. It has become increasingly difficult for people to cross borders as freely as they want to pursue economic desires. Watson argues "As far as labour mobility is concerned, it is hard not to conclude we are actually in a period of *de*globalization."[43]

While the international movement of capital has been liberalized greatly in the last quarter of the twentieth century, the movement of workers has not.[44] Take, for instance, a fairly liberal estimate of the number of people crossing international borders. S. Castles and M.J. Miller estimated that in 1993, there were as many as 100 million migrants in the world, if one includes all possible categories (refugees, migrant workers, etc.). This most generous estimate is equal to only 1.7 per cent of the world's population.[45] Yet as others point out, the greatest period of voluntary mass migration was undoubtedly the late nineteenth century and the first decade of the twentieth.

How does international migration currently take place? As are other international flows—of communication, goods or capital—most of it is regional in character, not global.[46] Migrant flows are concentrated towards North America, the Arab states, and Western Europe. While we might judge the other economic processes central in most descriptions of globalization to be concentrated among the most economically advanced countries, labour flows are in fact much more North-South in character. They represent a flow of labour from poorer countries to richer, with portions of the new wages often being remitted back to the poorer nations.

Perhaps more than any of the other areas we are considering, immigration may be influenced by a wider range of factors and of policies. Flows of people across borders are affected by a "web of other processes," including investment patterns, regional policies, trade patterns, security relations between states, employment levels, social welfare policies, citizenship rules, and so on.[47]

The political consequences of labour inflows may cause some people to become concerned when a great number of people with different religious or cultural traditions enter their country. In places such as Canada, Australia, or the United States, these tensions may not be as great, since most living in these countries trace their own heritage to immigrants. Countries where ethnicity or religion plays a central role in national identification may have more trouble accommodating newcomers. For the most part, Canadians view immigrants as additions to an already mixed society. The model most often espoused is that of a cultural mosaic, a mélange of differing customs that contrast and complement each other. Americans, on the other hand, speak of the "melting pot" where people from different backgrounds accept the dominant culture and subordinate their ethnic cultural differences to it. Thus, the children of immigrants to the U.S. view themselves as Americans first and foremost, and tend to lose more rapidly their ties with the country of their parents' origin.

Economically, labour inflows can have important ramifications. Many industrialized countries have experienced declining birth rates. As their populations age, the younger generations appear to be smaller, or simply maintaining population levels. Improvements in the medical field have extended life expectancy, allowing many more people to survive into old age. Since governments in industrialized societies have developed old-age pension schemes, the costs of these programs is going to grow considerably in the future—just at the time that the numbers of workers paying in to them will be flattening out or even falling. Concerns with the funding of these programs have captured political headlines for years.

In the U.S. and Canada, these pressures are actually lower than in other industrialized countries. Immigration is a key factor, since immigrants immediately add to the existing workforce. Immigrant families tend to have more children. These fresh inflows help to keep the average age in the population lower. This in turn makes the existing social programs easier to maintain. In Germany and Japan, two countries lacking a tradition of open immigration, old-age support schemes will have to be altered dramatically in the future. Immigration can have a very positive economic impact, even as many might argue that inflows of low-skilled workers undercut labour's wages in industrialized countries.

Finally, labour flows can directly influence the labour market. Labour is flowing to the very countries that lack unskilled workers compared to other productive factors: the scarcely populated, oil-rich countries of the Middle East and the industrialized countries of Western Europe and North America. In the Middle East, oil revenues help to pay immigrant workers. Western Europe and North America are rich in both capital and skilled labour, but relatively lacking in unskilled labour. (Remember, in these economic models, we are interested in looking at the ratio of these factors to each other, not the absolute amounts.)

Historically, immigration has added to the pool of unskilled labour. By increasing the supply, it usually reduces the wages these workers can earn. This can reduce the growth in wages of more skilled labour over time. The exact impact of immigration is difficult to discern, however, because its economic impact must be disentangled from the influence of general economic conditions, trade, and all the other factors that shape wages.

Compared to the other areas we have examined in this chapter, we can see that labour flows seem to be the least affected by globalization. Labour flows are not nearly as large (in percentage terms) as they once were. Rules limiting the movement of people over borders are not only strong, but they are being strengthened in many places. The flows that have taken place tend to be concentrated on a handful of rich countries. The impact of labour flows may also be quite different from one country to another, depending on existing economic conditions, its future needs, and its political settings. Our various paradigms are less useful for letting us understand this variation.

SUMMARY: EVIDENCE OF ECONOMIC GLOBALIZATION

Some have looked at these figures and concluded that globalization is less fact than fiction. Consider the position taken by Paul Hirst and Grahame Thompson: "as we proceeded our scepticism deepened until we became convinced that globalization, as conceived by the more extreme globalizers, is largely a myth." Hirst and Thompson took on the claims of globalization on five points.[48] First, the internationalization of the economy was not entirely unprecedented, they concluded, since the levels of international investment and trade of the 1870-1914 period were equally high. Second, evidence indicates genuinely transnational corporations remain fairly rare. Third, there is little evidence that higher capital mobility across borders actually causes investment and jobs to move from the economically advanced countries to the less economically developed ones. Fourth, trade and investment are still concentrated on the OECD countries, and in that sense are not "global" at all. Fifth—and something we have yet to explore—the U.S., the European Union, and Japan can, if they co-operate successfully, influence global markets, thereby achieving some sense of governance over the international economy.

Before we turn to questions about how well states can respond to the challenges of globalization and examine some of the political consequences more closely, we have considered some pieces of evidence regarding whether or not the chief elements of globalizing processes have really been growing in recent times. Our short look at communication patterns, trade, and capital flows tells us that the most economically advanced countries have in fact been experiencing some important changes in these areas. Trade and communication have been growing for some time. Capital flows have surged in recent years—though some parts of the financial systems of all countries remain surprisingly insulated from each other. These different forces have the potential to create the destabilizing consequences people fear from globalization, though the degree or pace of change does not seem to have reached critical levels yet.

Politics enters in two ways. The first is a recognition that globalizing processes are beginning to be felt. They are nowhere near the levels people often assume, however. That means we may be at the first stages of a longer process, in which we are in a position to make decisions about how these changes may proceed. We therefore need to evaluate the possible positive and negative aspects of globalization as we investigate further, in order to link these changes both with globalization's supporters and with its opponents.

Second, it is already apparent that the expectations we draw from the economic and social processes at work are very sensitive to political circumstances. Different political institutions will respond to these pressures differently; interests will be changed by globalization, but how those changes are expressed will vary considerably. Therefore, it is incumbent upon us to focus on the political dimensions of globalization, if we are to anticipate correctly the reactions likely to emerge, and if we are to make intelligent decisions about the future.

Rival Interpretations for Current Economic Changes

We must recognize also that some of the changes observed within societies that are blamed on globalization could be generated by different forces. Inequality can be produced by labour flows, but it would be foolish to conclude that all inequality can be explained by immigration. Much the same can be said for the other political and economic outcomes associated with globalization. Reductions in government services, changes in economic regulations, and other outcomes may be explained more effectively through consideration of other powerful political economic pressures.

EXPLAINING SHIFTS IN EMPLOYMENT

The most promising rival explanation for some of these economic patterns focuses on another powerful economic change sweeping across the most economically advanced countries: the shift from an industrial economy to one based on services. The most persuasive exponent of this view is Torben Iversen. Iversen and his co-authors have provided powerful arguments that some of the patterns of political economic change the opponents of globalization focus on really are caused by underlying changes within economies.

One of the more interesting arguments comes from Iversen and Anne Wren. They note that in the economically advanced countries, three common arguments about globalization are heard. First, global capital markets constrain the government's abilities to guide the economy. Second, pressures to attract and maintain foreign direct investment cause convergence in many social policies as states deregulate in "a race to the bottom." Finally, higher levels of trade allow into the country goods produced by cheap labour in the less economically developed countries, thus putting downward pressure on wages. But as Iversen and Wren see it, globalization is overemphasized in these complaints. The real culprit is the general shift in employment from manufacturing to services in the OECD countries. Fewer people are employed in factories, and more in restaurants and other parts of the service sector. This shift should be credited/blamed with the changes in labour markets, rather than any great surge in globalization.[49]

Similarly, Iversen argues with co-author Thomas Cusack that "most of the risks being generated in modern industrialized societies are the product of technologically induced structural transformations inside national labour markets."[50] Central to their argument is that the amount of labour working in both the agricultural and industrial sectors of the economy is on the decline throughout the economically advanced countries. Governments are responding to this shift with three different combinations of policies. First, some countries promote employment in the private service sector by deregulating product and labour markets. The government offers some compensation packages to ease adjustment out of economically declining industries, but these are limited in size and scope. The United States, Britain, and Canada have followed such a mix of policies. While these countries have been able to raise employment, inequality in wages has increased.

A second set of policies employed in response to the shift of employment out of agriculture and industry emphasizes a very different set of choices. Instead of deregulating private services, these countries have chosen to keep this sector regulated. Employment has been boosted through growth in the public sector. This is the pattern seen in Scandinavia. This mix of policies keeps wages from diverging, and employment levels are maintained.

The third mix of policies in response to the decline in employment in agriculture and industry emphasizes a stronger reliance on regulation than the previous two. The state attempts to heavily regulate labour and product markets, and winds up blocking the expansion of the service sector. A variety of techniques, such as shorter work weeks, early retirement, and other techniques are used to deal with employment concerns. The result, however, is for higher unemployment, and pressures building for greater inequality. This mix of policies is found in countries such as France and Germany.

Iversen and Cusack can describe these patterns, and offer explanations for them, based on domestic labour market practices and government regulatory patterns. Trade, international capital flows, or other globalizing forces do not come into play. They proceed to seek to correlate these patterns of response with variations in national ties to the international economy, but find little of obvious use. Therefore Iversen and Cusack conclude that greater openness to the international economy plays an insignificant role in their story. Rising inequality and persistent unemployment come more from the structural shift to a service economy—as well as how governments are responding to these changes—rather than from globalization, in their view.[51]

Those on the left of the political spectrum do not ignore such changes in the character of economies, but instead see these alterations working alongside the impact of globalization. As Boyer and Drache describe globalization, it causes the decline of older style "Fordist" mass production/assembly line industries. "Fordist" is a term employed by those from a more Marxist tradition, to describe the industrialized economies of the twentieth century. Henry Ford developed not only a new product, but a new model for stabilizing the economy when he introduced the Model T automobile. The Model T was mass-produced by assembly line, and for such a low cost that Ford's own workers could afford to buy it. The result was a stable economic system, where workers consumed their own production. Yet that stability seems to have ended, perhaps due to competition from globalization, or as part of this general shift towards employment in the service sector. As Boyer and Drache argue, "the painful restructuring of Fordist industries has left a void which the rapid growth of the service sector has not been able to fill."[52]

RIVAL EXPLANATIONS FOR REDUCTIONS IN GOVERNMENT SERVICES

On another front, it is easy to recognize that governments in the West, in order to deliver benefits to constituents, ran up considerable debts. States lived beyond their means by borrowing. In Canada, the federal government's debt rose from 11 per cent of GDP in 1981 to 49 per cent in 1991.[53] More broadly, net public debt as a proportion of GDP in the developed world shows that the level Canada hit was comparatively high, but not nearly the highest among OECD members, and certainly was not a unique experience. That same year (1991), Denmark, France and Germany recorded levels in the 20-30 per cent range, while the U.S. and Britain were in the 30-35 per cent range. The figure for the Netherlands was 55.9 per cent, while Italy hit 102.7 per cent, but Belgium was even more heavily indebted with 121.3 per cent. Japan was an outlier in the other direction, with a meagre 5.9 per cent.[54] If government spending on the welfare state was *based* on such high levels of borrowing, it is clear that the upper levels of borrowing were unsustainable in the long run.

Another way to consider these figures is that governments were trusted with very large debts by investors. Investors only limited governments' borrowing when debt reached levels thought to be unsustainable. They would be unsustainable when governments would not be able to raise taxes high enough to pay back those debts. According to Carles Boix, given the high level of accumulated debts plus the economic challenges of promoting investments, governments faced two broad alternatives. On the one hand, they could reduce taxes in hopes that extra money in the public's hands would encourage savings, directly add to investments, and also accelerate growth. With fewer revenues, however, the government would have to reduce welfare expenditures, thereby purchasing more growth and investment at the cost of higher inequality.

On the other hand, governments could increase their spending on human and fixed capital (i.e., education), as well as infrastructure. Investment would be supported by these additional government expenditures, so investments would continue even as tax rates remained high or even grew. The choice between these two broad strategies, Boix argues, comes down to ideological preferences more than anything else.[55] The choice of political party remains important, even in globalized national economies, because room to manoeuvre still exists. Parties represent packages of policy choices.

> As a matter of fact, the increasing globalization of the economy, which has forced the convergence of national macroeconomic policies, has, on the contrary, magnified the role of (competing) supply-side economic strategies and intensified the importance of parties and partisan agency in the selection of these policies.[56]

Thus, a new consensus may be emerging. As Kapstein outlines this consensus, "trade and immigration have had some effect on labor markets in the industrial countries, but they are not solely responsible for the problems we observe."[57]

Conclusions

As most of the indicators illustrated, ties between countries have advanced in recent years. Two more subtle points arise from this evidence. First, the globalizing processes are not all proceeding at the same pace, and certainly not at the same pace for all countries. The most economically advanced countries are the most integrated in the global economy; yet these may be much better positioned to harness the opportunities presented and deal with the negative aspects of globalization. Second, globalizing processes may be increasing in scale and volume, but it is harder to discern clear dramatic breaks in the trends observed. There are some exceptions, of course. For instance, international capital flows became more open in the late 1970s and early 1980s. But such breaks are less easily identified in the patterns of trade, foreign direct investment, or labour migration.

In order to go beyond some assessment of globalization occurring in the aggregate, we need to look more precisely at the differential impact globalization is having on specific countries. This will allow us to appreciate the differences in political environment within these countries, and also allow us to take into account possible variations in the political outcomes globalization likely will cause. There will not be one story told in the following chapters, but several.

NOTES

1 See, for instance, the questions posed by Geoffrey Garrett, "Global Markets and National Politics: Collision Course or Virtuous Circle?," *International Organization* 52, 4 (Autumn 1998): 790-91, as well as his answers.

2 Hence, we have seen strict regulation of certain forms of technology such as satellite dishes in countries such as China or Iran, let alone phone or fax connections as in Cuba or North Korea.

3 See, for example, Ingrid Bryan, *Canada in the New Global Economy: Problems and Policies* (Toronto: John Wiley & Sons, 1994), 2-3.

4 The levels for 1998 can currently be found at <www.worldbank.org/data/databytopic>.

5 Garrett, "Global Markets and National Politics: Collision Course or Virtuous Circle?," 795.

6 Robert W. Cox, "Political Economy and World Order: Problems of Power and Knowledge at the Turn of the Millennium," in Richard Stubbs and Geoffrey R.D. Underhill, eds., *Political Economy and the Changing Global Order*, 2nd ed. (Toronto: Oxford University Press, 2000), 27.

7 Torben Iverson and Anne Wren, "Equality, Employment, and Budgetary Restraint: The Trilemma of the Service Economy," *World Politics* 50, 4 (July 1998): 507; Garrett, "Global Markets and National Politics: Collision Course or Virtuous Circle?," 787-88.

8 Eric Helleiner, *States and the Reemergence of Global Finance* (Ithaca, NY: Cornell University Press, 1994), 1.

9 Paul Krugman, *Pop Internationalism* (Cambridge, MA: MIT Press, 1996), 62-63.

10 Martin Feldstein and Charles Horioka, "Domestic Savings and International Capital Flows," *Economic Journal* 90 (June 1980): 314-29.

11 Karl Socher, "Globalization and International Monetary and Capital Markets," in John-ren Chen, ed., *Economic Effects of Globalization* (Aldershot, UK: Ashgate, 1998), 33.

12 William Watson, *Globalization and the Meaning of Canadian Life* (Toronto: University of Toronto Press, 1998), 49-50. He cites the work of Maurice K. Levi, "Are Capital Markets Internationally Integrated?," in Thomas K. Courchene and Edwin H. Neave, eds., *Reforming the Canadian Financial Sector* (Kingston, ON: John Deutsch Institute for the Study of Economic Policy, 1997), 63-86.

13 Benjamin Cohen, *The Geography of Money* (Ithaca, NY: Cornell University Press, 1998), 98.

14 Ibid., 3.

15 Although we describe the current set of international rules on exchange rates to be a "floating" system, this may be an apt description only for the relations between the major economies. Most countries in the world tried to bind their own currency with that of their most significant trading partner, at least before 1998. After financial crises in 1997 and 1998 the picture has become more mixed.

16 Layna Mosley, "Room to Move: International Financial Markets and National Welfare States," *International Organization* 54, 4 (Autumn 2000): 739.

17 Ibid., 740-41.

18 Ibid., 743.

19 Ibid., 747-49.

20 John Goodman and Louis Pauly, "The Obsolescence of Capital Controls? Economic Management in an Age of Global Markets," *World Politics* 46, 1 (1993): 50-82.

21 Sebastian Edwards, "How Effective are Capital Controls?," *NBER Working Paper* #7413, Nov. 1999.

22 Paul Hirst and Grahame Thompson, citing UN statistics, in *Globalization in Question: The International Economy and the Possibilities of Governance*, 2nd ed. (Cambridge: Polity Press, 1999), 68.

23 Ankie Hoogvelt, *Globalization and the Postcolonial World* (Baltimore: Johns Hopkins University Press, 1997), 75-77.

24 Hirst and Thompson, *Globalization in Question*, 68.

25 Ibid., 76-77.

26 Ibid., 68.

27 Robert Boyer and Daniel Drache, "Introduction," in Boyer and Drache, eds., *States Against Markets: The Limits of Globalization* (London: Routledge, 1996), 7.

28 See the conclusions of Paul Doremus, William Keller, Louis Pauly, and Simon Reich, *The Myth of the Global Corporation* (Princeton, NJ: Princeton University Press, 1999).

29 These points are developed by Hirst and Thompson in *Globalization in Question*, 273.

30 Ibid., 96.

31 Krugman, *Pop Internationalism*, 76.

32 Ibid., 157.

33 Ethan Kapstein, "Winners and Losers in the Global Economy," *International Organization* 54, 2 (Spring 2000): 366.

34 Cited by Herbert Stocker, "Globalization and International Convergence in Incomes," in Chen, ed., *Economic Effects of Globalization*, 103.

35 This point and this example are made by Bryan, *Canada in the New Global Economy*, 11.

36 Dani Rodrik, "Sense and Nonsense in the Globalization Debate," *Foreign Policy* (Summer 1997): 25-26.

37 Ibid., 29-30.

38 Brian Burgoon, "Globalization and Welfare Compensation: Disentangling the Ties that Bind," *International Organization* 55, 3 (Summer 2001); 509-52.

39 Ronald Rogowski, "Trade and the variety of democratic institutions," *International Organization* 41, 2 (Spring 1987): 203-23.

40 Frances M. Rosenbluth, "Internationalization and electoral politics in Japan," in Robert Keohane and Helen Milner, eds., *Internationalization and Domestic Politics* (Cambridge: Cambridge University Press, 1996).

41 Miriam Golden, "International Sources of the Collapse of Rent-Seeking Regimes: Hypotheses Drawn from the Italian Case," paper presented at the Joint Sessions of the European Consortium for Political Research, Grenoble, France, 6-11 Apr. 2001.

42 See Mark R. Brawley, "Reexamining the Influence of Trade on the Variety of Democratic Institutions," forthcoming.

43 Watson, *Globalization and the Meaning of Canadian Life*, 48.

44 Ibid., 49; Saskia Sassen, *Globalization and Its Discontents* (New York: New Press, 1998), 12-15.

45 S. Castles and M.J. Miller, *The Age of Mass Migration* (Basingstoke: Macmillan, 1993). See Hirst and Thompson, *Globalization in Question*, 23.

46 Hirst and Thompson, *Globalization in Question*, 29.

47 This point is made very forcefully by Sassen, *Globalization and Its Discontents*, 12-13.

48 Hirst and Thompson, *Globalization in Question*, 2.

49 Iverson and Wren, "Equality, Employment, and Budgetary Restraint," 507-46.

50 Torben Iversen and Thomas Cusack, "The Causes of the Welfare State Expansion: Deindustrialization or Globalization?," *World Politics* 52, 3 (April 2000): 313.

51 Ibid., 320.

52 Boyer and Drache, "Introduction," 17.

53 Bryan, *Canada in the New Global Economy, Problems and Policies*, 44.

54 Ibid., 46-47.

55 Carles Boix, *Political Parties, Growth and Equality* (New York: Cambridge University Press, 1998), 3.

56 Ibid., 3-4.

57 Kapstein, "Winners and Losers in the Global Economy," 381.

5 | Globalization and Domestic Politics

In a review of the state of the field of international political economy, three of the best scholars in the area made it clear that in their view, international and domestic politics cannot be separated from each other.[1] Although political science tends to be divided up into component parts (such as comparative politics, international relations, or American politics) these are conceptual divisions made for our purposes. Typically, fields within a discipline are determined by the object of study. In political science, we are usually trying to understand how and why a state chooses to implement certain policies. Comparative or domestic politics is the study of policies aimed at the domestic sphere; international relations looks at policies the state pursues externally.

These two sets of policies are never entirely separate, however. A decision about exchange rates is intimately related to decisions about domestic monetary policy. Tariffs used to be a major component of tax policy; as tariffs were reduced, new taxes had to be brought in to replace them. The linkage between policies is much more complex than most of our models make them out to be. If we are to get a better understanding of globalization, we need to get a better grasp on these sorts of linkages. We especially need to appreciate how these linkages have increased in number and/or in importance over recent years, so that we may see how globalizing processes spark new politics. We also need to reach a better understanding of how domestic institutions and arrangements filter these globalizing forces, shaping political reactions.

Globalizing economic processes bring new pressures to bear on many actors. Greater economic competition translates into concerns over new factors (such as the exchange rate or transportation costs). Worries about additional factors increases the complexity of politics by integrating a higher number of policies and illustrating the linkages between them. As Milner and Keohane remark in the introduction to their edited volume on the subject, greater globalization or international economic ties "expands the tradeables sector within an economy, thus reducing the amount of economic activity sheltered from world market forces." They also point out, however, that "political institutions can block and refract the effects of internationalization."[2] In other words, globalizing economic processes alter the array of interests within states, change the salience of certain policy issues, present policy-makers with different choices, but all these changes are altered by the domestic political arrangements that vary from one country to the next. Let us consider each of these points in more detail.

Domestic Policies Become International—and Vice Versa

One of the clear consequences of globalization is that many more actors are involved in international political economy than before. Actors who have had little of such experience before find themselves involved in international markets and contracts. Their inexperience can lead to poor decisions, since a host of new factors may come into play, blind-siding some of the participants. Most notably in the last three decades, exchange rate movements have caught the uninitiated off guard.

Exchange rate movements may have been the most important factor in the miscalculations of both banks and debtors in the 1980s debt crisis, though to be sure there was a massive swing in the dollar's value. The U.S. dollar's value increased by 50 per cent in the span of only a couple of years. For those who borrowed dollars, but invested them in efforts to earn returns in another currency, the rising value of the dollar would have made it nearly impossible for them to meet their debts. Banks, too, did not enter such probabilities into their decisions concerning who or how much to lend. The movement in the dollar's value was compounded by other factors (such as the decrease in economic activity globally, poor information on total borrowing by sovereign actors, the shift to variable interest rate loans, and so forth) that also led to poor decisions by both borrowers and lenders.

Even more recent swings in currency values, though much smaller, have created unexpected losses for some actors inexperienced in such affairs. Consider, for instance, the Los Angeles Rapid Transit District Authority. When ordering new rail cars for the metro system being built in Los Angeles, they decided to diversify their suppliers. Some were purchased from a Canadian company, Bombardier. Others were bought from a Japanese manufacturer, Mitsubishi. Though the cars were priced at roughly the same exchange rate levels when the initial deal was inked, as payments came due the exchange rates had moved in unanticipated ways. The rise in the value of the yen drove the price of the Mitsubishi cars up to considerably higher levels. A more experienced purchasing agent might have set the price in dollars, or have also established a hedge investment of some kind to help recuperate any losses due to exchange rate movements.

As national economies open up, and as transportation and communication costs fall, more actors enter international contracts. They need to be experienced to be able to anticipate potential risks in these deals. As they become wiser, they also become interested in policy decisions they could afford to ignore in previous periods. Exchange rates may be the most obvious example for Americans. When only a portion of the American economy was engaged in trade (and this portion was controlled by large corporations) most businesses could afford to ignore what was happening to the international value of the dollar. Only large MNCs would lobby for changes in the value of the dollar. Today, much more of the U.S. economy is involved in international transactions, and therefore is affected by movements in the dollar's value versus other currencies. Exchange rate policy has become more salient as a result. Canadians, of course, have had to remain aware of the value of their currency vis-à-vis that of the U.S. and other trading partners.

Globalization and the Focus on National Competitiveness

As more of each country's economy becomes involved in international transactions, issues about international competitiveness gain greater prominence. Exchange rate changes, relative tax levels, pension schemes, health insurance, and a host of other policies suddenly are being scrutinized in light of new concerns. Do these policies make it easier to sell goods abroad? Do they draw in investment and skilled labour from overseas? Yet even as such debates draw attention, some scholars have questioned whether we are looking at these matters in the correct light. There are a number of people who have argued that focusing on national competitiveness as a goal is a mistake.

National competitiveness does not have to trump other goals. It can and should be viewed as one goal among many. Some economists have questioned whether "national competitiveness" has any real meaning in the first place, since competitiveness inheres in firms or individuals. The real sources of competitiveness may not be very closely related to the economic attributes—or ills—often attributed to it. In Paul Krugman's words,

> The idea that a country's economic fortunes are largely determined by its success on world markets is a hypothesis, not a necessary truth; and as a practical matter, that hypothesis is flatly wrong. That is, it is simply not the case that the world's leading nations are to any important degree in economic competition with each other, or that any of their major economic problems can be attributed to failures to compete on world markets.[3]

In Krugman's view, it would be much better for us to seek to improve domestic productivity. Increasing productivity is much more closely related to raising living standards than any increases in trade or competitiveness would be, at least for the most industrialized countries.[4] And what is the purpose of trade or international transactions, if not to raise our standard of living?

Krugman notes several reasons why international competitiveness has become the centre of so much debate. The term is appealing to the public mind. It offers some obvious policy conclusions, such as subsidizing high-tech industries, and introducing tough trade measures for those states with which your country may have trade imbalances, and means this concept is particularly appealing to politicians in the United States.[5] Yet in the end, what will these policies produce? Will they really improve the competitiveness of American industries? Even if they do, will that achieve higher standards of living for Americans?

Altering Domestic Policy Choices of Governments—Will Governments Shrink?

Perhaps the most fundamental and common argument we see about globalization today concerns the impact of global forces on policies that in the past were deemed to be purely domestic in nature. The social welfare policies implemented in many states in the post-World War II years came under attack in recent years, as governments claimed such policies undermined the fiscal health of the state. To express this in more sinister terms, international finance would no longer fund these states' welfare programs. Milner and Keohane formulate this argument as a hypothesis relating increased internationalization with reduced autonomy for governments. As countries open themselves to greater international economic interaction, Milner and Keohane expect states to find it more difficult to select or implement their preferred policies effectively.[6] This hypothesis has been subjected to empirical tests by several other economists and political scientists.

Dani Rodrik, also a proponent of this point of view, has looked at the evidence. He has argued that governments can no longer maintain one of the most common policy mixes in the domestic political economy: extensive social support programs paid for by progressive taxes. Rodrik argues such arrangements will erode, since the owners of capital (including both foreign and domestic investors) now have the option of placing their money elsewhere. Immobile factors of production will increasingly bear the tax burden, in Rodrik's view. In short, the compromise of "embedded liberalism" described by John Ruggie is under threat.[7]

We can break this line of argument into component parts. On a general level, there are questions posed about the simple ability of states to collect tax revenues in the new "globalized" economic environment. This in turn raises questions about the ability of the government to spend money. The general impression in the public is, as noted in earlier chapters, that states must reduce their taxes (and therefore their expenditures) as they liberalize their international economic policies. Has this been the case in recent decades?

Since trade in manufactured goods has been liberalized among GATT members since the 1960s, we might expect to see these pressures developing on the tax rates charged by GATT members. Watson, using data he gathered from various sources, shows that the difference in tax collected by the most economically advanced countries has widened since the 1950s, though within the last decade tax rates have started to converge again. Yet this convergence is very slight, and does not come close to countering the gap that developed over the decades when trade was already liberalized among these states. Among the OECD countries, the spread remains a very high 29.4 per cent of GDP.[8]

When we consider economic unions—instances where tariffs have been eliminated—tax rates do not seem to converge. For instance, the various states in the U.S. do not charge the same tax rates; the original 6 members of the European Economic Community (now the EU) have not experienced convergence in their tax rates, either. Watson concludes that there must be other factors at work that allow governments to select divergent tax policies. Simple trade liberalization, or even this in combination with open capital markets, does not necessarily drive tax rates to the same level. He concludes that the expectations of pressures for a "race to the bottom" in taxes or regulation are unfounded.[9]

Watson reaches similar conclusions about international economic liberalization leading to a decline in the size of the state in the domestic economy. If tax rates can vary substantially, so can expenditure levels. Moreover, Watson concludes that trade can and indeed has generated gains that could be taxed to pay for additional government services. The size of the government's role in the economy has grown among the OECD countries, even as their participation in trade rose since the late 1950s.

More specifically, Watson is interested in addressing questions about pressures being exerted on Canada's government to alter policies. Canadians often express fears about globalization threatening their country's impressive array of social services. Yet as Watson notes, Canada fits his description of the overall OECD pattern quite well. As Canada's trade increased, its government could provide greater services. Referring to the years since 1958, he writes:

> Despite what the globalization hypothesis predicts, growing trade competition from the United States and growing dependence on U.S. capital have not kept us [Canadians] from building a distinctive public sector. Quite the contrary, the period of our closest economic ties with the Americans has also seen our greatest fiscal difference from them.[10]

Watson concludes that Canadians need not fear greater international economic ties. Canadians still can choose whether or not they wish to continue the core services the government provides, such as national healthcare. Watson himself may not support all such policies in their current form, but concerns about competitiveness or the pressures of international finance are only indirectly involved in any decisions to maintain or reduce them. International factors enter in, but only in relation to how the government constructs its overall tax structure and borrowing.

Geoffrey Garrett has conducted a similar analysis of taxes, trade, and state spending, but on a broader basis. Garrett looks across all the members of the OECD from the 1960s to the 1990s. He finds that social democratic, corporatist practices remain common in the 1990s, despite the expectations of many who see globalization as the source of convergence in policies. He does note, however, that states implementing social democratic, Keynesian welfare policies tend to have higher interest rates, and therefore have to pay more to carry their public debt.[11] There is a cost to selecting such policies in a globalized economy, but it comes from the decision to carry more extensive debts. As more states balance their budgets, and reduce their debt burdens, these interest costs are reduced. Is international competitiveness the culprit in this story?

Garrett's statistical analysis of the relationship between increased capital mobility and government expenditures does provide greater support for the opponents of globalization. He finds that liberalization of capital markets has created downward pressure on government spending. This was not true of higher levels of trade, however. The impact of capital mobility was lessened or even reversed when one took into account political factors. If leftist governments (those supported by labour) were in power, then economic internationalization could lead to an increase in government expenditures.[12] He concludes that there is support for the argument that greater integration into the global economy can lead to greater economic gains that are translatable into higher levels of compensation for those whose interests might be hurt by globalization.

The logic behind endogenous growth theory, as it is called, is that any expansion of the state's role depends on economic growth.[13] Economic growth, in turn, depends on technology change. Technological improvements rest, in turn, on the development of human capital and skilled labour. The most economically developed countries are best at developing human capital and technology, and hence have the best chance of continuing to grow economically. On the other hand, this implies that globalization will lead to greater divergence between the less economically developed and most economically developed countries.

Many concerns about globalization are not about aggregate levels of government spending, but that specific globalizing processes challenge particular social programs found in most industrialized states. Rather than focus on the net levels of taxes or expenditures, they focus on particular actions governments undertake, and see the content of government action changing. In some respects, this takes us back to Krugman's comments regarding government policies and competitiveness. As Krugman noted, the real trick for governments is to improve productivity, since that is the true source for improvements in individuals' standard of living. Trading off other goals for competitiveness is a bit foolish, unless the actions also deliver increased productivity. Even then, the other goal might well be valued more highly than economic gain.

Social policies typically do not aim solely to improve economic productivity. They are created to achieve other ends, though they might also provide sources of economic growth or increased productivity. These goals always had the potential to clash. Now with globalization, these tensions may be especially powerful. As Phil Cerny put it, "globalization has had a severe impact on the potential for the state to provide redistributive public goods efficiently. Corporatist bargaining and employment policies are challenged everywhere by international pressures for wage restraint and flexible working practices."[14]

Cerny goes on to argue that this is not simply because international financial markets put pressures on states to lower their expenditures. Instead, Cerny sees the process of globalization as dramatically altering social and public functions, forcing a reconfiguring of political activity. He argues that "globalization entails the undermining of the public character of public goods and the of the specific character of specific assets, i.e., the privatization and marketization of economic and political structures."[15] This argument contains an additional angle. Cerny believes that technological change occurring in globalization is altering the political economic environment in ways that fundamentally change the sort of social problems the state must address. It is a bit harder to map out how and why some groups will be better positioned to organize for political action. Those issues will be given separate attention in the following chapters.

A critical outcome of globalization, in Cerny's view, is that the solution of problems via collective action is changing in character. The appropriate locale for such action is different; there is a mismatch between the sort of social and economic problems people face and the political structures under which they currently operate. This resonates strongly with the perspective of the greens described earlier. Perhaps states will recognize that they are no longer in the best position to respond to this situation. They would then be well advised to engage in greater international cooperation or to establish some sort of international rules to regain some of their lost capabilities. Cerny fears that greater political action at the inter-state level will be beyond the democratic or constitutional control citizens currently can exercise over states.[16]

Similar concerns are voiced by Benjamin Cohen, when he discusses the current state of monetary policy decisions. Monetary policy decisions are now influenced strongly by competition between currencies, Cohen maintains. This can have a positive aspect, since markets act as a check on governments, forcing them to manage their currencies responsibly. If a state can prevent its citizens from using alternative currencies, it has a tendency to abuse its monopolistic powers in the provision of currency. Yet there is a trade-off here, in Cohen's view. Against this benefit must be weighed the disadvantage that "market actors are less accountable than politicians to the general electorate, raising serious questions about legitimacy and representation in decision-making." Yet he goes on to point out that "Governments have not entirely lost their capacity to act on behalf of their own citizens."[17]

Jeff Frieden, also, has noted that not all forms of capital are equally affected by the liberalization of international capital markets. The option to move abroad is felt quite strongly by an investor who holds her money in a six-month government-issued bill. Every six months, she can evaluate where to invest her capital. Re-deploying her capital may not be as easy as you might think, but it can be moved at fairly low cost. A manufacturer who owns a factory, on the other hand, may find it quite costly to shut down an operation and move production abroad. These two investors' calculations are altered in different ways by the international liberalization of capital markets.

Capital can be very liquid or very fixed. Different economic models make different assumptions about how easily capital can be taken form one use and employed in an alternative use. Since some capital is relatively fixed in its current use, the liberalization of international markets will probably not open up any options that are economically viable. Frieden points out that these leave the state leverage in its policies—but these policies must be tailored to specific sectors. The state may be losing leverage via its broadest macroeconomic policy instruments, but policies defined along sector (or industrial) lines may still be potent.[18]

GLOBALIZATION AND THE RECONFIGURING OF DOMESTIC COALITIONS

Another one of the hypotheses that Milner and Keohane put forth regarding greater economic internationalization centres on the power of the forces unleashed in globalization. In their words:

> [M]ounting internationalization will increase the likelihood that polities experience large economic shocks that lead to political crises. These are the very same crises that, as institutionalists have noted, create the "political space" necessary for political entrepreneurs to fundamentally reorganize domestic politics.[19]

Considering the patterns discussed already, they have a strong point. The market forces unleashed in globalization can potentially upset many past social, economic, and political arrangements. When the markets cause negative disruptions, it creates doubts about the efficacy of existing arrangements. At such a point in time, when people's confidence is shaken, political operators may be able to convince people that old arrangements should be replaced by a better, as yet untried, alternative. Crises can open new opportunities for ideas to play a more powerful role in shaping political outcomes.

On the one hand, we would expect that political entrepreneurs would have greater opportunities to use international policies to play up different lines of division in politics. We have already seen how increased international transactions change the economic interests of some actors. Knowing this, political entrepreneurs can promote disputes over certain types of policies in order to divide their opponents, or create new coalitions. As more policies interact, the ability to package a set of policies together becomes more difficult in some respects, but more useful in other respects. These issues will become clearer when we explore the earlier episode of globalization (in the late nineteenth century), and examine the interrelationships between various policy choices in the next two chapters.

On the other hand, Milner and Keohane are suggesting that being open to the international economy leaves a state vulnerable to greater economic disturbances. If these economic shocks occur, existing political institutions or informal arrangements may be challenged. It is a broader way of thinking about the specific lines of argument we have been exploring in this chapter. Keynesian welfare policies are a form of institutional arrangement; international economic shocks could challenge these. But economic shocks originating outside a country could also challenge other institutional arrangements, if the shocks discredited the institutions or policy-makers involved.

Given the broad definition of institutions, increased globalization could account for change in important policy arrangements such as the strength of the welfare state. One can imagine more fundamental changes. In the 1870s, there was shift in the tariff policies of countries, which sparked shifts in styles of taxation, among other policies.[20] Some might link globalization to the spread of certain institutions (such as central banks, built along gold standard lines) with powerful implications for policy. Again, these issues are explored in more depth later when we focus more closely on the late nineteenth century. One thing is clear: globalization has the potential to shake up traditional political arrangements.

UNDOING "EMBEDDED LIBERALISM"?

Another way of framing the political impact of globalization on the domestic political economy is to consider the ways in which international economic regimes were established in the wake of World War II and the Great Depression. Historical factors shaped the evolution of international economic arrangements. State leaders had hoped to emulate the liberal economic practices of the pre-World War I period in the 1920s, but changed circumstances thwarted or deflected their aspirations. The New York Stock Market crash and the outbreak of the Great Depression encouraged states to implement protectionist policies in trade, erect barriers on capital flows, and control currency exchanges. The state intervened in both domestic and international economic relations. In some states these interventions did foster economic recovery, but that was not the case everywhere. Real economic recovery did not come to the U.S. for instance, until the outbreak of World War II.

As noted before, many liberals saw World War II as a consequence of the economic policy failures of the 1920s and 1930s. The Great Depression led to political instability in many countries, with the military taking power in Japan and Nazis seizing control in Germany. Protectionist trade practices encouraged these states to pursue autarkic, imperialist, expansionary policies. Thus, in some ways, World War II could be seen as a consequence of the inability of nations to deal with international economic issues in constructive ways. When allied planners set about designing the post-war rules to govern international economic matters, they sought to not replicate the pre-World War I regimes based on liberal principles (such as the gold standard). Rather they sought to emulate those results at the international level but combine that outcome with rules that would fit with the new array of practices at the domestic level.

The outcome of the discussions focused on reconciling the tensions of government interventions in the domestic economy with liberal practices internationally—what John Ruggie referred to as "embedded liberalism." Those tensions could not be eliminated, but were merely balanced. The balance came unstuck in the 1970s and 1980s, but many people now see liberal principles and practices at the international level overriding domestic concerns. As Rodrik puts it, "globalization presents this dilemma: it results in increased demands on the state to provide social insurance while reducing the ability of the state to perform that role effectively."[21]

Rodrik emphasizes this point—that while there may be a positive correlation between openness and the size of government among the OECD countries, it is largely the result of the compromise just described. Embedded liberalism meant that states intervened in their domestic economies to help shield segments of society from the disruptive impact international economic forces could unleash. As he notes, the correlation identified above isn't just about higher levels of trade; it is in fact stronger if you look more precisely at the exposure to external risks. (In other words, it isn't the level of trade per se that is driving the level of government intervention in the economy, but rather the combination of the level of trade and its volatility or fluctuation.)[22]

The relationship between domestic political institutions and the ability to persevere through international economic shocks has been observed more recently. Thomas Friedman has argued that the countries of Asia least affected by the financial crises of 1997-98 were those with the most democratic systems. Taiwan and Australia had the freest media and were not as badly hurt by the financial meltdown as other countries in the region.[23] Therefore Friedman stresses the importance of governance and political practices for a nation's being in a position to weather the buffeting that comes along with globalization. Democratic states may be less tolerant of corruption, making them less vulnerable to the sorts of problems underlying these international financial crises. Democracies also have to make broad commitments to the well-being of their citizens. They are much more likely to be engaged in the "embedded liberalism" Ruggie described. This means they are also vulnerable to shocks.

The "race to the bottom" thesis concerning regulation and taxes is important here, because the state must be able to garner revenues if it is to execute other functions. Marxists and other theorists on the left argue that globalization will necessarily limit governments' ability to tax capital. If a government cannot generate funds, then it cannot afford to undertake the domestic policies critical to the working of "embedded liberalism." Yet the evidence, as noted before, was that the race to the bottom had not actually affected the size of government despite some people's impressions. Regarding taxes, the available evidence is similar. For instance, as the European Union has come together, the most economically advanced countries, which began with the highest tax rates, did not reduce taxes as these national markets merged. Instead, the countries (on Europe's southern fringe) that joined the European community with lower tax rates raised the rates they charged upwards, closing the gap.[24]

While our impression may have been that economic globalization has altered the balance of goals in our policies, making the pursuit of economic competitiveness relatively more important, the truth may be somewhat different. The pressures to reduce taxes and the size of government involvement in the economy have called other policies into question. Still, in the words of Milner and Keohane, the final balance in these matters has not been struck:

> In effect, internationalization has called into question the "embedded liberalism" compromise in which extensive state involvement in the economy helped to generate support for openness in many advanced industrial countries. At the moment, the prevailing view seems to be that less intervention is desirable, and that economic growth will thrive in a less regulatory environment. In time resistance to the costs of rapid adjustment could increase, and new forms of government intervention—many of which seek to regulate and condition this openness—may be chosen. The declining policy autonomy of states as they cede control to markets may only be a temporary phase, until new forms of intervention are demanded and discovered.[25]

Similarly, Ethan Kapstein offers us some observations on the balancing of economic and social priorities. Kapstein notes that achieving economic justice domestically is much more complicated today. Globalization complicates the problems faced by governments in achieving this goal primarily because of one particular globalizing process: greater capital mobility. Capital mobility allows those who control capital to relocate away from those countries that impose higher taxes—and higher taxes are usually a critical tool for governments seeking a more equitable distribution of wealth.[26] Taxes are an important government instrument for taking money away from the wealthier, but also for providing funds to help those on the bottom of society.

On another front, Edward Luttwak has noted that freeing markets from regulation tends to create greater insecurity among society's members. Individuals who feel economically insecure seek security in other behaviours; society becomes less free overall as a result, as governments seek to curb drug use, political demonstrations, or other forms of behaviour. While Luttwak's argument is tenuous, it is interesting to note how often liberalization of the economy is combined with the enacting of conservative social policies.[27]

Certainly, American workers have the impression that their jobs are less secure than before.[28] Polling indicates that job insecurity has risen steadily in the 1990s—so much so that journalists and other observers discuss the career strategies of the younger generation as a constant shifting of employment from one firm to another. This hasn't created extreme anxieties largely because the job market in the United States has been particularly good for much of the 1990s. Will that pattern continue? In countries where job prospects have not been so rosy, workers have been much more worried about the threats posed by foreign competition.

Redistributing Wealth and Power within the Domestic Political Sphere

Another way of understanding the challenges to the welfare state is to look at how globalization redistributes power among domestic actors. All economic actors reside within national boundaries. Since the most important policy decisions remain in the hands of states, economic actors play politics first within the boundaries of states. Globalization does not have to be seen as a force reducing the power of the state, yet strengthening no other actors. Instead, as we saw above, globalization can be seen as a set of processes or forces that strengthen the hand of some players at the expense of others.

GLOBALIZATION AND INCOME INEQUALITY

Former Labor Secretary Robert Reich argued that globalization was creating a two-tiered economy and hence a two-tiered society. Reich observed that international factors were influencing the U.S. economy more than ever, and that such connections tend to create "winners" and "losers." Those with the skills and assets needed to compete internationally would do even better in the new global economy. Those who lacked these assets, however, would do worse. Unskilled labour, in particular, would be hurt. The increasing economic opportunities associated with globalization would heighten this division in society, Reich warned.

Edward Luttwak identifies other changes in society due to globalization, though these would have a similar result. Luttwak expects globalization to spark chain reactions within the domestic economy.[29] Globalization allows larger firms to increase their reliance on small suppliers. Outsourcing can even become international, as more and more inputs or components can be bought from foreign sources. As the larger firms increase their outsourcing, they can afford to downsize their own workforce. Downsizing undermines the strength of unions, as labour becomes more insecure and less willing to challenge management. Thus, management (or capital) gains advantages, while workers lose out.

Luttwak argues that globalization is creating more losers than winners. This raises a question, however. Why don't the losers challenge globalizing trends more often, or with greater intensity? Luttwak offers this answer:

> Were it not for the fact that most losers are also parents who may reasonably hope that their children will be gainers one day, the voting booth would soon stop the advance of turbo-capitalism, and even reverse it. That is what happened in France in 1997, after an exceptionally informative election campaign....[30]

Unfortunately, this argument cannot be tested, and thus few are swayed by it. Kapstein is less convinced of this argument, and points out that this view is widely held.

> Underpinning these analyses is a widespread view among economists that unskilled workers have become particularly vulnerable to economic and technological change and are "falling behind" their more highly educated colleagues in terms of earnings and job security. That development raises a political fear: that rising income inequality could spark a political backlash against free trade and the neoliberal economic agenda.[31]

Something like this has happened before, though the causal factors were probably much more domestic in nature than international. In the period of the late nineteenth-century internationalization, industrialization was also at work. Craftsmen were losing market share to cheaper manufactured goods from mechanized production. Their skills no longer were beneficial. They proved to be some of the most vociferous opponents to industrialization.

In recent years a parallel argument has emerged, though this is based on economic theories about the sources of trade, as well as the ways in which the gains from trade are distributed. The trade story has been seen before as well. In the late nineteenth century, after several decades of relatively free trade among the major economic powers, improvements in production, communications, and transportation combined to drive down the price of a number of commodities. Farmers especially suffered as the price for grain dropped; producers of commodities such as iron and steel also felt the effect of competition. Protectionist coalitions swept to power in several countries as a result. The political economic processes at work in this period will be scrutinized more closely in a later chapter, but it is quite possible that such patterns could be repeated.

Kapstein notes that these hypotheses tend to be poorly constructed when we examine each of the steps involved. Economists do an excellent job highlighting and underscoring diverging economic interests among various members of society. Yet there are other steps to model or theorize about before we link economic interests to political action, let alone a change in government policy.[32] As Kapstein points out, in most of the burgeoning literature on globalization "little if any attention is given to the role of domestic political and economic *institutions* in channeling the effects of trade or other economic changes (such as the introduction of new technologies) within societies."[33]

On the other hand, Kapstein realizes it is pointless to assume (as some elementary economic models of trade and its effect do) that factors of production could be easily re-deployed into other employment paying just as much. As he put it, "Trade would hardly raise a political eyebrow if the factors of production displaced by imports could make a frictionless transition to new and equally remunerative economic activities."[34] It is necessary to look more closely at the ability of economic actors to adjust to other activities, since not all can do so easily. After that, the ability to organize for political action needs to be studied, as does the access of different groups to political decision-making. Following that, coalition possibilities have to be modelled; the whole effort is quite complicated, but we shall endeavour to elaborate some of these issues in chapters that follow.

If we look at unskilled labour, the group everyone agrees is threatened most by globalization, it has the fewest options for finding alternative employment. Job retraining is often heralded as one way to help workers shift from employment in one sector to another. Actually, retraining also implies giving labour the necessary skills to find employment. Unfortunately, studies in the U.S. show that such efforts are not particularly effective.[35] Unskilled labour in the American economy seems to have found new jobs in the service sector, perhaps at lower pay, but this pattern does not hold in very many other countries.

When we look in other industrialized economies, unskilled labour seems to have suffered in terms of both pay and employment. According to the arguments above, we should expect labour to be weaker politically as a result. Garrett, in his examination of trends across the OECD countries, found some surprising statistics. For instance, Garrett compared the portion of union members in the largest confederation across 15 OECD countries, from 1970 to 1990. The figures reflected a stable pattern, not a changing one.[36] So why should we believe that labour is less politically powerful than it was 30 years ago?

THE INTERNATIONAL MOBILITY OF FACTORS OF PRODUCTION

Another way to study the variance in the impact of globalization on different groups within countries is to consider how easily certain factors of production (such as forms of capital, land, or labour) can move over borders. Globalization is supposed to make transportation and communication cheaper, so does this encourage producers to move from one country to another? Land can't be moved, but what about different forms of capital or labour? How does this alter political competition, or the ability of the state to regulate domestic relations or manage its policies? Internationally mobile factors of production are considered to have an edge over those that cannot flow across borders. Mobile capital, such as investments, can be moved over borders much more easily than machinery or factories. Under most countries' existing regulations, capital can enter much more easily than most labour. This can give a powerful bargaining advantage to mobile capital over the other factors of production: the option of exiting for more profitable arrangements in another country.[37]

As evidence that some holders of capital have in fact taken their money out of countries with high taxes, as a way to exert bargaining power, we can consider two types of evidence. First, we can look at interest rate differentials across economies. Are these large? Do large interest rate differentials persist over time? If they have, then the expected advantage of mobile capital would be theoretical rather then practiced. Evidence on interest rates does indicate that the removal of capital controls by the United States, Germany, and other major European powers in 1974-75 has made a difference. Prior to that time, significant interest rate differentials between the U.S. and Europe existed, and persisted over time. Interest rate differentials among the major financial powers largely disappeared by the early 1980s, however.[38]

Of course, to be more certain of the political leverage gained by having the option to move, one would like to observe the holders of mobile capital issuing their threat to move capital internationally, and then observe cases illustrating variation in how states respond to this threat. Capital flight from Latin American debtor states, or from countries experiencing high inflation may be evidence of this kind. Inflation may be a greater threat than tax on the returns to capital, so it sparks international movements of capital more quickly than tax differences.

Garrett's statistical analysis again provides us with some results that challenge commonly held expectations. According to his figures, increasing levels of trade and capital market liberalization have not led to lower taxes on capital—if anything they might be higher in general. Political differences come into play, as well. Where leftist governments are in power, however, increased levels of trade are associated with lower levels of taxation; and greater capital mobility internationally is associated with lower interest rates, in general.[39]

Another way to think about the domestic divisions generated by greater exposure to the international economy is to look at the ways in which elements of capital and labour share interests. The capital and labour combined in the production of one good or service will share an interest in trade liberalization, or monetary policy, based on the ability to market that good or service abroad, or to have foreign producers sell their goods or services into their home market. If intermediate goods are being widely traded, and commodities and factors of production can flow across borders with ease, then there will be increased demands for state intervention, at least by those factors of production which are not mobile over borders. They will ask for some forms of protection, or cushioning.[40]

This sort of political split—the tradeables versus the non-tradeable sectors—may become more common in the future. Frieden has already identified one way in which this plays out. The tradeables producers will place a priority on exchange rate policy. They wish to ensure that the exchange rate helps them in their competition against foreigners. The traders may be those who compete against imports, or those who export to foreign markets. In either case, the producers of tradeable goods and services will want to make sure that the exchange rate does not rise too high, affecting the price of their output. Nor will they want the exchange rate to be too volatile. This group is now larger, as globalization brings more and more producers into international markets. International capital market liberalization brings more holders of capital into this category as well, as they begin to consider making investments abroad.

Producers of non-tradeable goods and services, on the other hand, will place greater import on the domestic monetary policy. They will gladly sacrifice exchange rate policies to achieve desirable domestic outcomes.

Thus the two sides will come into conflict over which should dominate when formulating the monetary side: external goals or internal.[41]

One important point to remember, however, is that the mere opportunity to engage in greater economic activity over international borders does not in itself alter domestic political coalitions. Domestic groups may realign themselves in response to these opportunities, but several other factors are at work. Some groups are better able to get organized, and or are better able to express their demands. Political entrepreneurship also matters: to quote Milner and Keohane, "the entrepreneurship of a Deng Xiaoping, Gorbachev or Salinas may be needed to galvanize the potential beneficiaries of reform into a winning coalition."[42]

It is also important to remember that the processes of globalization can create a backlash just as easily as it produces economic rewards for integrating into the international economy. The backlash will come from "those brutalized or left behind by this new system."[43] Globalizing processes can provide the means to greater political power for some, but it can also provide the motivation for those who are hurt to organize or work harder at changing policies.

Resistance and Promotion

We laid out our primary task in this text by posing a question concerning the political consequences of globalization. Will globalizing forces build increased support for globalization or will they create forces resisting globalizing processes? The challenge for political scientists is to develop a better understanding of how these political conflicts will unfold. There are a number of ways to model these different pressures.[44]

Daniel Verdier has argued that much hinges on political centralization. Verdier examines reactions to previous episodes of globalization, in order to develop his theoretical argument. Economic interests are divided between those who can compete internationally and those who are competitive only locally. In countries where political power is centralized, the internationally competitive interests have a much greater chance of dominating decision-making. Where political power is subdivided, locally competitive interests have an easier time getting their narrower interest enacted, at least at the local level. This argument parallels theoretical arguments about liberalization; when domestic institutions force decision-makers to think about the broadest possible interests, economic openness is more likely to result. When decision-makers only have to answer to narrow portions of the national constituency, they are more easily captured by narrow interests.

Hudson Meadwell and I have argued that the best way to approach this situation is to model the politics in terms of the problems groups themselves identify. To illustrate our points, we have begun describing how globalizing economic processes in the late nineteenth century affected farmers.[45] Rather than seek to explain results in a single issue area, such as agricultural tariff policies in the late 1800s, or monetary and credit policies, or regulation of transportation, or some other isolated policy, we intend to show that these were related in understandable ways. The trick is to think in terms of the problem, not the result. Some policies were clearly substitutes for each other, as means of providing relief to farmers (e.g., lower transportation rates or tax breaks could reduce farmers' costs). Others were clearly complements (e.g., lower taxes could only be provided to farmers if new streams of revenue were found elsewhere, or government expenditures were cut).

How policies were packaged together makes a difference—it makes little sense to discuss tariff changes without also discussing state revenues and expenditures more broadly, or to examine demands for economic regulation of transportation without also reflecting on calls for changes in monetary policy. And in our view, it would be more fruitful to begin with the underlying problem, and then examine why one form of relief was pursued rather than another. The answer, we will argue, can be found in the specific aspects of the various policy options: in the utility of the policies for mobilizing farmers, the sorts of complementary policies that can be used to draw in political allies, and their tactical value in policymaking. Also, by setting off with this step, we generate questions that would otherwise never arise.

Such studies as this or Verdier's are important not only as points of comparison with the current period, but also because they helped shape arrangements that have evolved into those we currently live with. Milner and Keohane suggest that past practices, institutions, and decisions may matter greatly in any attempt to predict how globalization will affect a country today. While the same sets of international factors may be pressuring polities and their governments in particular, some may be better conditioned or prepared to face these choices. Domestic institutions can filter or shape these forces, as much as be shaped by them.[46]

As noted earlier, globalization allows for the tactical and strategic linkage of policies by political entrepreneurs. This was true for those trying to help farmers in the late nineteenth century, but it may also be true for those trying to help unskilled labour, or other groups adversely influenced by globalization today. Increasingly, trade, monetary, and investment policies are intertwined in the conflicts over globalizing processes. For example, protectionist trade policies are thought to generate inward foreign direct investment. When foreign producers can no longer penetrate a market from outside due to barriers to trade, they "jump" behind the tariff wall and build or purchase factories inside the country. Domestic actors affected by globalization will try to use these interacting policies to their advantage.[47] Recent patterns in international investment into the U.S. or Europe, and the resulting mergers between large corporations, may be explicable through an analysis of such cross-pressures.

Such approaches to the study of globalizing processes still need to be elaborated. These are merely the first steps to coming up with a convincing political analysis useful for describing a broad number of cases. It is already clear, however, that the complexity of the processes, and the interaction of the various policies involved, will make it difficult for us to develop a simple story about the politics sparked by globalization. Instead, the complexity actually allows for greater discretion in how political actors manipulate the situation. This may make it very difficult indeed to model the politics.

Conclusions on Globalization and Domestic Politics

One important conclusion is to recognize that as globalizing processes proceed, economic interests become more ambiguous. The demands for change in economic policies reflect political factors as much as, if not more than economics.[48] The two cannot be divided up as neatly as the preceding arguments illustrate. Instead, there are powerful feedback loops. Globalizing economic processes alter interests and capabilities of domestic actors. Domestic political contests result in different goals being pursued, and power and interests are shuffled in turn.

Stanley Hoffmann worries that in the push to implement globalization in recent years, the economic aspects are being emphasized over other goals. While economic liberalization is usually connected in our minds with follow-on effects held to be positive, the causal connections are not all that well supported by social science findings. Political repercussions are not being considered, as they should.

It should not be surprising that in the drive to create a global economy through the dismantling of state barriers, concerns for human rights, democracy, or self-determination have often been submerged or twisted, according to the highly debatable assumption that free economies must "ultimately" lead to free politics as well. The assumption may turn out to be correct, but it is fair to say that the jury is still out."[49]

Hoffmann wants us to think more closely about the politics generated by globalizing economic processes. Whether globalization is likely to build its own support by providing economic rewards to powerful constituencies in participating countries, or whether it is just as likely to motivate those hurt by such trends to mount more effective resistance are questions we still are unable to answer. Our inability should make us think twice about the decisions we still face concerning specific globalizing processes.

NOTES

1 Peter Katzenstein, Robert Keohane, and Stephen Krasner, "International Organization and the Study of World Politics," *International Organization* 52, 4 (Autumn 1998): 670.

2 Helen Milner and Robert Keohane, "Internationalization and Domestic Politics: An Introduction," in Milner and Keohane, eds., *Internationalization and Domestic Politics* (Cambridge: Cambridge University Press, 1996), 5.

3 Paul Krugman, *Pop Internationalism* (Cambridge, MA: MIT Press, 1996), 5.

4 Ibid., 8-9.

5 Ibid., 16.

6 Milner and Keohane, "Internationalization and Domestic Politics: An Introduction," 16-17.

7 Dani Rodrik, *Has Globalization Gone Too Far?* (Washington, DC: Institute for International Economics, 1997), 19.

8 William Watson, *Globalization and the Meaning of Canadian Life* (Toronto: University of Toronto Press, 1998), ch. 4.

9 Ibid.

10 Ibid., 43.

11 Geoffrey Garrett, "Capital mobility, trade, and the domestic politics of economic policy," *International Organization* 49, 4 (Autumn 1995): 659.

12 Ibid., 673.

13 The connections to debates on globalization are neatly summarized in Dimitri Landa and Ethan Kapstein, "Inequality, Growth, and Democracy," *World Politics* 53, 2 (January 2001): 275-76.

14 Phil Cerny, "What Next for the State?," in Eleonore Kofman and Gillian Youngs, eds., *Globalization: Theory and Practice* (London: Pinter, 1996), 128.

15 Ibid., 130.

16 Ibid.

17 Benjamin Cohen, *The Geography of Money* (Ithaca, NY: Cornell University Press, 1998), 5.

18 Jeffry Frieden, "Invested interests: the politics of national economic policies in a world of global finance," *International Organization* 45, 4 (Autumn 1991): 429-31.

19 Milner and Keohane, "Internationalization and Domestic Politics: An Introduction," 16.

20 See the various papers of Mark Hallerberg, as well as Mark R. Brawley and Hudson Meadwell, "Tariffs, Taxes and Transportation: The Politics of Agricultural Relief," paper presented to the annual meeting of the American Political Science Association, Boston, 1998.

21 Rodrik, *Has Globalization Gone Too Far?*, 53.

22 This is what Rodrik explores in Chapter 4 of *Has Globalization Gone Too Far?*

23 Thomas Friedman, *The Lexus and the Olive Tree* (New York: Anchor Books, 2000), 184, 188, 455-56.

24 See the evidence presented in Richard E. Baldwin and Paul Krugman, "Agglomeration, Integration and Tax Harmonization," unpublished paper, draft of Sept. 2000, 4-5. They provide an interesting way of explaining this outcome, focusing on the economic advantages of having industries concentrated geographically.

25 Helen Milner and Robert Keohane, "Internationalization and Domestic Politics: A Conclusion," in Milner and Keohane, eds., *Internationalization and Domestic Politics* (Cambridge: Cambridge University Press, 1996), 249.

26 Ethan Kapstein, *Sharing the Wealth* (New York: W.W. Norton, 1999), 28.

27 Edward Luttwak, *Turbo-Capitalism* (London: Weidenfeld & Nicolson, 1998), 71-75.

28 Rodrik, *Has Globalization Gone Too Far?*, 21-24.

29 Luttwak, *Turbo-Capitalism*, ch. 4 describes the process.

30 Ibid., 6.

31 Ethan Kapstein, "Winners and Losers in the Global Economy," *International Organization* 54, 2 (Spring 2000): 360.

32 See James Alt and Michael Gilligan, "The Political Economy of Trading States: Factor Specificity, Collective Action Problems, and Domestic Political Institutions," *Journal of Political Philosophy* 2, 2 (1994): 165-92.

33 Kapstein, "Winners and Losers in the Global Economy," 361.

34 Ibid., 363.

35 Ibid., 378.

36 Garrett, "Capital mobility, trade, and the domestic politics of economic policy," 667.

37 Milner and Keohane, "Internationalization and Domestic Politics: An Introduction," 19.

38 For an overview of this evidence, see J. Lawrence Broz, "International Capital Mobility and Monetary Politics in the U.S. Congress, 1960-1997,"paper presented to the 1998 annual meeting of the American Political Science Association, Boston.

39 Garrett, "Capital mobility, trade, and the domestic politics of economic policy," 675.

40 See the argument made by Ronald W. Jones in "Private Interests and Government Policy in a Global World," *Tinbergen Institute Discussion Paper* T12000-051/2, esp. 13.

41 Frieden, "Invested interests," 450.

42 Milner and Keohane, "Internationalization and Domestic Politics: A Conclusion," 255.

43 Friedman, *The Lexus and the Olive Tree*, 9.

44 Alt and Gilligan, "The Political Economy of Trading States."

45 See Mark R. Brawley and Hudson Meadwell, "Protection or Inflation? Politicians, Farmers' Demands, and Forms of Agricultural Relief in the late Nineteenth Century," paper presented at the International Studies Association meeting, 2000, Los Angeles, and Brawley and Meadwell, "Tariffs, Taxes and Transportation: The Politics of Agricultural Relief," paper presented at the American Political Science Association meeting, 1998, Boston.

46 Milner and Keohane, "Internationalization and Domestic Politics: An Introduction," 22.

47 Jonathan Crystal, "A New Kind of Competition: How American Producers Respond to Incoming FDI," *International Studies Quarterly* 42, 3 (Sept. 1998): 513-14.

48 Ibid., 539.

49 Stanley Hoffmann, "The Crisis of Liberal Internationalism," *Foreign Policy* 98 (Spring 1995): 174-75.

6 | How Globalization's Impact Varies

Not surprisingly, globalization has had a varied impact in different places. This has partly to do with policy choices, as outlined in the previous chapter. Initial choices concerning whether to resist globalization or to embrace it will lead to different outcomes. Moreover, we have already "unpacked" this term somewhat, to find globalization is composed of some very different processes that may have reinforcing effects, but can also have isolated consequences as well. States may try to differentiate between these processes, blocking some but accepting others. We examine in this chapter how these different globalizing processes affect countries with different levels of economic and political development.

All states do not begin in the same position vis-à-vis globalizing processes. Consider the position in the past decade of less economically developed countries and the former members of the Soviet bloc. Many of these countries had few international economic ties, since they lacked efficient industries or strong export sectors. They need foreign capital to retool existing productive sectors, or to develop wholly new sectors. Many countries had high levels of dependence on imports of raw materials, capital goods, and intermediate inputs, combined with low domestic savings.[1] Communication links vary widely as well.

Industrialized countries, for the most part, were already open to high volumes of international trade by the 1980s, let alone the 1990s. They removed most barriers to capital flows in the 1980s. They already have more advanced technology, industrial sectors capable of competing internationally, and good levels of saving. Many would think, therefore, that they could do well during globalization—though we have already focused on some of the fears citizens of these states have about their jobs, government social policies, and other aspects of their lives these citizens feel are at risk.

For one or two industrialized countries, globalization does represent something comparatively new. The United States and Japan, the two largest national economies in the last decade or two, were also the most insulated economies of the industrialized Western countries. Measured by trade (exports plus imports) as a percentage of GDP, both these countries went from fairly low figures—less than 10 per cent in 1970—to considerably higher levels (nearing 20 per cent) by the late 1990s. These two countries have felt economic globalization in some powerful ways.

Some observers maintain that globalizing trends actually extend only a single national model to which all must conform. They argue that market and political trends promote an American economic and cultural model on a global scale. This helps explain a great deal of the hostility to globalization—or at least it gives those who wish to oppose globalizing forces an excellent tool for mobilizing actors. Those who turn to the politics of identity to gather political power for opposing globalization consider these trends to be quite acceptable for the U.S., or for states culturally and economically similar to the U.S. (perhaps including Canada and Australia). Yet there are good reasons to question this view.[2] In the latter half of this chapter, we shall take a closer look at how globalization represents something new for the United States.

In places we will also contrast the U.S. and Canadian experiences. As an industrialized country that has historically been dependent on trade, some would argue that globalization represents little new for Canada. Canada may in fact be more threatened by changes, because it is both exposed to more trade and international flows (including immigration) than most other countries, and because it has as much to lose as any other country.[3] Since Canada has a significantly higher level of welfare policies in place compared to the United States, if the "race to the bottom" were to take place, Canada would be forced to undergo some dramatic changes.

The U.S. on the other hand, will be experiencing many globalizing effects for the first time. It is only now becoming much more integrated into the international economy, therefore the changes it will be going through are unprecedented. Canada will more likely be feeling more of the same old sorts of pressures it has always been under—a change in degree—whereas the United States will be under pressures representing a change in kind.[4]

Considering the Impacts Associated with Globalization

There are states that continue to resist the forces of globalization fiercely. Though they might be missing out on economic opportunities, some governments are willing to pay this price for other advantages they are attaining. For instance, the North Korean government still practises state socialism. It does not wish to share control over political and economic decision-making with anyone else (internal or external). It also does not wish to allow its citizens access to rival sources of information. It therefore uses its sovereignty and coercive authoritative powers to block globalizing processes. As the needs of its society go unmet, however, even this government will have to re-consider its decisions.

North Korea is an extreme example. The government there still hopes to exercise near-total control over its society. The government of the People's Republic of China aspires to less extreme ends. The country still is ruled by the top leadership of a single party, but the party's grip on the economy, media, and population has slackened in recent years. Through the exercise of its sovereignty, the government is selectively participating in globalizing trends. It wishes to participate in international trade, receive international investments and technology, but is less certain about flows of people and information. Of course, one of the great questions to be answered in coming years is whether these changes will overcome the government's control, or whether the government will seek to halt these trends. The recent crackdown on the Falun Gong movement shows how intolerant the government remains.

On the other end of the spectrum we might imagine a democratic country that embraces liberal economic practices to the fullest. Countries such as Japan or the United States appear to be completely engaged in international trade, with few barriers to the flow of goods over their borders. The sheer size of these countries' economies actually shielded them from some of the influences of trade. International economic instabilities could never cause much disorder if the countries had comparatively little at stake in international markets. Yet trade is only one facet of the economic processes associated with globalization. Japan is not known for its acceptance of international investment in most areas, and allows only small amounts of many services to be provided by foreign firms. Neither the U.S. nor Japan allows very free flows of people over its borders, either.

Finding a current example of a country that has allowed free movement of goods (including capital) and people over its borders is in fact

FIGURE 6.1 | DECISIONS INSIDE GLOBALIZING PROCESSES

harder than you might think. Even though we describe the current period as a time when "free trade" is the norm, no country allows foreign goods unfettered entry into its markets. Few are very accepting of large numbers of immigrants. That means all states make choices about how much of their sovereignty to concede in responding to the opportunities and choices of globalization. Building on the diagram in Chapter Four, we might introduce policy choices into each step.

HOW GLOBALIZING PROCESSES FILTER THROUGH A COUNTRY

As noted in the previous chapter, globalization, perhaps more than any other issue presents us with the need to consider theories and findings from both comparative politics and international relations. Comparative politics typically confines itself to the study of domestic political outcomes, whereas international relations usually focuses only on the study of outcomes in foreign policy or the level of international interactions. These divisions are necessary to delimit areas of study that are in fact closely related. Globalization represents a wonderful example of how decisions on international matters can have fundamental and powerful influences on domestic outcomes, which in turn shape how further decisions about international affairs will be made. We could accept these artificial, abstract divisions because for many of the most economically advanced countries, the impact of international political economic ties on the domestic political economy was fairly weak. That may no longer be true.

Domestic political institutions critically filter the way international forces are felt in politics. The last chapter emphasized how these changes alter state policy decisions. But what is the impact of globalization on other actors? Economic influences, exerted through markets, alter people's views and interests. People organize to engage in political activity based on their interests and perceptions. If they cannot come together to work towards a common goal, they are unlikely to have a political voice. Their ability to refashion government policies in their pursuit of their interests depends on how well their political power can be felt through institutional arrangements,[5] so we will still need to keep an eye on how politics is played in different settings.

Geoffrey Garrett and Peter Lange have made the case that knowledge of some very basic domestic political characteristics can provide us with information about how states will handle pressures from outside. As Garrett and Lange suggest:

> [T]he responsiveness of governments to changes in domestic pref-
> erences will vary significantly with regime type. The easier it is for
> opponents to challenge the policies of the incumbent government,
> the more responsive will the [domestic] system be to changes in soci-
> etal preferences.... One should thus expect—in the wake of a sim-
> ilar change in domestic preferences—political change to be faster
> and smoother in stable democracies than in more authoritarian
> regimes (where the entry barriers to politics are higher).[6]

In short, democracies may be better at making the adjustments necessary to harness the benefits associated with globalization. They are certainly less likely to pass up the opportunities for the economic gains globalization represents.

One major problem confronting public decision-making in democracies, however, is that globalization is blamed for rising income inequal-
ity. This is one reason why we might well expect a political backlash against globalization to occur. In the wake of the Great Depression, Western democracies everywhere relied on government intervention to manage the economy. Governments did not intervene simply to stabilize their economies. They began to manage their economies with other goals in mind, such as promoting security in employment, and greater equality.

The 1930s and 1940s were decades when democracies were challenged by both communist and fascist regimes, so Western democracies instituted a number of programs designed to achieve both macroeconomic stability *and* greater equality in their societies.

In the post-World War II years, each of the dominant democracies chose to defend these arrangements. Economic difficulties due to adjustments in the return to peacetime production had created intense international competition in the years just after World War I. Many feared that these same problems would recur in the late 1940s. The leaders of the Western democracies wanted to create international economic rules that captured the benefits of freer trade, but without threatening the success of the domestic interventions they had implemented. The balance they struck has been labelled "embedded liberalism," as discussed earlier. Open markets internationally would be embedded in domestic markets that were still subject to government intervention.

Globalization threatens this balance. The unleashing of international markets forces alterations in how governments intervene domestically. Most people fear that the changes will undercut the governments' aims of greater stability, increased equality, and so on. In particular, increased exposure to international markets seems to be associated with these two problems. "Embedded liberalism" could be "disembedding." That would have an effect on equality within the economically advanced democracies.

Paul Krugman challenges those who blame international trade and investment for increased inequality, however. He offers an alternative explanation for increasing earnings inequality in the industrialized countries: technological change. Skilled workers, and more educated people, earn more than less-skilled workers.[7] Any long-term economic growth is ultimately based on increased productivity. Each worker must be able to produce greater wealth in the same amount of time. Technological improvements make that possible, so as greater skills and technology enter into the economy, those who control the technology or have these skills can produce more, and therefore earn more.

Those on the left of the political spectrum, and even some Keynesians, worry that greater exposure to the international economy threatens the welfare policies aimed at attaining greater equality. The logic here, however, is tied to the "race to the bottom" argument, which we have already investigated. In the closely integrated economies of the U.S. and Canada, Canadians fear that free trade and other forms of economic integration are creating pressures to undercut Canada's generous welfare state. Canada has several policies in place differentiating it from the U.S., most notably public health care. How have the pressures of international competition, primarily with the U.S., affected Canada's social policies in recent decades?

One area of concern is employment. Prior to 1982, the two countries exhibited similar trends in unemployment. The two countries' rates were usually not that far apart, and they moved approximately together. After 1982, however, Canada's unemployment rate has remained steadily higher than the American rate, typically by about 3 per cent. The explanation may lie in the different regulatory and institutional frameworks in the two countries. Or, it could be created by the different policies being implemented in Canada. Or, it could be because of differences in the labour market itself. The U.S. labour market is notoriously more flexible than those of other countries. Unions are more prominent in Canada, the country has a higher minimum wage, and unemployment benefits are more generous here.[8]

Although there have been cutbacks in government expenditures in both countries, these have been felt more strongly in Canada. The public health-care system remains in place, though in several parts of the country there is growing pressure to allow a greater range of private services to complement or to compete against publicly provided services. Government expenditures on health and education have been reduced across the country. There are different points of view as to what caused these cutbacks.

Non-democracies may be able to ignore their citizens' interests in tapping into international economic opportunities. At least, non-democratic governments may choose to block globalization's impact because that maximizes these governments' *own* interests. The same is not likely to hold for democracies, however. If democracies are interested in seizing some of the potential economic benefits from globalization, yet not accept too much risk at the same time, or lessen the negative impacts of globalization, how are they going to respond to globalization? Several paths have been suggested. One is to band states together in regional organizations.

THE HOPES AND DANGERS FOR DEMOCRACIES PURSUING REGIONAL CO-OPERATION

If democratic governments are having the effectiveness of their policies undercut by market dynamics, how might they be able to regain some of their power? Institutionalists suggest that states may be able to gain greater control over their situation by co-operating more effectively. Since their fates are intertwined, and the effectiveness of their decisions linked, they need to do a better job communicating with each other, sharing information, and reducing uncertainties in how each will behave to affect others. Institutionalists tell us that international institutions or organizations can achieve these solutions.

Martin and Schumann are among the many Europeans who see regional co-operation as the only way to vest more authority in governmental actors in their confrontation with markets. Since they viewed globalization as the result of technical progress that enabled other actors to evade government control, governments would need to develop some new capabilities to recoup some of their lost powers. For governments to reassert control over markets and economic actors, their strength versus market pressures must be increased, Martin and Schumann argue. European integration offers such a path, they suggest.

> There is need of a countervailing state power against the corporations, cartels and criminals, one which can support itself on the will of a majority of citizens. In the borderless market, however, no European state can achieve that alone. The European alternative to the Anglo-American style of laissez-faire capitalism will either develop within a democratically legitimate union, or not at all.[9]

As this illustrates, however, Martin and Schumann perceive problems with the legitimacy of the EU at this stage. Though the European Union institutions strengthen the hands of the member governments, it does so without building political loyalty among the citizens. Co-operation through the EU strengthens the governments' abilities to make their policies more effective, but democratic control cannot be as effectively executed. Accountability to the public remains a problem. Martin and Schumann therefore see a trade-off being made, one they would rather avoid.

Some other observers fear that this dangerous trade-off is occurring. Robert Boyer and Daniel Drache, for example, see the shift in decision-making to regional organizations as an attempt to evade national political processes. This is their judgement of NAFTA and EMU.[10] Such arrangements prevent domestic checks on globalizing processes from being exerted. Rather than applying a brake on globalizing trends, regional economic agreements may actually be accelerating them!

Regional trade agreements have certainly been much more popular in recent years. Europe has long had the European Common Market, alongside other smaller, regional agreements such as EFTA (European Free Trade Area). Most of these have been incorporated within a single structure. The EU has also increased in membership, and promises to grow further. Perhaps more importantly it has moved much closer to becoming a single market, especially now that monetary union has been implemented. North America has its own free trade zone, NAFTA. South America has developed Mercosur, which encompasses Brazil, Argentina, Paraguay, and Uruguay.

Asia seems largely to have escaped formal regional organization. Some people argue that regional co-operation is taking place there, too, but in a less easily identified form. There is no formal organization comparable to those mentioned above. There are informal arrangements, including ASEAN, APEC, and others, but these do not have the constraining rules or powerful decision-making capabilities of the formal regional institutions. As the East Asian financial crisis illustrated, these countries have extensive economic ties that already bind their destinies together.

The pattern of past Japanese FDI has already constructed an integrated regional economy in East Asia. Some argue that Japanese foreign direct investment has a distinctly different impact both on the countries receiving the investment as well as on Japan itself. This unique impact is described as the "flying geese" model. Geese fly in a "vee" formation—the bird in the front breaks the air, creating a draft that the other birds can exploit. They are able to ride along the first bird's wake using less energy than they would flying alone. Japan's pioneering development of certain sectors, followed by purchases from foreign suppliers, and then its foreign direct investment, allows for its neighbours to climb in industrial development as Japan moves out of production in those same sectors. The result is an array of industries integrated across borders, but also constant progressive economic development for all involved.

Richard C. Hill and Kuniko Fujita argue that this pattern of investment means that Japan will not lose its industrial base in the same way that the U.S. and Europe have. Instead, Japan's industry will remain at the cutting edge, with older technologies being shared with neighbouring countries.[11] Every nation can draw benefits from this investment pattern, because every country's industrial development continues to move forward. Regional co-operation is taking place, but it does not have to have a recognized political structure. This raises some important issues about the appropriate structure or organization for mutually beneficial regional co-operation.

One question that arises in this context is whether regional arrangements should be pursued at all. Regional agreements often fit uncomfortably with broader multilateral institutions. Which sort of arrangement promotes globalization more strongly? Which sort allows for states to best "unpack" globalization, therefore meeting the desires of those who support globalization, while also shielding others who need protection from negative consequences? Does the existence of NAFTA or the EU alter the functioning of the WTO? Do these different forums offer states different trade-offs? Economists (holding liberal values and beliefs) may see little difference in these agreements; if anything, they would expect greater gains to be generated by the broadest arrangements. But if broad arrangements are not forthcoming, regional agreements might be the more practical route to gaining the benefits of international economic interactions. Are regional free trade zones more effective in achieving the gains from trade and international investment without threatening the control or effectiveness of national governments? Further study needs to be made before these political questions can be truly answered and in detail.

Often unnoticed, there are a number of sectoral international agreements in Asia. These sectoral agreements are often popular because they are more easily negotiated than the broader regional or multilateral deals. Sectoral agreements govern the international economic activities of a single industrial sector. They determine the degree of free trade for a small range of goods. Vinod Aggarwal, in studying the trade of East Asia, has drawn some conclusions about the politics generated by so many sectoral agreements. Smaller in scope, these agreements can satisfy the needs for groups interested in a small range of products or services. Yet when a number of small groups interested in liberalizing trade have their own immediate needs met, the political interests required to push through broader trade agreements won't be there—they'll already have had their goals met. Aggarwal therefore worries that more sectoral agreements in East Asia will leave the region without the constituencies motivated to achieve a regional free trade zone. There economic globalization may be proceeding in such a fashion that momentum will not build over time in the same fashion as it has in other regions.

We are not usually offered a clean way of understanding where regionalization ends and globalization begins. What exactly is regionalization, as opposed to globalization? Is increased American investment in Canada evidence of the former or of the latter? Are the NAFTA side protocols an example of balancing liberalization in the economy with enforceable regulatory standards, or an example of globalizing forces getting the upper hand? Couldn't similar protocols be embedded in WTO practices? In trying to answer some of these questions, let us turn to the oldest regional economic institution, the European Union. Is it a device created by states to shield themselves from the buffeting of international forces? Or is it promoting globalization? If we think of economic internationalization (rather than "globalization") we would probably realize that the sorts of pressures we are interested in can come either from broad multilateral arrangements or regional agreements. Some regional agreements could be viewed as attempts to counter or control broader international forces, however. The best of these examples is the European Union.

EUROPEAN INTEGRATION—CAUSE OR EFFECT?

According to historians Alan Milward and Vibeke Sorensen, European integration was pursued by national governments as a way to make their policies more effective. Rather than a sign of the weakening of states, integration was a strategy for overcoming weaknesses. This can be seen in the limitations states placed on the integrating institutions themselves, and also in how states' own agendas still dominate policy-making within the integrationist framework.[12] This challenges the view of neo-functionalists, who understand integration to result from states ceding their individual powers to a higher authority. As Milward and Sorensen put it, it is "oddly contradictory" that the period of European integration is a time when European states gained greater control over various other parts of society and the welfare state grew in size.

Because of these perspectives on the evidence, Milward and Sorensen see integration as the alternative to increased interdependence. Interdependence would require national adjustment to international practices, whereas integration offered the possibility of continuing to pursue national policies in spite of international pressures.[13] Moreover, states prefer integration to interdependence because integration emphasizes law over other factors.

To put it another way, Federico Romero claims that European integration "seems to embody a negotiated international co-ordination and expansion of parallel domestic strategies, all of which were aiming rather at the economic and political consolidation of the nation-state."[14] As Alan Milward agrees in his conclusion,

> Nation-states since the late nineteenth century have been increasingly held together not by traditional symbols of allegiance nor by repressive force but by national policies designed to secure material benefits for large social groups. As these policies have evolved, the reality has had to be faced that to be fully effective many need some form of international agreement, or occasionally even depend

absolutely on the international framework, for their effectiveness. Integration, the surrender of some limited measure of national sovereignty, is, we suggested, a new form of agreed international framework created by nation-states to advance particular sets of national domestic policies which could not be pursued, or not be pursued successfully, through the already existing international framework of co-operation between interdependent states, nor by renouncing international interdependence.[15]

These descriptions underscore the contradictory pressures states currently experience. Nation-states face threats to the effectiveness of their policies, which we described as pressure on their sovereignty in the previous chapters. But democratic states are also under pressure to increase democratic access, and improve participation by citizens, as well as offer improved economic performance over time. These demands have to be met even as globalizing trends might exacerbate economic and social dislocations.[16] Regional or international co-operation offers one way to seek a balance in this situation.

Identifying Where Globalization Will Soon Have a Strong Impact

Although states may try to shield themselves by turning to regional or international arrangements to control the impact of globalizing trends, ultimately the impact of globalization will alter the balance of political forces within these countries. The economic component of globalization will always create some winners, as well as likely produce losers. The question is where the balance between these interests fall, who can organize their interests to be heard, and who can get the state to respond to their demands. The state's own interests enter the picture, of course. Globalizing trends in culture, in communication, and elsewhere help shape how this political clash will unfold.

As the first step in this analysis, we have to consider whether a constituency for globalization has already been created by past policy choices. Unsurprisingly, globalization has proceeded much more quickly in some places rather than others. As earlier chapters suggested, states have choices regarding participation in globalizing processes. A few states have resisted the processes at the core of globalization, such as trade, international investment, or improved external communications. Cuba is a good example of a state whose leadership has struggled with the decisions to allow these processes to affect their country; North Korea is an example of a state that has refused to engage in these processes. Choices remain. As globalization proceeds the opportunity-costs associated with refusing to participate may rise. Technology, decisions by other states, and globalizing trends may be changing the terms of those choices, however.

Milner and Keohane framed internationalization as about choices; more technically, internationalization is about opportunity-costs. As the benefits to opening up to the world economy rise, the decision to stay largely closed off becomes relatively costly. Viewed in these terms, globalization is important perhaps especially so, for those states that have attempted to separate themselves from global economic forces.[17] We should think that globalization only has supporters in those places already tightly integrated into the international political economy.

In making those choices, we should expect states to keep their own interests in mind, including defending their own independence. They may trade that independence for other goals, of course, but independence won't be given away without the expectation of something in return. Sovereignty may be under threat, but states can respond in ways that help them retain some of their powers. Stephen Krasner has noted that even as globalization may be undercutting certain aspects of sovereignty, other international norms and practices bolster it.[18] States with very limited resources and capabilities find support for their claim to sovereignty from the recognition and aid they receive from other states.

What bothers many people—not just Marxists and greens, but even some Keynesians—is that in the face of integrated capital markets, countries positioned at a disadvantage may be faced with such constraints that their choices are extremely limited. Whereas liberals focus on voluntary choices as the route to achieving mutual benefits, Marxists and others on the left are more likely to view some actors on capital markets as having no real choice at all. Economically developing countries, in particular, face the choice of trading off stability for growth, since low interest rates to stimulate growth may lead to capital flight once countries have relaxed capital controls in order to join the international financial system. Expanding government expenditures to stimulate growth may actually increase consumption of imports, depreciating the currency and driving equity capital out.[19] Currency markets remain a source of instability, even though states may want to encourage investors to come into the country freely. What policy choices do states actually have, once they've decided to open themselves up to international capital markets?

Richard Rosecrance, having chosen to emphasize how technological changes are driving globalization, has coined the term "virtual state." He wants to stress that technology has made the knowledge component of production (and of goods and services themselves) more important (and more profitable). States are rewarded in this new environment by allowing greater flows of the factors of production. (He is somewhat unclear on how labour flows fit in, however.) States may choose to impose regulations domestically, which can vary from state to state, but what is important in his eyes is that the state implement these regulations impartially.[20] Technology has made it more attractive to open up countries' borders to flows of capital, in particular.

Even among the most industrialized states, different sets of countries face different trade-offs when considering whether to participate in globalizing economic trends. Robert Boyer and Daniel Drache draw a distinction among the industrialized Western countries between those they describe as "market-driven" and those they term "social democracies." Among the first group are the United States, Canada, Britain, Australia, and New Zealand, while classic examples of the latter group are Germany, France, and Sweden.[21] Each set reacts to globalization differently because they are coming from different starting points.

Boyer and Drache employ concepts from the French *régulation* school of political economy. This approach views markets as inherently destructive, but can be tempered by government policies and agreements reached by the state and prominent social actors/groups. Markets are merely one economic mechanism for allocating resources—one among many from which society can choose. Markets are not necessarily the best mechanisms. Thus in Boyer's and Drache's view, the free-market-oriented countries will not be able to withstand the destructive aspects of globalization.

> Free-market-oriented nations such as the U.S., the U.K. and Canada have not been successful in coping with innovation and market variability, i.e., structural competitiveness. Conversely, where market forces have been kept under control as in Japan, Germany and Austria, their individual economic performances have been far superior in terms of growth, unemployment and innovation.[22]

This conjecture was published in 1996. Their expectations certainly can be challenged, for the United States, Britain, and Canada have done tolerably well in the late 1990s. Japan remains mired in economic recession and, with Germany and other European countries, has been facing very slow productivity growth and persistently high unemployment.

One can raise a different line of inquiry about economic performance, as to which of the countries controlling market forces may have done better. If we concede that globalization may be delivering benefits to society overall, there remains a question as to how this wealth is spread around. Ethan Kapstein, in several works, has posed just this question: "After all if globalization and technological change are making countries so much richer, we might well ask how societies are sharing the wealth."[23] Kapstein examines the evidence, and finds that while more wealth is indeed being generated, labour is not receiving much of this new wealth. As he asks, "If our economic policies do not help working people enjoy a decent way of life, and instill hope for a better future, what is the point?"[24]

CONCLUSIONS: TRADING SOVEREIGNTY AWAY

In the end, Krasner may have the best assessment of the wide array of evidence on how different states are exposed to globalizing trends. On the one hand, indicators show that transnational flows of a variety of items (ranging from messages in various media to capital) have steadily increased since 1950. On the other hand, states seem to have been able to pursue their own individual definitions of interests, and their own policy agendas in that time. This would include wide variation in the levels of taxation and government expenditure.[25] Nonetheless, there may be pressures now emerging for states to reconsider many of their choices. As he concludes,

> I do not want to claim that globalization has had no impact on state control, but these challenges are not new. Rulers have always operated in a transnational environment, autarky has rarely been an option; regulation and monitoring of transborder flows have always been problematic. The difficulties for states have become more acute in some areas, but less in others. There is no evidence that globalization has systematically undermined state control or led to the homogenization of policies and structures. In fact, globalization and state activity have moved in tandem.[26]

In general, we have seen two positions proposed in this and the previous chapters. On the one hand, increased globalization is seen as causing convergence in policies states pursue, which puts pressure on the Keynesian welfare practices of the most economically advanced countries.

On the other hand, it is argued that cross-national differences are not disappearing, and that increased trade and international investment brings enough increased wealth that states can afford to continue to support the Keynesian welfare state.[27] While current statistical evidence supports the latter position, concerns about the veracity of the former in the future continues to fuel policy debates.

Considering How Recent Globalizing Forces Look in Two Different Settings: the United States and Canada

How has the world's largest economy, that of the United States, been affected by globalization? Perhaps surprisingly, integration into the world economy is a fairly new force for the United States to accept.[28] This can be contrasted with the experiences of Canada, which has relied heavily on trade, foreign capital, and inflows of labour for decades. As Bill Watson points out, U.S. imports relative to America's GDP climbed only to 14 per cent in the mid-1990s—while Canada's never fell so low in the entire twentieth century.[29] We might expect globalization to register as a more serious set of new issues in the United States—but has this been the case?

INDICATORS OF AMERICA'S DEEPENING RELATIONSHIP WITH THE GLOBAL ECONOMY

As mentioned earlier in this chapter, the United States economy has long been insulated from the global economy. The sheer size of the American economy has ensured that trade has been of marginal importance to the U.S.—even if the amount the U.S. exports or imports actually makes up a large portion of global trade flows. The best way to understand this is to consider some of the statistics on trade. As a percentage of GDP, American exports and imports prior to the 1970s typically were below 10 per cent. This has grown steadily, however, over the past two decades. In 1985, exports and imports combined to account for some 17 per cent of GDP, rose to 21 per cent in 1993, and then 25 per cent in 1997.[30]

One obvious impact of globalizing trends for the United States, then, is the increased importance of trade policy in political debates. As Geoffrey Garrett observes:

It is thus not surprising that trade issues dominate contemporary economic relations between the two largest (but smallest trading, as a percentage of GDP) Western nations—Japan and the United States. The debate within those countries on how best to compete can be expected to grow more heated as their trade exposure increases.[31]

Trade liberalization has enjoyed a sheltered position in American policy-making circles. This is probably due to a variety of circumstances, outlined succinctly by Michael Hiscox.[32] Hiscox suggests that the best explanation for America's consistent support for free trade is a combination of the interests voiced by important groups, as well as the institutional interests expressed by the American President. As the one political voice for the entire country, the U.S. President appreciates the possible gains from liberalizing trade, while the Congress is divided.

Trade is not only more important, but as tariffs and other barriers fall, and the pressures to compete become clearer and stronger, concerns about economic regulation bubble to the surface. Dani Rodrik makes a similar point: "Trade becomes contentious when it unleashes forces that undermine norms implicit in domestic practices."[33] Rodrik uses the example of child labour to underscore his point. If a factory in Ohio closed and the firm involved moved its production to Texas, where it hired 13-year-old children to work on an assembly line, most Americans would be outraged. So why shouldn't we be upset if the same action takes place but the firm involved has moved its plant to another country? This is why political disputes are more and more over "fair trade" as opposed to "free trade."

Another way to interpret the impact of globalization on the U.S., however, is to note other changes occurring in the American economy. Americans now spend more on services and other non-tradeables than on manufactured goods. Expenditures on non-tradeables refers to money spent on health care, travel, entertainment, and legal services, for example. As industrial productivity increases, the prices of manufactured goods fall. If productivity in the service sector hasn't increased as rapidly, then the price of manufactured goods will fall in comparison.[34]

As the U.S. becomes more economically engaged with the world, other parts of the political agenda beyond trade change. Different aspects of economic policy gain salience. In the area of monetary policy, for instance, greater economic internationalization shifts the cleavage on policy from a focus on interest rates to the exchange rate. The two are related, to be sure, yet there are important differences. The key political cleavage over monetary policy in a more closed economy pits creditors against debtors; in an open economy, the division is determined by exchange rate preferences.[35]

For instance, in the early 1970s, when the Nixon administration was trying to decide how to handle problems with the value of the U.S. dollar and a commitment to fixed exchange rates internationally, domestic goals came into conflict with international obligations. On almost all sides, priority was given to domestic targets.[36] Now we can more easily observe differences between international interests and domestic interests. While further empirical work needs to be done,[37] preliminary evidence indicates such divisions can be seen in how much support there is for U.S. government funding of the IMF or international bailouts.

The role of the U.S. dollar in the world economy and in world finance remains dominant.[38] By almost any measure, whether it be the percentage used in international trade payments, the amount held as foreign exchange reserves by governments, the number of currencies tied to it, or currency used for pricing commodities, the U.S. dollar plays the dominant role in international affairs. In fact, a number of countries experiencing difficulties with their own national currencies have decided to base their own money entirely on the U.S. dollar. "Dollarization" takes management of the monetary supply out of local political hands and puts it entirely in the hands of the leadership of the U.S. Federal Reserve.

This pattern could change in the near future, though expectations differ widely. Some expect the U.S. dollar to continue to be the most important currency internationally, so long as current market practices continue. Benjamin Cohen has stressed how existing "network externalities" make it unlikely that another currency will dethrone the dollar. On the other hand, there is at least one other currency with the potential to make serious inroads into the dominance of the dollar: the euro. Because the euro is used by a major trading bloc, and because Europeans save large sums (making it likely that extensive lending in euros will develop), rivalry between the two currencies could easily develop.

For the U.S., competitive pressures may not matter much yet. But if they do develop in the future, they could have serious ramifications for how the dollar is managed. When two currencies are in competition for widespread international use, the issuers have to worry about maintaining confidence in their money. The best tool for convincing others to hold onto a currency is to raise interest rates. Raising interest rates can depress economic activity in the domestic economy, however.[39]

Monetary policy can clash with other interests in a number of ways. In an economically open economy, monetary and trade policy become potential substitutes, whereas in a closed economy they are not. While the U.S. economy could be considered an open economy from the time of the Civil War until the 1930s, it has been so actually only in the last two decades.[40] We saw in the 1980s attempts to substitute trade and monetary policies. Those hurt by foreign competition make demands in both areas, and strategize between using policy in the two. As the U.S. is increasingly affected by globalization, such interactions can be expected to increase. The opportunities to substitute monetary policy for trade policy will grow. The ability to construct viable political coalitions in the United States on the basis of either trade or monetary policy will grow as well.

Globalization or Americanization?

Many authors note that U.S. government policies seem to be one of the prime factors behind the spread of globalization. Edward Luttwak identifies a new package of economic practices: "turbo-capitalism." This includes an emphasis on technological change, privatization of social services, deregulation of markets, and liberalized international trade. These overlap most definitions of globalization, and Luttwak titled his book *Turbo-Capitalism: Winners and Losers in the Global Economy.* The spread of this form of capitalism, Luttwak argues, is the set of policies the U.S. implemented beginning in the late 1970s, which forced other states to follow suit.[41]

This argument had been made earlier by Eric Helleiner, if in a more limited form. Helleiner noted that both the U.S. and Britain had allowed or even supported the development of the lightly regulated Euro-dollar market during the 1960s. Euro-dollars are American dollars held outside the United States. Prior to the 1960s, such deposits were small, but a burgeoning market developed. It was significant because local governments left this business largely unregulated, with dangerous consequences in the 1980s.

Both Britain and the United States deregulated their financial systems, and then liberalized their international financial linkages in the 1970s and 1980s. These moves gave their financial services an edge against foreign competitors. In order to maintain the competitiveness of their own banks, other countries then followed suit. Helleiner therefore describes the 1980s as a period of "competitive deregulation."[42] John Goodman and Louis Pauly elaborated on this logic by showing the impact these decisions had on other major players.[43] Goodman and

Pauly illustrated how the decisions by the U.S. and Britain on capital controls reconfigured the domestic interests within other major economies, and soon drove them to make similar decisions about ending capital controls. The international use of the dollar (since at least the 1940s) has given the United States specific advantages in international monetary affairs. "At least on the money markets, globalization so far means little more than Americanization of the world."[44]

Importantly, American practices in labour markets may also be spreading internationally. This is one of the most contentious aspects of globalization, in fact. American labour markets are among the most liquid and fluid in the world. It is not unusual for firms to experience high turnover rates in their workforce. It is also not unusual for Americans to travel great distances in search of employment. Families pack up and move across state lines surprisingly often. Knowing that they can draw on labour flows, American firms do not have to work so hard to retain workers (except when unemployment falls to extremely low levels). The result is a labour market characterized by fluidity. This is quite different from labour markets in Europe and elsewhere. In these countries, labour cannot readily flow from one region to another for a variety of reasons. Also, traditions tend to keep people bound more closely to home. Europe's labour markets do not exhibit the same turnover rates, and social policies create incentives to stay put. Pressures to lower social policies are therefore seen as the first step towards undermining this whole arrangement, and are fiercely resisted.

Many therefore see the current international economic practices as a set of rules and norms largely fashioned by the United States. Liberalized trade, more open capital markets, and more open foreign direct investment have been policy goals pursued by the U.S. for several decades, if not longer. Why, then, should the U.S. be worried about the consequences of these policies being adopted elsewhere? Shouldn't these policies enable the United States to compete more effectively in the international realm, relying on its advantages? If not, why would the U.S. be promoting these policies in the first place?

As noted in earlier chapters, globalizing processes don't have to be limited to the economic sphere. In cultural terms, globalization may not be so difficult for the U.S. to face, either, if only because globalization seems to promote American products and American ways. As proof of globalization, many would point to the ways in which cultures seem to be homogenizing. If one travels to Warsaw or Beijing, what does one see? Michael Jordan t-shirts, kids listening to Janet Jackson and munching on McDonald's hamburgers—pretty much the same as one would see in Chicago or New York.

If, on the cultural front, globalization is really Americanization, how does this affect the United States? One might think it doesn't affect it at all. America's culture is being exported—in the form of movies, music, clothing styles, and so on. On the other hand, American culture is a very fluid. Foreign content in American culture is difficult to judge. Who owns America's largest movie studios and recording companies? Even American television channels are not entirely owned by Americans. Still, the products made for the American market seem to dominate the products for other markets.

If globalizing affects trends in cultural affairs, should other countries be worried? If it is an American culture that is being promoted via global communications and global markets, should other countries fear such influences? For Canadians, such fears are anything but new. Since Canadians see important differences between their culture and that of the United States, and wish for those differences to be maintained, Canada has long had policies aimed at controlling cultural matters. Government support for broadcasting through the CBC, legislation regarding content, and other rules are important elements of these policies. American rules on these matters are quite meagre in contrast.

Many Canadians feel this is a merely a rearguard action. Even though the Canadian government has fought hard to treat cultural goods differently in NAFTA and multilateral negotiations, ever greater pressure is coming from the U.S. to do the opposite. Since exports of cultural goods account for more and more of American trade, this pressure is not likely to go away. Canada feels the brunt of these pressures because its media markets are so close to America's—close both in a physical sense, making it easy for American broadcasts to serve Canada's major metropolitan markets, but also in the sense that language and income levels are quite similar in many of these instances as well.[45]

Canadian Bill Watson offers another prescient point. He observes that the lack of serious ideological debate these days represents a victory for essentially American positions.

> It is ironic, but true, that the end of a Cold War that required an ideological chafing has given way to a more relaxed but even greater ideological conformity into which we have entered freely. We and the Americans and everyone else in the respectable world now hold essentially the same truths to be self-evident.[46]

Watson's observation, while meant to refer to Canadians, may well be speaking for the citizens of some other countries.

IS GLOBALIZATION CHANGING THE FACE OF AMERICA'S DOMESTIC POLITICS?

If globalization is finally having an impact on the United States, what changes can we observe? What sort of effects will surface first? As noted earlier, the relevance of exchange rate and trade policies should be rising. Other changes in the domestic political economy should become apparent.

Unionization rates in the U.S. have been steadily declining for some time, but are now hitting record low levels. This can be attributed in part, at least, to globalization. The opportunity to invest abroad gives American firms the option of moving their operations to foreign soil. This threat alone can shift the balance against labour's interest.[47] The same threats, plus the weakening of labour's organization, combine to put downward pressures—or at least a cap—on wage demands. This may help explain why the United States has experienced the pattern of economic changes it has in the 1990s. There has been high growth combined with low inflation, usually thought of as the best possible combination. These positives, however, come along with a major negative: rising inequality.[48]

Another important change for the United States, as a result of its greater integration into the global economy, has been the flow of capital coming in to the United States. How much foreign direct investment is coming into the United States? In the late 1980s there were growing concerns voiced about foreign ownership in certain sectors. Some of these concerns reflected confusion and the absence of accurate information. Concerns also were expressed by those who knew that other countries exercised some constraints on incoming investments while the United States did not. The result was the empowerment of legislation.

Analyses intended to answer some of these questions founder on some fundamental issues. What counts as foreign ownership? Does the foreign investor have to own the company in question in full? Or own a controlling share? Or simply own a significant percentage of the firm's shares? Depending on which measure you use, you will get very different results. U.S. legislation actually focuses on the last of these definitions. Yet even using the looser definition, the figures on foreign ownership are surprisingly small. Foreigners owned between 11 per cent and 19 per cent of U.S. manufacturing in 1992; they owned between 16 per cent and 23 per cent of the banking sector.[49] These levels are low compared to other OECD countries.

Another area of concern expressed in the late 1980s was that foreign ownership of real estate was on the rise. This evaluation was perhaps based solely on impressions rather than facts, since Japanese investors had purchased a large number of golf courses in Hawaii and on the west coast, as well as several prominent buildings in city centers. (Rockefeller Plaza being the best known.) Figures do not support the overall impression. Edward Graham and Paul Krugman found foreign ownership of real estate to be extremely low.[50] Japanese investment in the banking sector was higher than expected in those years, but not in any other part of the economy.

The legislation passed in the late 1970s, when international security concerns were still a factor for the United States. The legislation was inspired by two relatively strong surges in FDI coming into the United States. The first surge peaked in 1979-1981, the second in 1986-1990. Interestingly, since 1990 FDI flows into the United States have "virtually dried up" according to Graham and Krugman, who have studied this issue extensively.[51] This remains true despite the legislation passed in this area. The U.S. remains very open to foreign investment.

From their studies, Graham and Krugman also conclude that fears voiced about foreign investment are unfounded. "The main conclusion of this study is that there is little evidence to support concerns about the negative effects of FDI in general."[52] In other words, the levels are low, the benefits are obvious, and the problems largely imaginary.

CONCLUDING REMARKS ON GLOBALIZATION AND THE U.S.

Evidence suggests the United States is only now finding itself under the influence of powerful globalizing trends. To a great extent, those who seek to understand the forces behind globalization look to the U.S.—to its government, its major firms, or its economic interests more broadly. If the United States were to discover that globalization would be costing it its own independence, would it change its attitudes? Do we already have indications of that, with the resistance of American policy-makers to submit American policies to control by international institutions or multilateral organizations (whether we are talking about the UN or the WTO)?

A few people actually hold out the hope that such things will occur. If the U.S. discovers it doesn't like globalization, it might stop promoting it, and even lead in developing co-operative measures to reduce globalization's impact. As Martin and Schumann put it:

Across the whole spectrum of commercial, social, financial and monetary policy, it is ultimately Washington's politicians and their advisors who set the rules for global integration, even if they are often not themselves aware of it. Neither a quest for colonial supremacy, nor actual military superiority, but the sheer size of the American economy makes the USA the last factor of order amid the chaos of global entanglement. It is therefore quite possible that an American government will also eventually be the first to break out of the global trap.[53]

They add that the U.S. led the way in establishing the Keynesian welfare state and helped insulate that welfare state from international markets in the Bretton Woods negotiations in 1944. American desires were fundamental in how the balance of "embedded liberalism" was struck at that time. American decisions appear to have played a fundamental role in altering this compromise with the unleashing of capital markets and the consequent "disembedding" of liberalism. The U.S. could conceivably lead the way in fashioning a different compromise in the future. Watching how the U.S. experiences globalization, and how it responds to it in the coming years, will be of great interest to us all.

Variations in Globalization's Impact

This chapter has illustrated how the same stresses and strains of globalization present very different decisions before states and their citizens. Some states have already been exposed to these forces for some time, whereas others may be experiencing changes in politics as these forces gather strength. Some states have decided to forgo participation, and therefore will be affected by opportunity costs associated with their decisions. Most democracies have already decided they would participate but they seek to balance that participation in some manner. Regional or multilateral institutions have been developed to help states maintain the effectiveness of their policies, even as they relinquish some of their decision-making independence when they join in on globalizing activities.

Even recognizing how all this variation can be playing out, we still need to figure out another set of complicating issues. How can the proponents of globalization, or their opposition, organize to make their demands felt? When should we anticipate that the opponents of globalization will be able to link their issues with others? Since so much of the argument so far has focused on economic issues, one gets the impression that those who garner the economic benefits of globalization will be positioned to use those benefits to further their interests. Those hurt by globalizing trends may lash out, or seek compensation from the state, but would such groups ever be politically powerful? Would they ever be able to portray themselves as more than the economic losers in the new world of global economic competition? To answer these questions, we need to address the politics of identity. The cultural dimension of globalization may play a prominent role in shifting some of the terms of political conflict over globalization.

NOTES

1 Kwan S. Kim, "Global Economic Integration: Issues and Challenges," in John-ren Chen, ed., *Economic Effects of Globalization* (Aldershot: Ashgate, 1998), 118-19.

2 Alan Scott, "Globalization: social process or political rhetoric?," in Scott, ed., *The Limits of Globalization: Cases and Arguments* (London: Routledge, 1997), 5.

3 Sylvia Bashevkin, "Rethinking Retrenchment: North American Social Policy during the Early Clinton and Chrétien Years," *Canadian Journal of Political Science* 33, 1 (Mar. 2000): 15.

4 Ibid.

5 For an excellent overview of the basic choices we can make when modelling these various steps together, see James Alt and Michael Gilligan, "The Political Economy of Trading States: Factor Specificity, Collective Action Problems, and Domestic Political Institutions," *Journal of Political Philosophy* 2, 2 (1994): 165-92.

6 Geoffrey Garrett and Peter Lange, "Internationalization, Institutions and Political Change," in Helen Milner and Robert Keohane, eds., *Internationalization and Domestic Politics* (Cambridge: Cambridge University Press, 1996), 53.

7 Paul Krugman, *Pop Internationalism* (Cambridge, MA: MIT Press, 1996), 195-96.

8 Ingrid Bryan, *Canada in the New Global Economy: Problems and Policies* (Toronto: John Wiley & Sons, 1994), 160-61.

9 Hans-Peter Martin and Harald Schumann, *The Global Trap: Globalization and the Assault on Prosperity and Democracy*, trans. Patrick Camiller (Montreal: Black Rose Books, 1998), 226.

10 Robert Boyer and Daniel Drache, "Introduction," in Boyer and Drache, eds., *States Against Markets: The Limits of Globalization* (London: Routledge, 1996), 19.

11 Richard C. Hill and Kuniko Fujita, "Product Cycles and International Divisions of Labor: Contrast between the United States and Japan," in David A. Smith and Jozsef Böröcz, eds., *A New World Order?* (Westport, CT: Praeger, 1995), 91-108.

12 Alan Milward and Vibeke Sorensen, "Interdependence or integration? A national choice," in Milward and Sorensen, eds., *The Frontier of National Sovereignty: History and Theory, 1945-1992* (London: Routledge, 1993), 4.

13 Ibid., 12, 18.

14 Federico Romero, "Migration as an issue in European interdependence and integration: the case of Italy," in Milward and Sorensen, eds., *The Frontier of National Sovereignty,* 35.

15 Alan Milward, "Conclusions: the value of history," in Milward and Sorensen, eds., *The Frontier of National Sovereignty,* 182.

16 For a discussion of these conflicting yet interconnected pressures, see Ramesh Mishra, "The Welfare of Nations," in Boyer and Drache, eds., *States Against Markets,* 328.

17 Helen Milner and Robert Keohane, "Internationalization and Domestic Politics: An Introduction," in Milner and Keohane, eds., *Internationalization and Domestic Politics,* 19.

18 Stephen Krasner, *Sovereignty* (Princeton, NJ: Princeton University Press, 1999), 3.

19 Kim, "Global Economic Integration," 118-19.

20 Richard Rosecrance, *The Rise of the Virtual State* (New York: Basic Books, 1999), 89.

21 Boyer and Drache, 5-6.

22 Ibid., 6.

23 Ethan Kapstein, *Sharing the Wealth* (New York: W.W. Norton, 1999), 7.

24 Ibid., 8.

25 Krasner, *Sovereignty,* 13.

26 Ibid., 223.

27 Geoffrey Garrett, "Capital mobility, trade, and the domestic politics of economic policy," *International Organization* 49, 4 (Autumn 1995): 658.

28 For a discussion of this comparison, see Bashevkin, "Rethinking Retrenchment."

29 William Watson, *Globalization and the Meaning of Canadian Life* (Toronto: University of Toronto Press, 1998), 23.

30 These figures are from the U.S. Department of Commerce, as given in "American Trade Policy: Throwing sand in the gears," *The Economist,* 30 Jan. 1999, 63-65.

31 Garrett, "Capital mobility, trade, and the domestic politics of economic policy," 682.

32 Michael Hiscox, "The Magic Bullet? The RTAA, Institutional Reform and Trade Liberalization," *International Organization* 53, 4 (Autumn 1999): 669-98.

33 Dani Rodrik, *Has Globalization Gone Too Far?* (Washington: Institute for International Economics, 1997), 5.

34 Krugman, *Pop Internationalism*, 36-38, 40.

35 Jeffry Frieden, "Economic Integration and the Politics of Monetary Policy in the United States," in Milner and Keohane, eds., *Internationalization and Domestic Politics*, 111.

36 For a review of the literature on this subject, see Mark R. Brawley, *Turning Points: Decisions Shaping the Evolution of the International Political Economy* (Peterborough, ON: Broadview Press, 1998), ch. 17.

37 Lawrence Broz is currently undertaking this sort of analysis.

38 This is a conclusion held by practically all sides. See Paul Hirst and Grahame Thompson, *Globalization in Question: The International Economy and the Possibilities of Governance*, 2nd ed. (Cambridge: Polity Press, 1999), 58-59; Benjamin Cohen, *The Geography of Money* (Ithaca, NY: Cornell University Press, 1998).

39 For a discussion of how this dilemma affected Britain in the 1920s, but has not yet affected the United States, see Mark R. Brawley, *Afterglow or Adjustment?* (New York: Columbia University Press, 1999).

40 Frieden, "Economic Integration and the Politics of Monetary Policy in the United States," 112-14.

41 Edward Luttwak, *Turbo-Capitalism* (London: Weidenfeld & Nicolson, 1998), 1.

42 Eric Helleiner, *States and the Reemergence of Global Finance* (Ithaca, NY: Cornell University Press, 1994). The argument is first presented on p. 12, and then laid out in detail in Chapter 4.

43 John Goodman and Louis Pauly, "The Obsolescence of Capital Controls? Economic Management in an Age of Global Markets," *World Politics* 46, 1 (1993): 50-82.

44 Martin and Schumann, *The Global Trap*, 74.

45 As much as francophones in Quebec like to think they have a distinct culture, their distinction rests largely on one dimension—language. I have often asked myself what is so distinct about *The Simpsons* dubbed in French?

46 Watson, *Globalization and the Meaning of Canadian Life*, 230.

47 Kapstein, *Sharing the Wealth*, 99.

48 Ibid.

49 Graham and Krugman, *Foreign Direct Investment in the United States*, 2.

50 Ibid., 31, 33.

51 Ibid., 12-13.

52 Ibid., 149.

53 Martin and Schumann, *The Global Trap*, 216-17.

7 | Globalization and the Politics of Identity

How has globalization affected culture? How do these changes affect the way people think about themselves, and their relationship with people elsewhere? Improvements in transportation and communication can make it easier for us to learn about others, but how will that knowledge affect us? Will we become more cognizant of our similarities, or our differences? Will we build bridges tying us together, or will we learn how hard it may be to connect people from many different cultures and traditions?

To begin to answer these questions we have to consider the direct ways in which globalizing processes influence issues of identity. Globalizing processes, particularly economic changes that are reshaping the way cultures are generated and transmitted across generations, can have a direct influence on the politics of identity. But after reviewing these possible linkages, we need to turn to a second way in which the politics of identity get intertwined with issues about globalization: as a tactical or strategic manoeuvre by political entrepreneurs. Those who wish to oppose globalization are quite likely to turn to the politics of identity, in order to mobilize support for their cause. This is not the only reason why the politics of identity may become contentious in coming years, but it certainly points out one way the politics of identity may be a crucial factor in determining whether globalizing processes proceed, or are slowed by a political backlash.

How Globalizing Processes Ignite the Politics of Identity

Globalizing processes can be thought of as having a direct impact on the way people think of themselves, the groups they identify with, and the sorts of political bodies they turn to for assistance or to which give their loyalty. The term "globalization" implies a decline in the importance of the national. This holds for people's political affiliations, too. If globalizing economic processes are making national governments less effective, then will people focus their political activities on other levels of government, or other political authorities? As we saw earlier, this is a pivotal element in the greens' political perspective.

Ankie Hoogvelt argues that the current set of processes in globalization promote the politics of exclusion rather than incorporation.[1] She claims that globalization in markets is reconfiguring domestic political economic practices in ways that make people see each other differently than before. In particular, globalization brings greater economic inequalities, causing internal divisions in societies to grow. Others second this finding, arguing that global processes (especially the economic ones) spark racism and ethnocentric political reactions.[2] The connections are not always so direct, however, in these other analyses. Sometimes ethnocentric or nationalistic responses are merely the result of tactical decisions by political leaders.

William I. Robinson suggests that the economic changes we associate with globalization are causing deeper social disruptions in many societies around the world. Sometimes the connections are indirect; the changes also have the potential, in his view, for reconfiguring both inclusive identities and exclusive ones.

> Economic globalization brings with it the material basis for the transnationalization of political systems, civil society, social classes, and cultural life. As a new global social structure of accumulation transforms existing national ones, integration into this emergent global economy and society is the causal macrostructural dynamic that underlies recent social change worldwide.[3]

Williamson continues this line of argument by drawing out parallels to Polanyi's *The Great Transformation*, a work referred to often in previous chapters. This line of argument suggests that societies are unlikely to accept too much disruption of social institutions by economic forces before there is a backlash. That backlash may well take a nationalistic or ethnocentric form, as it often did in the 1930s.

For those who see the nationalist upsurge and consequent political conflict as a direct result of globalization, there are questions as to whether this is something entirely new. Is the resurfacing of the politics of identity a sign of some countries just passing through a stage that Western Europe went through more than a century ago? Or is it something very different that needs to be seen as unique? As Cesare Poppi forcefully put it:

> Far from being the resurgence of obsolete, "archaic" or "primordial" feelings, as some liberal thinkers in despair still appear to think in the face of the onslaught in Bosnia and Rwanda, ethnicity is but one specification of the contemporary renegotiation of the terms of engagement between the local and the global, the specific and what used to be called "the universal."[4]

Poppi would therefore expect the politics of identity to be played out differently these days than previously, as those who seek to resist globalization employ the politics of identity as part of their bargaining over the terms of their participation in global political and economic systems.

Robert W. Cox also refers to Polanyi's arguments. Cox argues that the politics of identity are important as an element shaped by globalization —and critical for how far globalization itself will proceed, but also as an important force to be reckoned with in understanding the longer-term consequences of globalization. As he put it:

> Economic globalization is generating sources of conflicts and cleavages that are working their way slowly but surely into the foundations of world politics. The politics of the superstructure—U.S. military power and coalition politics in support of economic globalization—are challenged by emergent social forces and social tensions, which are evident in both poor and rich countries. To understand these social forces it is necessary to reflect on the formation of identities that give meaning and orientation to people and on the forms of knowledge capable of explaining how to cope with the challenges of the future.[5]

In other words, Cox foresees growing conflict between the globalizing forces and the images of culture they promote, backed by those countries that can accept such ideas, versus the forces that may be bubbling up in those countries that will have a harder time accepting them. This is certainly a useful framework for considering the roots of Islamist political movements, or for considering why the terrorist network headed by Osama bin Laden could receive support from people dispersed in so many countries.

In many ways, Thomas Friedman, a journalist who has long covered the Middle East for the *New York Times*, has come up with a simple yet compelling imagery to describe this sort of conflict. He uses this imagery as the title of his book *The Lexus and the Olive Tree*. The Lexus represents the potential rewards from participating in economic globalization. But this often comes at a cost, represented by the olive tree. Here is how he describes the other things at risk when economic globalization proceeds:

> Olive trees are important. They represent everything that roots us, anchors us, identifies us and locates us in this world—whether it be belonging to a family, a community, a tribe, a nation, a religion or, most of all, a place called home.[6]

For a healthy society, Friedman argues that economic goals must be met, but not without close tending to "the olive trees" as well. Identity cannot be lost in the trade-off for economic improvement. If economic advances come at the cost of a society's roots, if it destroys individuals' identities and sense of community, then there will be political turmoil. Note that Friedman did not pose the title his book as a choice, using the word "or"—he clearly argues that in a functioning society, individuals demand both economic progress and a sense of belonging.

TWO SCENARIOS: CONVERGENCE OR FRAGMENTATION?

Although we have so far suggested that globalization will lead to clashes between different cultures or identities, there are logical alternatives. One is conflict-ridden, but the other is that some will find it possible to adopt a more global or universal identity. After referring to W.B. Yeats on the "eternities of race and soul," Benjamin Barber laid out these two possible prospects, which he labelled "Jihad" and "McWorld." The former outcome is described as holding

> the grim prospect of a retribalization of large swaths of humankind by war and bloodshed: a threatened balkanization of nation-states in which culture is pitted against culture, people against people, tribe against tribe, a Jihad in the name of a hundred narrowly conceived faiths against every kind of interdependence, every kind of artificial social cooperation and mutuality; against technology, against pop culture, and against integrated markets; against modernity itself as well as the future in which modernity issues.

Barber goes on to describe the alternative outcome.

The second paints in that future in shimmering pastels, a busy portrait of onrushing economic technological, and ecological forces that demand integration and uniformity and that mesmerize peoples everywhere with fast music, fast computers, and fast food—MTV, Macintosh, and McDonald's—pressing nations into one homogenous global theme park, one McWorld tied together by communications, information, entertainment, and commerce. Caught between Babel and Disneyland, the planet is falling precipitously apart and coming reluctantly together at the very same moment.[7]

Barber's description, then, is that both sets of changes or challenges are occurring simultaneously. What is not clear from his description, however, is whether these processes are occurring in different locales, or pushing against each other in the same places at the same time.

Barber goes on to argue that globalization represents a threat to democracy: "Can it be that what Jihad and McWorld have in common is anarchy: the absence of common will and that conscious collective human control under guidance of law we call democracy?"[8] Just as Cox suggested, Barber sees issues of identity spilling over into other dimensions of politics. As Friedman also fears, when the fragmenting politics of identity get tied up with other issues, the results will not be positive. Friedman draws from his own experiences reporting on the Middle East. In the end, he wants to strike a balance between the need for an identity rooted in the local community and the ability to participate in global economic and political processes.

Friedman's experience and knowledge of the Middle East provided him with an important insight, however, on when the backlash against globalization is likely to be most successful. Conflict over identity plays an important, perhaps necessary role in the equation. An alternative ideology to globalizing capitalism is unlikely to develop, he believes, because there is no compelling alternative out there that can offer to improve people's lives economically in a less painful fashion.[9] The existing backlash in the economically developed countries lacks a coherent ideology, evidenced in the demonstrations against the WTO in Seattle in December 1999 and in Quebec City against free trade in the Americas in April 2001. The backlash will be severe only when it combines groups' economic, political, and cultural grievances.[10] This has been most apparent in the Middle East, Friedman argues. As the events of 11 September 2001 illustrate, those who use the politics of identity to motivate their followers are much more likely to wield power than those who do not.

While Barber may not want the "jihad" outcome, he is also unhappy with what the "McWorld" outcome means. Since it represents a world where economic forces wipe away national differences, thereby weakening national political institutions, "McWorld" contains the sort of conflicts between the market and society Polanyi described: the dominance of the market over all else, which cannot work for long. We can dispute this description of "McWorld," since many observers would suggest that the emerging global culture has some identifiable cultural characteristics. We have also seen the evidence that states can and do retain valuable differences in setting their domestic policies. Yet for or better or for worse, most writers and thinkers around the world would describe the new global culture that seems to be evolving as distinctly American in flavour.

NATIONALISM, CULTURAL PRODUCTS, COMPETITION

In recent times, French intellectuals have been at the forefront of those arguing that globalization really represents the imposition of American culture on everyone else. French political leaders second these opinions, though economist Paul Krugman has remarked that the French seem more attracted to a dashing turn of phrase rather than arguments grounded in economic theory and logic. Lionel Jospin, French Prime Minister in 1999, spoke of his fears about the crushing effects globalization can have on national cultures. In his view, "Nothing would be more dangerous than a world where globalism rhymed with uniformism."[11]

While Barber implied that his vision of "McWorld" was one of anarchy, in cultural terms his "McWorld" is clearly rooted in American culture. McDonald's is after all a symbol of American culture, even if it has been transplanted to dozens of countries around the globe. This has made the chain the target of anti-globalization protesters in country after country, too. Barber also expects the "McWorld" outcome to outlast other possible eventualities. Global culture, fuelled by global communication and resounding with American symbols and styles, will override existing diverse identities. As he poses it, "Over the long haul, would you bet on Serbian nationalism or Paramount Pictures? Sheik Omar Abdul Rahman or Shaquille O'Neal? Islam or Disneyland?"[12]

Of course, there are more viable candidates one may want to bet against in a challenge to American culture than Serbian nationalism. The French government continues to wish to use subsidies and other measures to support its cultural industries, despite the opposition (or at least lack of support) other EU members express. As France's Foreign Minister,

Hubert Védrine has stated, "Others do not have this vision because they have nothing left to defend."[13] France is not alone in using government resources and economic regulation to foster or protect cultural industries; Canada and many other countries also implement such policies.

Of course, we should remember the difficulties in defining the precise origins of most cultural products. In reference to a movie, globalization can refer to production, distribution, or consumption.[14] Nothing requires that these be similar in pattern. Most people would be concerned about production only—where is a particular cultural product made? That turns out to be a difficult question sometimes. Production may have been disaggregated into various locations and activities: where was the film shot, then edited? Who starred in it? Who directed? Who owns the film?

Canadians are familiar with these sorts of issues through the rules about "Canadian content" governing radio and television broadcasts. This has generated complaints in the music industry, since many Canadian artists have been very successful, but produce their songs in the United States. If Céline Dion records a CD in Los Angeles using American musicians and backup singers, but the songs are also written by Canadians, is this an American product or a Canadian one? Or should we look instead to the music company she performs for, which could be owned by citizens of a third country?

Perhaps the most contentious aspect of cultural conflicts and competition in Canada swirls around the use of language. The French-English conflict plays out primarily in Quebec, but has important ramifications for political identity within the country as a whole. What would a Canada Day celebration be without a mixture of Celtic music from the Maritimes, country music, and ballads in French? Yet when we turn to the phenomenon of globalization, we immediately think of English—if American English. Language use, therefore, becomes a battleground for those wishing to resist globalization via the politics of identity.

Why is language used as the "marker of cultural distinctiveness" so often? Poppi claims it is because "all other cultural traits have become widely homologated to the wider context."[15] To put this more simply, culture shouldn't really be defined in terms of a single dimension. Culture means much more than language, just as political identity is based on much more than the language one predominately uses. Yet when we look at, for example, Quebec in cultural terms, how different is it? Poppi is suggesting that thanks to the progress globalization has already made, people in many countries already dress alike, watch similar TV shows, listen to similar music, drive cars styled in similar ways, and so on. Language remains one of the last ways of defining separateness in cultural terms.

Boundary markers, such as language, are promoted by those with their own particular agendas. To really use the politics of identity to define separateness, such as ethnicity, political operators need some way of defining who is "in" and who is "out." Language is a very convenient marker, because it is readily apparent to anyone coming in contact with a stranger. Physical characteristics are very unreliable as markers, since the genetic basis for ethnic or racial differences is infinitesimally small.

Often such boundary markers have to be invented, as in the Bosnian civil war, where linguistic divisions are not so apparent. Divisions in Bosnia were supposedly based on a combination of linguistic and religious factors, but in fact the Muslim population had not been particularly ardent in its pursuit of Islam. Today there are as many Mosques in Bosnia as a decade before, but there is little reaction to prayer calls. Intermarriage between Bosnian Croats, Serbs, and Muslims also makes it difficult to think through how ethnic divisions actually mattered before Yugoslavia broke up. Once the country was falling apart, however, political operators tried to use ethnic divisions for their own purposes. Historic claims or grief were selectively picked up, dusted off, and used. As Poppi puts it, it is "the agenda of the present that shapes up an image of the past."[16]

UNDERSTANDING THE SALIENCE OF THE POLITICS OF IDENTITY IN TACTICAL TERMS

These observations suggest that the politics of identity increasingly will be employed as globalizing tendencies proceed. Saskia Sassen notes that in many countries, the winners and losers produced by globalization are already engaged in political conflict. Their battleground, for tactical reasons as much as because of the true origins of their differences, is over issues of identity. As she puts it, "actors with little economic and traditional political power have become an increasingly strong presence through the new politics of culture and identity, and an emergent transnational politics embedded in the new geography of economic globalization."[17] Again, those who feel they are losing out culturally as a result of globalization can use the politics of identity to mobilize their side in resisting its processes.

In the minds of Hirst and Thompson, globalization therefore sparks a nationalist response in many countries. Nationalism is played up by those who feel they cannot succeed in global economic or political competition. Relying on nationalism is not a winning strategy, however, because they feel it is not sustainable in the longer-run.

> Complete cultural homogeneity and exclusiveness are less and less possible. "National" cultures that aim to be dominant over the individuals who belong to them are increasingly projects of resistance to and retreat from the world. Inward-looking nationalism and cultural fundamentalism are, to put it bluntly, the politics of losers.[18]

There are many who would dispute this conclusion, among them French government officials, China's current political leaders, and Quebec intellectuals. Certainly, Hirst and Thompson are overstating their position. There are many reasons for the rise of fundamentalist religious practices one finds in a number of countries, and among them globalization is only a minor factor. Scholars such as Hirst and Thompson also ignore the fact that among the citizens of industrialized countries, those in the United States are particularly religious, and quite patriotic. They also are quite ignorant of the outside world—does that make them inward-looking nationalists? Are they likely to oppose globalizing trends?

What we should note from this discussion, however, is how attractive an emphasis on nationalism will be to those who choose to resist globalization. Even those who lose in purely economic terms may tend to turn to nationalism or ethnic disputes as a political manoeuvre. Ethnic divisions within societies often explode into violence. While it is probable that even in Yugoslavia in the mid-1980s, the politicians who were using ethnic divisions to promote their own agendas did not intend to unleash the violence that followed, they pushed their country down that path. The politics of identity can lead to particularly violent intra-state conflict.

Globalization may decrease the chances of future conflicts between states, by making it costly to disrupt international economic ties. At the same time, globalization may increase the probability of intra-state wars. But if intra-state wars include genocidal violence, the rest of the world may not stand aside. The events in the former Yugoslavia led to NATO's first combat operations. Operation Allied Force, the air campaign for Kosovo, also refuted Thomas Friedman's Golden Arches theory of conflict prevention. Friedman had pointed out that no two countries that operated McDonald's restaurants had ever gone to war against each other. (Barber's "McWorld" was a world of international peace, if not yet one of shared culture.) Now Friedman argues that "globalization is going to sharpen civil wars within countries between localizers and globalizers."[19]

Experiences in the former Yugoslavia suggest that other countries can easily get drawn into these domestic disputes.[20] The war on terrorism that the U.S. is currently leading can also be thought of in these terms, since Islamists have long sought to resist or even reverse many of the modernizing changes we would relate to globalization.

NATIONALISM VERSUS CLASS CONFLICTS?

Conservative leaders in the late nineteenth century, such as Bismarck, adeptly used nationalism to counter the emergence of other identities. In particular, Bismarck and his counterparts in France, Italy, and elsewhere used nationalism and foreign policy to undercut the formation of class identities. The rulers of many European countries were faced with the political consequences of industrialization and international economic integration that left many people resentful and unhappy. Those people, often labourers forced from the countryside and into urban settings, where they could find only low-paying, difficult jobs, were drawn to revolutionary ideologies such as Marxism. Nationalism was taken up by the conservative elite in several countries in an attempt to foster the formation of a different identity, to reduce the emerging sense of class difference.

In this earlier period, it was the traditional elite who chose to employ nationalist identities, in order to prevent the formation of different political identities. Class conflicts in those days threatened to undermine existing political arrangements and also to draw new political lines across international boundaries. Where have class conflicts gone in the current period? As international markets have developed, we might have expected the class conflicts to develop international linkages, too.[21] These arguments are rooted in Marxist analyses that emerged in the late 1960s and early 1970s. These arguments provided the basis for the evolution of dependency theory. Yet dependency theory is now largely out of favour, since it predicted that economically developing countries would be harmed by participating in international markets.

Robert W. Cox notes that "The newly affirmed identities have in a measure displaced class as the focus of social struggle; but like class, they derive their force from resentment against exploitation."[22] That also implies, in his view, that while some of these identities seem narrowly defined at first glance, they have the potential to be much broader because the underlying forces propelling their popularity are also quite broad. Nationalism in a single country may seem to have little to share with nationalism in another, but in fact, if they are both triggered by globalizing economics or an infusion of American culture via global channels, these two nationalisms may be linked by more than emulation.

This is certainly true of religious fundamentalism. Religious movements can easily cross national boundaries. Thus, in Huntington's perspective, we will soon be experiencing a deeper "Clash of Civilizations." His definition of cultures emphasizes the religious dimension over other possible factors. National conflicts carry less weight. Already some see NATO's actions in the Balkans as the basis for united action—based on a shared identity—as the beginning of broader co-ordination by the Western countries. Religion does not seem to be a very useful device for understanding how these clashes over identity become externalized into international conflicts, however.

These sorts of analyses share a basic assumption. They see one form of identity dominating others. You cannot be both an Islamic fundamentalist and a nationalist, in these analyses—though we see plenty of examples to suggest that such identities can overlap. Whether identities can be shared, or whether they create tensions that need to be resolved, are difficult questions to answer. Simply raising them suggests that we pose some more basic queries about the possible changes in identity generated by globalization.

COMPETING PRINCIPLES FOR IDENTITY, OR CAN IDENTITIES OVERLAP?

This last point has been made by V. Spike Peterson. As she sees it, the discussion so far misses entirely the impact of globalizing processes on identity. It is not so much that globalization is shattering national identities by eroding sovereignty, as some propose, but rather that identities are influenced by factors causing people to reconsider the principles their identities are based on. States are no longer the exclusive actors staking a claim to peoples' identities. In Peterson's words,

> state-centric political identity no longer monopolizes but shares the stage with a growing number of non-territorial claimants. Subnational and transnational social movements transgress territorial boundaries in favour of identities "grounded" on ... non-state based communities.[23]

This position is echoed by many others. Yale Ferguson and Richard Mansbach, for instance, also talk about the increasing salience of non-state identities.[24]

Eric Helleiner has noted the recent surge in green political groups in many countries. The basis of green political and economic philosophy is "think globally, act locally." In his view, this philosophy offers a guiding principle for reconciling local diversity, such as the distinctiveness of local preferences on social policies, or sensitivity to locally specific problems (perhaps having to do with the environment, for example), with global economic processes.[25] The philosophy of the greens makes it possible for people to place greater faith in or give greater allegiance to local political authorities. Such changes might force us to consider the increasing importance of municipal, state/provincial, or regional political agencies.

Another dimension to globalizing forces is how they affect the construction of gender as a dimension of identity. Gender roles reflect a complex mix of sources, but economic changes can be a powerful element. For example, the development of the welfare state in the industrialized economies in the 1930s and 1940s led to a redefinition of the identities of workers and of the workplace itself. Industrialization had reorganized where work was done, allowing for a separation between workplace and home. Women's roles became more tightly connected to the home, as male employment was related to the industrial workplace. This evolution was then recognized in welfare policies adopted in the interwar period and thereafter.[26] "Embedded liberalism"—both its international and its domestic dimensions—constructed specific meanings for gender, homeworkers, as well as the social responsibilities of the state.

As globalization proceeds, gender is being reconstructed in the various countries tied together by the international economy. The erosion of "embedded liberalism" in some countries is directly related to changes in female participation in the industrial workforce in others. As Eileen Boris and Elisabeth Prügl describe it:

> This international restructuring leads to changes in class because, by resorting to "flexible" subcontracting arrangements, companies are gradually eliminating a middle class of (largely male) production workers in center economies who in the post-World War II era had achieved wages that supported a family, job guarantees, and benefits assuring their social security. In place of this middle class, a disproportionately female work force is taking over jobs in export processing plants in newly industrializing countries.[27]

Since gender is typically a major component in one's definition of identity, these changes may be having powerful and unintended effects. This does raise an interesting question, however, concerning how different elements of identity interact.

One way of thinking about the way these dimensions of identity may interact is to picture them as being "nested."[28] Persons may comfortably think of themselves as part of a broad group based on a nation-state, but still feel like part of a distinct subnational group, and even a historical group. For example, someone living in New Brunswick might feel strongly Canadian, but think of herself as distinctly a Maritimer, New Brunswicker, or even Acadian. These may fit together comfortably because each identity is a component of the next one in the hierarchy. That does not always happen, and in such cases, politics will be disruptive as political identities clash.

To add to this complicated picture, one can also consider how globalizing trends—particularly the unleashing of market forces—can provoke the formation of new groups. We have already seen how the opponents of globalization might choose to turn to identity as a technique for mobilizing support, so these new groups spawned by globalization are unlikely to promote broad, inclusive concepts of identity. As Boyer and Drache put it,

> Xenophobic social movements are a direct reaction to the global bulldozer. On the left side of the spectrum, women's organizations, environmental activists and popular sector organizations are examples of the kinds of social groups which have been battered by highly volatile markets. They will not accept their fate passively.[29]

Similarly, Robert W. Cox fears that such dangerous social movements can be generated by globalizing processes. Authoritarian populism, or even fascist-style national movements may emerge from situations where groups have materially based resentments and political structures and institutions are being undermined,[30] such as in the case already cited of the break-up of Yugoslavia. The international economic pressures on the country in the 1980s played a pivotal role in pushing the country down the path of ethnic national competition and violence.[31]

Yet Peterson's point is somewhat different. She seems to be thinking about identity considered on new planes. As Peterson puts it, "identities conventionally 'grounded' in state territoriality are losing ground to a politics of new, or even non space(s)."[32] Membership in NGOs could be the basis of such new identities. Someone in Toronto might discover being an environmentalist is more important than being Canadian; this could become the basis for a career evaluating environmental consequences of political decisions by governments around the world, regardless of where these consequences are felt. Someone in Los Angeles, the son or daughter of a political refugee from Central America, might begin to think of him/herself as a strong proponent of human rights; this would frame his/her view and the many decisions he/she makes in politics or economics. Peterson is suggesting that these new principles for political identities matter much more now than they did before.

We may be seeing more fragmentation of political identities, but we may also be seeing overlapping and sharing of identities. Most writers on the subject haven't given enough thought to such issues. Among those who have are Ferguson and Mansbach. Since they readily admit they are unable to predict how these identities will work in conjunction with each other—whether they will coexist smoothly, become "nested," generate intense conflict, or whether one identity will emerge as dominant—Ferguson and Mansbach are hesitant to predict how current trends will unfold.[33] At a minimum, however, they have suggested that this is an area to watch for greater changes.

Summary: How Globalization Leads to Clashes over Identity

There is a powerful logic running behind the thinking of Barber, Friedman, Huntington, and others, regardless of the perspectives or paradigms these authors draw on. They all see economic and technological changes unhooking people from the cultures presently anchoring people's lives. As Ankie Hoogvelt writes, "precisely because of economic modernisation and social change throughout the world, people are being separated from long-standing local identities while at the same time the nation-state is weakened as a source of identity."[34] One can expect other forces, such as religion, increasingly to fill the gap created. "Jihad," to use Barber's metaphor, gives meaning and purpose to political life in a way that nationalism no longer can.

We should remember that similar sorts of activities have erupted in the past, and not always in conjunction with globalizing processes. As some would remind us, new social movements have to have their own social and economic bases, and can be motivated by a range of factors, not only globalization.[35] That also means that those who wish to counter the development of these politics of identity, perhaps to head off ethnic conflict, or to prevent nationalism leading to interstate wars, need to worry about more than globalization.

Also, it is important to remember that the views of Peterson and others remain largely conjectural. Some people may be adopting identities based on new principles, but our evidence is somewhat weak. Most of these forms of identity easily observed in the political sphere still seek to be identified with a state—or see the state as the proper place to pursue their agendas. As Richard Rosecrance affirms:

> Despite economic globalization, religious fervor, and ethnic claims, the state has not succumbed to transnational or localist influences. It provides an arena in which individuals can decide or at least influence their collective fates. No other institution performs this paramount function.[36]

However, Rosecrance goes on to add that states must co-operate to succeed economically. So whatever identities emerge, they still have to be matched with international policies that aid in the economic progress of societies. As Friedman put it, most people want both "the Lexus" and "the olive tree."

Our chief concerns about the future of globalization, then centre on whether there are opportunities for those hurt by globalization to turn peacefully to the politics of identity. As both Sassen and Friedman argued, without a potent ideological counter to globalizing forces, those who oppose globalization will employ nationalism and other forms of identity to mobilize their forces. Only in those places where such identities are viable should we expect the opponents of globalization to be truly successful.

Let us now turn to historical cases to see how these claims may work out. How did previous eras of globalization unfold? Did globalizing trends in the past build upon themselves to sustain their effects for long periods of time, or did they generate backlashes? We might automatically expect the answer to that to be varied, given the arguments of previous chapters—which is why this chapter focused on the chief tool the opponents to globalization may turn to: identity issues. Did the politics of identity play a role in the previous eras of globalization?

NOTES

1 Ankie Hoogvelt, *Globalization and the Postcolonial World* (Baltimore: Johns Hopkins University Press, 1997), 67.

2 Philip McMichael, "The New Colonialism: Global Regulation and the Restructuring of the Interstate System," in David A. Smith and Jozsef Böröcz, eds., *A New World Order?* (Westport, CT: Praeger, 1995), 37.

3 William I. Robinson, "Latin America in the Age of Inequality: Confronting the New 'Utopia'," *International Studies Review* 1, 3 (Fall 1999): 42.

4 Cesare Poppi, "Wider Horizons with Larger Details: Subjectivity, Ethnicity and Globalization," in Alan Scott, ed., *The Limits of Globalization: Cases and Arguments* (London: Routledge, 1997), 286.

5 Robert W. Cox, "Political Economy and World Order: Problems of Power and Knowledge at the Turn of the Millennium," in Richard Stubbs and Geoffrey R.D. Underhill, eds., *Political Economy and the Changing Global Order*, 2nd ed. (Toronto: Oxford University Press, 2000), 30.

6 Thomas Friedman, *The Lexus and the Olive Tree* (New York: Anchor Books, 2000), 31. The description of what the Lexus stands for comes on pp. 32-33.

7 Benjamin R. Barber, *Jihad vs. McWorld* (New York: Ballantine Books, 1995), 4.

8 Ibid., 5.

9 Friedman, *The Lexus and the Olive Tree*, 334.

10 Ibid., 244-45.

11 Quoted in "France and world trade: Except us," *The Economist*, 16 Oct. 1999, 53-54.

12 Barber, *Jihad vs. McWorld*, 82-83. This is curiously reminiscent of a similar bet put in print by Kenneth Waltz. Waltz suggested that states would outlive economic agents such as MNCs, which they certainly have. Yet the particular country he referred to was the Soviet Union—which has not survived!

13 Quoted in "France and world trade: Except us," *The Economist*, 16 Oct. 1999, 53-54.

14 John Street, "'Across the Universe': The Limits of Global Popular Culture," in Alan Scott, ed., *The Limits of Globalization: Cases and Arguments* (London: Routledge, 1997), 77.

15 Poppi, "Wider Horizons with Larger Details," 291.

16 Ibid., 289.

17 Saskia Sassen, *Globalization and Its Discontents* (New York: New Press, 1998), XXXIV.

18 Paul Hirst and Grahame Thompson, *Globalization in Question: The International Economy and the Possibilities of Governance*, 2nd ed. (Cambridge: Polity Press, 1999), 266.

19 Friedman, *The Lexus and the Olive Tree*, 252.

20 Any reader who thinks that there is little connection between globalizing economic trends and the development of ethnic frictions in the former Yugoslavia, or the breakup of that country more generally, should read Susan Woodward's *Balkan Tragedy: Chaos and Dissolution after the Cold War* (Washington: Brookings Institution, 1995).

21 Stephen Hymer's works from the early 1970s depicted such a possibility. International alliances of different elements of classes are also important in the conceptual frameworks referred to as dependency and post-imperialism.

22 Robert W. Cox, "Political Economy and World Order," 29.

23 V. Spike Peterson, "Shifting Ground(s): Epistemological and Territorial Remapping in the Context of Globalization(s)," in Eleonore Kofman and Gillian Youngs, eds., *Globalization: Theory and Practice* (London: Pinter, 1996), 11-12.

24 Yale H. Ferguson and Richard W. Mansbach, "Global Politics at the Turn of the Millennium," *International Studies Review* 1, 1 (Summer 1999): 79.

25 Eric Helleiner, "New Voices in the Globalization Debate: Green Perspectives on the World Economy," in Stubbs and Underhill, eds., *Political Economy and the Changing Global Order*, 2nd ed., 64-66.

26 For a discussion of these issues, see Elisabeth Prügl, *The Global Construction of Gender* (New York: Columbia University Press, 1999).

27 Eileen Boris and Elisabeth Prügl, "Introduction," in Boris and Prügl, eds., *Homeworkers in Global Perspective* (New York: Routledge, 1996), 6. Similar arguments were made by Jan Jindy Pettman, in "Gender Issues," in John Baylis and Steve Smith, eds., *The Globalization of World Politics* (New York: Oxford University Press, 1997), 483-97.

28 For more on this idea, see Guntram H. Herb and David H. Kaplan, eds., *Nested Identities: Nationalism, Territory, and Scale* (Lanham, MD: Rowman & Littlefield, 1999).

29 Robert Boyer and Daniel Drache, "Introduction," in Boyer and Drache, eds., *States Against Markets: The Limits of Globalization* (London: Routledge, 1996), 20.

30 Cox, "Political Economy and World Order," 29.

31 See Woodward's excellent description, *Balkan Tragedy*.

32 Peterson, "Shifting Ground(s)," 12.

33 Ferguson and Mansbach, "Global Politics at the Turn of the Millennium," 101-02.

34 Hoogvelt, *Globalization and the Postcolonial World*, 183.

35 This point has been made by Timothy Scrase, "Globalization, India, and the Struggle for Justice," in Smith and Böröcz, eds., *A New World Order?*, 147-61, esp. 158.

36 Richard Rosecrance, *The Rise of the Virtual State* (New York: Basic Books, 1999), 211.

8 | Putting Globalization in Historical Perspective

According to Kenneth Waltz, many of those who argue that globalization is something quite new underestimate the extent to which the present looks like the past.[1] Is globalization all that new? What might we learn from previous episodes of globalization? In this chapter we do our best to look at elements of economic globalization that might have occurred in previous centuries. Several eras can indeed be seen as periods when globalizing processes created powerful political responses. If we can understand how these events unfolded, and examine these patterns in terms of the theoretical perspectives raised in earlier chapters, we will perhaps be in a better position to consider future developments and opportunities.

If we examine the same three areas of economic integration identified earlier, trade, production, and finance, then we should heed Geoffrey Garrett's comments: "contemporary arguments about these globalization pathways are nothing new."[2] Consider, for instance, one of the opening observations of Ingrid Bryan in *Canada in the New Global Economy*: "Canadian events, problems and policies can no longer be discussed in isolation from those affecting other countries. It is, of course, unlikely that they ever could but recent changes in the human and physical environments have created an entirely new, different, and interdependent world."[3] It sounds somewhat contradictory to assert that Canadian issues should never have been viewed in isolation, but that this is also something new for Canadians to worry about.

How do today's levels of trade or financial integration compare to past levels? Is globalization a new phenomenon or simply the latest academic fad? In Chapter 2 we examined some of the evidence about present internationalization. Now we're looking into specific historical periods of economic globalization. We will begin with the sixteenth century.

177

Globalizing Processes in the Sixteenth and Seventeenth Centuries

Long-distance trade in highly valued materials, the development of transport of bulky commodities across regions, and the development of greater complexity in the international division of labour emerged in the sixteenth century. Historians provide several reasons why this was so. Improvements in sailing equipment and navigation made it possible to pursue opportunities in trade. The centralization of political authority in the hands of monarchs broke down the local trade barriers that had grown up during feudalism. Centralized state organs were able to finance expeditions exploring trade routes. Urbanization fomented a need to expand trade. Facets of international economic development other than trade did not proceed as quickly, however.

TRADE IN THE SIXTEENTH AND SEVENTEENTH CENTURIES

Advances in transportation were vital during this period. Improved techniques in handling ships helped reduce the cost of transporting goods. It took fewer men to crew a ship, cutting expenses. Advances in navigation improved the likelihood of a ship completing a long-distance trip. These improvements combined with the development of better ship designs, such as the Dutch *fluit*, or fly-boat, made it possible to increase the number and type of goods involved in international trade, at least within Europe.

Though the volume of goods involved in long-distance trade remained much smaller, it too was on the rise. Trade over longer distances brought entirely new goods into international exchange. These trips were still dangerous, so items taken such long ranges were valued very highly. From Asia, spices such as pepper, cinnamon, and cloves were transported and among the bulkier commodities, were silk, cotton, and tea. None of these items could be produced in Europe, so they were in high demand. From the Americas, ships brought gold and silver, then later tobacco, cotton, and sugar.

International markets could develop because of improvements in technology involving transportation, but also because Europeans demanded such goods. Europeans also had to have the ability to pay for these goods. Europeans sent silver to Asia and to the Baltic region (where it then found its way into the Russian hinterland). Silver paid for the spices, cotton, and other products from the East, and for grain from what is now Poland, Russia, and Ukraine. Timber and furs also were purchased from the East, as well as from North America.

Wheat and other products were often purchased by merchants in Northern and Western Europe, only to be resold to cities in Southern Europe. The wheat or timber was paid for by earnings from the trade of other items. Salted fish, produced along the Atlantic seaboard, was a popular export item. Northern Europe also produced woolen and linen textiles exported and sold to Spanish or Mediterranean markets. The Spanish had large amounts of silver and gold flowing into their ports from their overseas empire. Silver from South America would come into a port such as Seville, only to be used to pay for fine linen lace produced in Flanders; Flemish businessmen might finance a trip to the Dutch East Indies, which would bring tea or spices to Europe. These items might earn further silver for the merchants in the North of Europe. The silver could then be used to pay for wheat and timber from the Baltic; some of this timber might be turned into further ships. Some of the wheat would be consumed in the Northern ports, but some exported to cities in Italy or elsewhere in the South. The Mediterranean merchants would trade salt or wine to pay for the wheat.

In short, a complex pattern of trade developed in the sixteenth century. It was centred around Europe, and the ports of Northern Europe in particular. The development of overseas empires helped fuel these developments by injecting precious metals into the trading system. Specialized equipment and merchants developed, too, since transporting wheat around Europe presented different requirements from shipping silver or spices around the world. To make the most of these arrangements information about markets, prices, or supplies needed to flow, and means of payment had to be improved.

INTERNATIONAL INVESTMENT AND PRODUCTION IN THE SIXTEENTH AND SEVENTEENTH CENTURIES

While there were many developments in trade, several problems prevented this trade from blossoming completely. International payments were difficult to arrange in anything other than precious metals, simply because monetary standards were not well developed. Legal standards varied considerably, creating additional risks. These issues significantly limited international investments. It would be some time before large-scale international investments could be spread around many countries.

There were international investments taking place, but these were very focused. One way to undertake investments but trust in their security, was to keep them within one political system, and therefore one legal system. So international investments, including investments designed to encourage production for international markets, was to invest in a country's colonies. The great expansion of raw materials production, including plantations and extractive mining operations, was financed in this manner.

A second way to overcome the problem of ensuring the safety of an international investment was to find some other method of enforcing security of ownership. This could be done in several ways. Investment took the form of establishing a completely separate business operation in another country. That operation would be run by someone the investor could trust due to some other link. Kinship would be one such tie. A father could set up a branch of his business in another country by setting up his son or son-in-law in that foreign land. Using ethnic or religious ties might also work in this manner, since anyone violating a contract could be sanctioned through group behaviour, as opposed to legal action. A merchant would not want to be cut off from his community.

Finally, despite the risks, some international investment took place without these extra measures in place. Most often, the hope of extraordinary rates of return inspired the international investment. If someone intended to open up new trade routes, or if a monarch was temporarily in a fix and willing to pay very high interest rates, international investors might step up to seize the opportunity. As often as not, these opportunities to make a lot of money were coupled with the risk of complete loss.

INTERNATIONAL FINANCE IN THE SIXTEENTH AND SEVENTEENTH CENTURIES

There were a couple of international monetary and financial links that grew to prominence in the seventeenth century, after getting their start in the late sixteenth century. The most prominent of these was the tie between the Dutch and the English capital markets. The Dutch had pioneered several techniques for raising capital from both the elite and the masses, and for employing this capital to finance both business and government. This capital remained focused on Dutch business and governmental authorities until 1688.

That year is remembered for the Glorious Revolution in England. The Glorious Revolution sealed Parliament's control over the monarch, as it intervened in the royal succession. William, Prince of Orange, political and military leader of the Dutch Republic, gained the English crown. The

Dutch government and public backed this move because they wanted to develop an alliance between their country and England. One of the spinoffs was the spread of Dutch financial practices to Britain. Dutch investors also had new confidence in the English government.

These investments grew in size over the early decades of the eighteenth century. Larry Neal has concluded that international capital markets were as integrated in the eighteenth century as in the twentieth, if we are to judge by the ties between London and Amsterdam. The interest rates in these two markets reacted strongly to each other. He includes analyses between other European financial markets, and shows they were sensitive to each other as well.

SUMMARY: A FIRST WAVE OF GLOBALIZATION?

In the words of Michael Ignatieff, "We have lived with a global economy since 1700, and many of the world's major cities have been global entrepots for centuries."[4] This is undoubtedly true. Yet the development of globalizing processes has not occurred in any single smooth trajectory. The advances of the sixteenth and seventeenth century were largely curtailed by the development of mercantilist policies in the seventeenth and eighteenth centuries.

Mercantilism reflected the decision by governments, and by monarchs in particular, to take advantage of these economic developments. International trade grew, and governments were not content to sit back and let this trade proceed unfettered. Monarchs, in particular, were caught up in domestic struggles. All states were threatened with international conflicts. Every government needed additional tax revenues. Monarchs were claiming absolute authority, by divine right, and one of the immediate benefits of sovereignty was to tax international trade.

Mercantilism developed as a set of practices geared towards achieving a positive balance of payments. The goal was to accumulate gold and silver. Precious metals were desired by governments because that was the necessary ingredient for hiring mercenaries. Without mercenaries, states were vulnerable. Power also could be turned into further wealth, if one could capture imperial possessions that generated further economic activity. Yet as mercantilism spread, and almost all the major military powers implemented policies based on its precepts, trade flows grew more restricted, international payments became more difficult and international investments dried up.

Globalizing Processes in the Late Nineteenth Century

Mercantilism did not last forever. It was challenged by the ideas of the liberal political and economic writers of the late eighteenth and early nineteenth centuries. More importantly, the economic success of Britain, as that country implemented liberal policies, brought others around to the liberals' way of thinking. Governments in other countries experimented with liberal policies, in order to achieve similar economic successes, or to win favour with Britain. British economic success, combined with its industrial strength, made it a powerful actor internationally. Others tried to emulate its experiences.

By the middle of the nineteenth century, mercantilist barriers to international trade were being knocked down. Technological improvements were again making dramatic advances as industrial techniques changed production, and the development of new forms of energy revolutionized transportation.

> In place of old wants, satisfied by the productions of the country, we find new wants, requiring for their satisfaction the products of distant lands and climes. In place of the old local and national seclusion and self-sufficiency, we have intercourse in every direction, a universal interdependence of nations. And as in material, so also in intellectual production. The intellectual creations of individual nations become common property. National one-sidedness and narrowmindedness become more and more impossible, and from the numerous national and local literatures, there arises a world literature.[5]

These concepts are recognizable as descriptions of the current period, but in fact the authors are Karl Marx and Friedrich Engels, writing in the *Communist Manifesto*.

Note all the elements they identify in this brief passage. They see the impact of changing preferences, increasing trade levels. They even use the term "interdependence." They describe the spread of intellectual creations. Finally, they also discuss how cultural differences are overcome by globalizing forces. They clearly see economic factors as the ultimate cause of these changes.

There is in fact broad agreement among economic historians that the world was economically quite integrated in the three to four decades prior to World War I.[6] During this period, globalizing trends included not only trade but other facets, too. Advances in transportation were matched by advances in communication as the telegraph came into wide use. Payments across borders were made much simpler by the spread of the gold standard. This also reduced the risks in international investments, so that the late nineteenth and early twentieth centuries were periods of high transnational investments.

TRADE IN THE LATE NINETEENTH CENTURY

Interestingly, some economic historians argue that trade one hundred years ago represented a higher degree of interdependence than trade today. In 1913, about half of the volume of trade was exchanged between the regions of the world we today call the North (the industrialized countries) and the South (or economically developing countries). In other words, a century ago trade consisted of manufactured goods exported from the industrialized countries being exchanged for raw materials produced in the less economically developed countries. That type of exchange would compare with only about 22 per cent of total trade today.[7]

At the end of the nineteenth century, only a handful of countries had mastered industrial technologies. These produced the bulk of the world's manufactures, producing for home consumption as well as for export. Today, industrial technology is much more diffuse. The range of goods in trade is much more elaborate these days, but even now, most goods are manufactured items, and most of these are being traded between the most economically advanced countries. Trade is very important, but much of this trade we could survive without. One hundred years ago, trade was much more necessary for economies to continue to flourish. Trade was more likely to be in goods that local economies could not produce, at any price.

Such evaluations stress that the content of trade matters. But for evaluating the degree of "globalization" in trade, we should consider some other dimensions. When we turn to statistics on the impact of trade on domestic economies, we start to find greater similarities between the decades just before World War I and the current period. World War I reversed these globalizing trends, and there was little recovery after that war before the Great Depression and World War II once again reversed these tendencies.

Hirst and Thompson clearly find that evidence of globalization in trade statistics would indicate that only in recent years are they re-approaching the levels reached in the period just before World War I. They compare the ratio of merchandise trade to GDP of the most economically advanced countries (i.e., those most "globalized" by most accounts). It was consistently higher in the years prior to World War I than in 1973, with only (West) Germany exhibiting as high a level in the second period as in the first. When comparing the statistics from the pre-World War I era to 1995, several countries remained less engaged in trade in the "globalization" period of the 1990s than before. These include Japan, the Netherlands, and Britain. France and Germany were only slightly more open in the more recent period than almost a century before. The U.S. was the only major economy much more open in the mid-1990s than it had been in this previous era.[8]

Trade can be critically important in economic development. Since trade has grown faster than production in the post-World War II period, some economists argue that expansion in trade is pivotal for overall economic growth. Was this also true for the last decades of the nineteenth century? The research of Simon Kuznets completed some time ago illustrated that this had indeed been true for the period between 1800 and 1913.[9] Where rapid economic development took place in that period, as in Britain (or later in the United States, Germany, and elsewhere) trade had played a role—though we shall return to this idea in a moment, since other observers would argue that the most economically successful countries in the years leading up to World War I were practicing protectionism, as opposed to opening themselves up to the international economy.

The role of technology in improving trade mirrors the description provided for the earlier time period. Shipping prices fell drastically, particularly for bulky commodities such as wheat, iron, and steel. Steam power tied together markets that had previously been difficult to connect. Getting wheat from the interior of North America to urban centers before it spoiled had been a challenge before railroads penetrated those regions. Steamships did not have to follow the winds, and could go directly from one continent to another. Telegraph cables made it possible to communicate vast distances at previously unheard of speeds— close enough to be considered instantaneous.

A dramatic increase in the integration of commodity markets in the late nineteenth century resulted. The spread of free trade in Europe opened up previously closed markets as well. As the price declined for shipping bulky items such as wheat by railway and steamship, producers could sell their goods in more and more markets. Since these commodities are by definition largely indistinguishable, prices in markets around the world began to converge. Trade was pivotal in shifting prices downward. The price for wheat in European markets, for instance, fell by some 45 per cent in the late nineteenth century.[10] Prices around the world began to move in step as markets became more tightly intertwined.

INTERNATIONAL INVESTMENT, PRODUCTION, AND FINANCE IN THE LATE NINETEENTH CENTURY

International investment patterns did not tie together production, except for a few specialized products. Multinational production of some goods did take place, but for the most part, this did not spur international investment. In a few isolated industries, such as cigarette production and oil refining, international investment in production did occur. Economies of scale in production led to the development of large monopolistic firms or cartels in a couple of countries. In order to head off foreign competitors, or to penetrate new markets in trade, these firms purchased existing producers in other countries. Integrating or streamlining production processes across international boundaries was secondary to defense of monopolistic profits.

There were extensive flows of capital internationally in the pre-World War I period, but this primarily took the form of portfolio investments. These investments are usually in the form of a loan from the original owner of the capital in one country to a borrower in another. The borrower manages the investment directly. This allows foreigners to start up operations to compete against business in the country where the capital originated. Rather than have production integrated, there should be greater competition internationally, as a result of this form of investment.

Indirect or portfolio investment was enormous in the decades before World War I. According to the IMF's statistics, net flows of capital in the 1990s are still only about half the size of those prior to World War I. Gross movements of capital over borders has risen dramatically in the last decade, but these movements largely cancel each other out over the course of a year. The resulting *net* balance is not nearly so large as a result.[11] Portfolio investments, on the other hand, tended to be long-term loans, in forms such as 20-year bonds. In the late nineteenth century, portfolio investments dominated international capital flows.

Another measure for comparing these two eras is to contrast the current account balance to the GNP. That ratio is a measure economists use to gauge financial openness. If 1875 is compared to 1975, no increase in openness can be detected. Indeed, some countries, including the financial powerhouse of the previous period, Britain, but also countries such as the United States, Italy, Sweden, Norway, and Denmark indicate *less* openness in 1975.[12] The overall pattern indicates decreasing openness after 1913, but then an opening up after 1970, so that countries are now *returning* to high levels of financial openness.

On another measure, Larry Neal tried to gauge how quickly crises were transmitted from one market to another. He was interested in finding a measure that would allow him to make comparisons across long spans of time, but using only limited data, since he has an interest in putting the seventeenth and eighteenth centuries into context. He therefore compared interest rate differentials across financial centres, to see how quickly shocks spread from one to the next. The closest integration of all was in the gold standard period,[13] when between the major economies interest rate differentials were quite low. Even in the post-World War II period, substantial differences in interest rates between the Western powers remained in place.[14]

Michael Bordo, Barry Eichengreen, and Jongwoo Kim also conducted some comparisons between the pre-World War I and the post-World War II periods. They examined the historical literature on each of these time periods, and noted that those who had applied the Feldstein-Horioka test showed that only in the 1990s were we approaching levels of integration comparable to the years prior to 1914.[15]

They also suggest that interest rate differentials might be a better tool for looking at capital market integration, though they seek to control for other elements of risk that interest rates are meant to capture. Using covered interest rate parity as a measure, they find that capital markets were well integrated in the decades before World War I, but were also well integrated during the Bretton Woods regime and afterwards.[16] Much the same results are generated if one considers the real interest rate parity between capital markets.

Bordo, Eichengreen, and Kim emphasize an important distinction between the gold standard years and the current period. In the pre-World War I years there was indeed a large amount of international investment taking place, so that measures such as net flows of capital as a percentage of GDP look similar to today's levels. Yet the range of these investments was quite limited. The vast majority was held in railroads, municipal and national bonds, and a few other types of assets. Bordo, Eichengreen, and Kim note that the breadth of international capital investments today is much greater.[17] Such distinctions are often overlooked by those who merely examine the gross statistics.

In sum, international capital markets were well integrated and "global" in the late nineteenth century, as well as today. Differences exist between the ways in which national financial markets were integrated, and in the ways capital flows influenced national economies. In the earlier period, capital flows were longer term. Investment was primarily portfolio, rather than direct investment. Production processes were not as highly integrated as today. The volume of international investment was great then, as it is today, but these investments focused on a narrow range of clients, which would have limited the influence of international capital on national economic development. Lending was concentrated on governmental authorities.

LABOUR AND MIGRATION IN THE LATE NINETEENTH CENTURY

From the similarities we can find between the late nineteenth century and the current period in global capital markets, we turn to international labour flows and discover dramatic differences. Those who note that the nineteenth century represented an earlier wave of globalization can make the case, using evidence from this issue area, that the earlier period may have represented an even greater degree of globalization than today.[18] It is fairly hard for people to move over borders these days, even after the fall of the "Iron Curtain." A century ago, millions of people crossed borders in the search for a better life. Not only did the United States and Canada receive these immigrants, but so did Australia, the countries of South America, and several others.

These flows of labour have been studied for some time. Economic historians questioned whether the movements of labour and capital were substitutes for trade. This possibility is suggested by the Heckscher-Ohlin model of trade, which bases comparative advantage on differences between countries in their relative endowments of factors of production. William Collins, Kevin O'Rourke, and Jeffrey Williamson compared trade flows with those of both labour migration and capital flows in the late nineteenth and early twentieth centuries. They discovered that trade and capital flows, as well as trade and labour migration, were rarely substitutes. Flows of capital and labour over borders were often complementary to trade flows, according to their evidence.[19] The usual interpretation for these patterns is that labour and capital went to those countries where arable land was still available. Immigrants and investment turned this open land into agricultural export zones, stimulating trade.

To be more accurate, what happened in the quarter-century before World War I was more complicated. The story of immigrants coming to settle the frontier is certainly part of what occurred. Yet many immigrants came to the western hemisphere in search of employment—not necessarily land. Many of these people came to earn money to send to family members back home, or to save up for some other goal. Once the immigrants had earned enough, they often returned to their homeland. Thousands of immigrants came to the U.S., Argentina, Canada, and elsewhere to work, but in less than 10 years they went home again.

SUMMARY OF EVIDENCE ON THE LATE NINETEENTH CENTURY

Observers today argue that globalizing economic trends are forcing countries to pursue similar policies, and are putting all states at the mercy of international markets. After studying the overall pattern of international and national economic changes from the late nineteenth century to the late twentieth, Jeffrey Williamson concluded that there was an "unambiguous positive correlation between globalization and convergence" in certain specific national economic characteristics in two periods. That is, national economies behaved similarly in that time period. The comparison was strongest in the years prior to World War I, and also in the decades after 1950. Moreover, when he looked more closely at this correlation for the years before 1914, he found the connection to be causal: "globalization served to play *the* critical role in contributing to convergence; it took the form of mass migration and trade."[20]

Of course, there are various interpretations of this evidence, and its political and economic consequences. For instance, Paul Bairoch has shown that inequality among nations, as measured by per capita income, has increased since 1860.[21] Do advances in trade exacerbate existing inequalities, or is such a pattern caused by technological improvements—advances that have been concentrated in a handful of countries? If we consider the two periods when globalization was said to have occurred in previous periods, the latter is certainly closer to what we consider to be happening today. What sort of politics emerged from the globalizing economic forces of the late nineteenth century?

The Political Consequences of this Past Globalization

One of the most important results of the globalization that occurred in the late nineteenth century, was its impact on equality. Williamson finds that globalizing economic forces in those decades caused inequality in the richest countries to rise, while inequality fell in the poorer countries. That matches some of the evidence concerning the impact of greater integration of economies in the late twentieth century.[22] At the same time, Williamson is quick to note that technological change—especially the use of machinery to replace unskilled labour—probably accounted for much of the rising inequality observed in the rich countries prior to World War I, not international trade or investment.

That inequality in earnings shows up in some of the legal changes introduced just prior to World War I, but continued quite strongly in the 1920s and 1930s. Unskilled labour in the industrialized countries tends to feel first the competition of additions to the pool of labour. As inequality increased, less skilled labour began to ask for limits to immigration. Such policies started slowly, but had become widespread by World War II. The barriers to flows of labour remain largely in place, making it quite unlikely that we will soon observe levels of labour flows over borders equalling those of the late nineteenth century.

Most commentators would identify a set of political reactions emerging from the globalization of the late nineteenth and early twentieth centuries that would limit the impact of these international flows over time. Yet things happened at different paces. Immigration flows were reduced before World War I. Prior to that time, tariffs had already been raised on numerous items, especially for agricultural goods. Capital markets remained open to international flows, right up to the outbreak of the war.

We can make out some clear geographic patterns to these reactions. In Europe, the backlash to globalization took the form of tariffs—blocking, or at least reducing the impact of trade. In the Americas and also Australia, the response to globalization's impact was to restrict immigration.[23] Earlier historical interpretations viewed the restrictions on immigration in other terms, stressing racial aspects. This is critical, for it illustrates how important the politics of identity are used as a catalyst for mobilizing political forces. Political entrepreneurs played up racial and ethnic differences between immigrants and receiving countries in order to build support for barriers to immigration. The economic interests behind such actions are evident. Both the United States and Australia were suffering from economic recessions and high unemployment in the 1890s, which was when the first big pushes for immigration restrictions took place.[24] (The U.S. House of Representatives first voted on this issue in 1897.)

Ashley Timmer and Jeffrey Williamson interpret these restrictions on labour flows as attempts to control the effects of immigration on the wages of unskilled labour. Immigration tends to lower the wages of the least skilled first. Restrictions on labour inflows could maintain the relative economic position of the unskilled workers compared to those in the workforce with better skills, as well as with those who controlled other factors of production.[25]

Free trade policies had begun to erode much earlier, precisely because those who controlled certain forms of production found they could not compete in the new global markets. Agricultural producers played a central role in this drama. As noted before, agricultural products are largely commodities; the developments in transportation helped drive the prices of such goods as beef or grain down by enormous amounts. Farmers everywhere faced falling returns. In countries where farmers wielded political power, they sought some form of relief. In Germany, where grain was grown on large estates owned by the aristocratic elite, the powerful landowners pushed government to raise tariffs that helped these individuals to maintain their wealth. Political compromises were made with another set of commodity producers: iron and steel mills. These industrialists' output suffered from the same problems as the grain growers.

Commodity producers felt the impact of increased competition in trade more fully than other producers. The nature of their goods helps explain why. Commodities are characterized by the fact that they are indistinct. Grain from one country could just as well be replaced by grain from another. Other products, such as coal, raw iron, and steel, have similar characteristics. As transportation costs fell, these goods flooded international markets. The producers of these goods sought relief from this competition.

Even in democracies agricultural producers might dominate other interests. In France, for instance, the division of the country into so many small districts allowed farmers to control many seats. All parties had to cater to their interests, to a certain extent. Agricultural tariffs went up in many countries in Europe. In the U.S., farmers were interested in expanding exports in the face of these new tariffs. They suffered from low prices, but also found it increasingly difficult to sell their produce abroad. They sought some form of relief, too, just not in the form of a tariff.

American farmers asked for a variety of policies to ease their economic circumstances. Sensitive to every little cost, they led the movement to regulate railroad rates. This in turn led to regulation of large businesses in general. They demanded, but could never win broad support for, inflationary monetary policies. This would have eased farmers' debts, but also made their exports more competitive. Their efforts to attack the tariff led to the advent of the income tax in the United States. These political positions, looked at together, show how globalization can influence a host of other policies.

Perhaps just as amazing is that the demands of American farmers were far from unique. Germany's aristocrat landowners, the Junkers, made similar demands on their government. They, too, asked for special rail rates for their grain, for inflationary monetary practices, and so on. Because they were no longer competitive internationally, however, they also wanted a tariff. Numerous other countries adopted tariff protection for agriculture, often because the tariff would generate revenue the government needed. The way such policies got packaged together—regulation of transportation, tariffs, monetary policies, availability of agricultural credit, increased agricultural research and training, and so on—and the political coalitions such melding of policies would support—have rarely been studied in ways that would illustrate the interconnectedness of the policies and the powerful insights possible from making such comparisons across countries.

Projecting from Past Experiences to the Present

Geoffrey Garrett argues that globalization remains more myth than reality. International integration of markets heightens insecurities in society, but governments do still use policies to offset negative aspects of these market outcomes. Moreover, we have also seen how he argued that these very government actions, as well as government spending in general, can attract international investors and skilled workers.[26] The issue for Garrett is to reframe these questions into slightly less sensational terms than so many others have used. He asks more specific questions about the factors shaping investors' decisions, and how these are affected by societal demands for redistributive policies, as well as other government interventions in the economy. These dynamics play out differently in different political and institutional contexts.

We can see that in how different countries experienced globalization in the late nineteenth century. Some, such as Britain, and perhaps Denmark, rode through the turmoil by specializing their production and exploiting opportunities. Others, such as France and to a certain extent Germany, resisted elements of globalization via trade policy. Others, such as the United States, experienced important political divisions due to globalizing trends. Where trade policy remained fairly open, as in the U.S. or Canada, immigration policy tended towards closure. Globalizing economic processes sparked a variety of understandable political counteractions.

Having identified similarities in the earlier period of globalization and the current period, Williamson goes on to note how the earlier period of globalization generated a political backlash. In his work with Timmer on immigration policy prior to the 1930s, they sound one sort of alarm.

> The parallels are clear. Inequality has been on the rise in the OECD economies since the early 1970s, especially the gap between unskilled and skilled workers, just as it was in the New World economies in the late nineteenth century. We should therefore not be surprised by the renewed interest, both in the United States and Europe, in reducing the flow of immigration. Labor-scarce economies have been sensitive in the past to trends of greater inequality in their midst, using restrictive immigration policy to offset these trends.[27]

We should remember, however, that such pressures are filtered through the particular political systems each country employs.[28] Countries today are much more democratic than they were in the years before World War I, even in democracies such as the U.S. or Britain.

The decades of the earlier globalization were followed, after World War I, by several decades of rising barriers between economies. These barriers only came down with the development of the compromise of "embedded liberalism" and the extension of government activity to shield citizens from the more disruptive elements of the international economy. Economic globalization has returned only in recent years. The earlier experience suggests that political forces eventually will offset these economic changes. This causes Williamson to conclude one of his studies by posing the following question about the future: "Will the world economy retreat once again from its commitment to globalization?"[29]

NOTES

1 Kenneth N. Waltz, "Globalization and Governance," *PS: Political Science & Politics* 32, 4 (December 1999): 695.

2 Geoffrey Garrett, "Global Markets and National Politics: Collision Course or Virtuous Circle?," *International Organization* 52, 4 (Autumn 1998): 795.

3 Ingrid Bryan, *Canada in the New Global Economy: Problems and Policies* (Toronto: John Wiley & Sons, 1994), 1.

4 Michael Ignatieff, *Blood and Belonging* (Toronto: Penguin Books, 1993), 12.

5 Karl Marx and Friedrich Engels, "The Communist Manifesto," in Arthur R. Mendel, ed., *Essential Works of Marxism* (New York: Bantam Books, 1961), 16-17.

6 Dani Rodrik, *Has Globalization Gone Too Far?* (Washington: Institute for International Economics, 1997), 7-9.

7 See World Bank figures cited by Ankie Hoogvelt, *Globalization and the Postcolonial World* (Baltimore: Johns Hopkins University Press, 1997), 14.

8 Paul Hirst and Grahame Thompson, *Globalization in Question: The International Economy and the Possibilities of Governance*, 2nd ed. (Cambridge: Polity Press, 1999), 27.

9 Hoogvelt, *Globalization and the Postcolonial World*, 69-75.

10 Jeffrey G. Williamson, "Globalization and Inequality Then and Now: The Late Nineteenth and Late Twentieth Centuries Compared," *NBER Working Paper* #5491, Mar. 1996, 8-9.

11 See the discussion by Karl Socher, "Globalization and International Monetary and Capital Markets," in John-ren Chen, ed., *Economic Effects of Globalization* (Aldershot, UK: Ashgate, 1998), 32. See also Michael Bordo, Barry Eichengreen, and Jongwoo Kim, "Was There Really an Earlier Period of International Financial Integration Comparable to Today?," *NBER Working Paper* #6738, Sept. 1998, 16.

12 See S. Grassman, "Long term trends in openness of national economies," *Oxford Economic Papers* 32, 1 (1980): 123-33.

13 Larry Neal, "Integration of international capital markets: quantitative evidence from the eighteenth to the twentieth centuries," *Journal of Economic History* 45, 2 (1985): 219-26.

14 Stephen Krasner, *Sovereignty* (Princeton: Princeton University Press, 1999), 221.

15 Bordo, Eichengreen, and Jongwoo Kim, "Was There Really an Earlier Period of International Financial Integration Comparable to Today?," 7-8.

16 Ibid., 8-10.

17 Ibid., 26.

18 See, for example, Ethan Kapstein, *Sharing the Wealth* (New York: W.W. Norton, 1999), 44.

19 William J. Collins, Kevin O'Rourke, and Jeffrey Williamson, "Were trade and factor mobility substitutes in history?," in Riccardo Faini, Jaime de Melo, and Klaus Zimmermann, eds., *Migration: The Controversies and the Evidence* (New York: Cambridge University Press, 1999), 227-60. Their findings are summarized on 252-53.

20 Williamson, "Globalization and Inequality Then and Now," 1.

21 See the discussion of Bairoch's statistics in Hoogvelt, *Globalization and the Postcolonial World*, 85-86.

22 Williamson, "Globalization and Inequality Then and Now," 20. Williamson is comparing his findings with those of Adrian Wood.

23 This observation was made most cogently (and supported by evidence) by Collins, O'Rourke, and Williamson, "Were trade and factor mobility substitutes in history?," 248.

24 Ashley Timmer and Jeffrey Williamson, "Racism, Xenophobia or Markets? The Political Economy of Immigration Policy Prior to the Thirties," *NBER Working Paper* #5867, Dec. 1996, 5.

25 Ibid., 30.

26 Garrett, "Global Markets and National Politics," 788-89.

27 Timmer and Williamson, "Racism, Xenophobia or Markets?," 30-31.

28 This point is nicely illustrated by Jeannette Money, "The Political Economy of Immigration Control," *International Organization* 51, 4 (Autumn 1997): 685-720.

29 Williamson, "Globalization and Inequality Then and Now," 20.

9 | Future Scenarios: Political Backlash, or Global Governance?

Almost every author who has tried to describe globalizing processes has emphasized the declining role of the state in regulating these processes. They may disagree on whether states willingly relinquished their ability to control some of these, or had the ability to regulate these processes seized from them. Yet in the end they all see political consequences to these changes. One of the principal consequences most agree on is that political backlashes against the impact of markets will develop. They disagree however, on how the state will respond to new demands for regulation, let alone whether states can respond effectively.

The chances of states reasserting their authority over international economic processes hinge not simply on their capabilities, but on the pressures from within that would push them to use those powers. As Robert W. Cox wrote "states can also become agencies for bringing the global economy under social control. The state remains a site of struggle for those who would challenge the social consequences of globalization."[1] Yet what would the reassertion of political authority look like? Would we be returning to something recognizable, or would we be entering some entirely new arrangement? Having discussed how different economic and social relations have become, we might need to create entirely new political arrangements to regain any political authority lost.

Let us consider three possible scenarios of the future. In one, a political backlash emerges within several countries, challenging globalizing trends.

In the second scenario, dissatisfaction with globalizing pressures leads to political pressures for states to react, but in this case, the states try to maintain the benefits associated with globalization while reducing damaging effects. This could be done through several methods: "re-embedding liberalism" (where domestic policies managing the economy are used, but international economic relations are left to be market-driven), or trying to control those international market forces through international institutions. There are variations in the ways these can be done, of course.

The third scenario is that the political opponents of globalizing trends will be too weak to make much difference in the future. Their wishes and desires will be swamped under a wave of positive support for globalization.

Each of these scenarios has so far focused on individual countries. Different countries are going to react differently to globalization. These different reactions will interact to produce international outcomes. Bringing states closer together economically does not always bring them closer together politically. The economic integration of the former states of the Soviet Union, or Yugoslavia, did not prevent them from pulling apart politically.[2] So each scenario of the future may bring rather different results at the international level.

Domestic Interests and the Future Pace of Globalization

One specialist in international political economy, Eric Helleiner, expects globalizing trends to abate. An expert on international finance with a deep knowledge of economic history, Helleiner reminds us that in the area of international finance, states chose the policies that created global finance. He rejects the argument that technology has driven globalization in finance. Because of these assessments of the sources of globalization, he concludes "a reversal of the liberalization trend is more likely than is often assumed."[3]

WHY WOULD GLOBALIZATION SLOW DOWN?

There are several reasons globalization might slow down, especially because globalization can spark political opposition. As mentioned in the previous chapter, earlier waves of economic internationalization generated sufficient opposition to slow them down. The impact of internationalization of markets on farmers and commodity producers generated strong political reactions in a number of countries in the late 1800s. Tariffs went up, followed in later decades by regulation of the movement of people over borders. The social and economic disruptions generated by the unfettered market sparked these political reactions.

Moreover, economic downturns tended to strengthen this opposition. Economic recessions, or more severe depressions, cause people to lose faith in markets. The supporters of trade or other international economic ties lose their interests in promoting such links when opportunities dry up. Tariff barriers are raised in one country, and this sparks retaliations in others. This process occurred not only in the late nineteenth century (especially in the 1870s and 1890s) but also in the late 1920s and 1930s. The tendencies have also been observed in the 1970s and 1980s, though in those years special efforts were made to keep tariffs down.[4] The 1990s have been a time of economic growth—especially among the most economically advanced countries—so these negative circumstances have not been widely met yet.

Globalization might spark its own downfall, then, by hurting groups who then turn to politics to redress their injuries. In an economic downturn, these groups will grow in size and number; in a severe downturn, these groups would be even more vocal. If the downturn were to grip the U.S., not only would that create opposition to globalization in one of the countries most in favour of globalization, but it would also create ramifications overseas. Those countries whose economic gains depend on exporting to the American market would find themselves dragged into the same downturn. A national economic problem in the U.S. could easily turn into a more widespread problem. That is perhaps the most likely way for globalizing trends to slow down.

Economic globalization could also slow down without experiencing such a dramatic crisis. With regional crises such as the East Asian financial crisis, renewed international efforts to control the risks of globalization might impede globalization's progress. Helleiner points out that the U.S. has helped organize collective action by states to regulate certain aspects of global finance activities. After liberalization was promoted, and market instabilities erupted, the U.S. led some regulatory efforts. International standards on capital adequacy, regulations on what counts as capital for reserves, as well as rules on money laundering have been implemented. While these rules do not overturn the liberalization trend, they illustrate that the mechanisms for organizing and employing regulations reversing globalization remain available.[5]

WHY WOULD GLOBALIZATION CONTINUE APACE?

While Helleiner has written that he expects a backlash against globalization to develop over time, he has also provided us with some reasons why this backlash may take quite some time to develop. One of the important aspects of globalization is the integration of economies across great distances. Helleiner notes that this increase in distance obscures the consequences of one's actions (or better yet, obscures the consequences of one's economic transactions).[6] This is why he appreciates the perspectives of the greens, and urges others to apply the ideas greens have been developing.

Purchasing a particular pair of basketball shoes rather than another may not seem like such a big deal, but the accumulated effect of many such decisions could have serious implications for supporting labour practices of one sort or another in distant countries. Protesters against globalization may know this, but then some are still observed wearing trendy brands of clothing nonetheless. The power of multinational corporations in their advertising may be the single most important factor at work, not the MNCs' lobbying efforts. After all, a reduction in sales would hurt them much more than limits in lobbying, yet widespread boycotts have not had much effect.

Some argue that this is for a simple reason: greed. Economic globalization offers material gains. Thomas Friedman, for one, expects globalization to continue. It may not be a smooth path, of course, but since globalization is driven, in his view, by the "basic human desire for a better life," he expects people to continue to demand the specific policies that comprise globalization.[7] The difficult problem is to strike the balance between economic progress and society's other needs, as Friedman stresses. Yet people everywhere, he argues, want a better life—if not for themselves, for their children. Economic advancement is critical. Internationalization and market liberalization are widely recognized as the best path to those ends, at least for now.

WHY WOULD GLOBALIZING PROCESSES ACCELERATE?

There is no clear, coherent alternative ideology that can counter globalization. Thomas Friedman reported that he thought the most important news out of Asia in the late 1990s was the domestic responses to the East Asian financial meltdown: "the relative silence with which the lower and middle classes in Thailand, Korea, Malaysia, Indonesia, and the former Soviet Union accepted the verdict of the global markets—that their countries had fundamental software and operating system problems—and were ready to take the punishment and are now trying to make the necessary adjustments."[8] In such an environment, what is to stop globalization—at least economic globalization—from speeding up? Both those who expect globalization to wreak havoc with society and those who endorse the changes it brings about expect it to speed up. On the one hand, there are those who decry globalization's impact, yet expect it to proceed. These include many of the activists who protest against the WTO, IMF, and other organizations or institutions they view as symbols of globalization.

The opponents of globalization feel that they are locked in a battle of "David and Goliath" proportions. The supporters of globalization include international institutions and government bureaucracies unhindered by accountability. Protesters have focused their energy on these actors. Whether or not globalization is popular, it is impossible to have a popular "referendum" on the subject because the key decisions are made in intergovernmental institutions beyond the reach of democratic elections. Or, so the opponents of globalization claim. Globalization will probably continue, they feel, precisely because its opponents have so little political power in the settings that count.

The logic political routes for the opponents to take include doing more than demonstrating outside international meetings or engaging in publicity stunts. Using the media is an obvious choice. Terrorism is another tool of the politically weak that might prove attractive; terrorism has to have an audience, however. The actions of September 2001 could be seen in terms of anti-globalization, but if so, they have hardly garnered support. Indeed, many groups that had wished to use confrontational tactics in subsequent meetings of the G-8, or international economic forums, have found they needed to tone down their tactics. Still, in places where globalization is particularly disruptive, and where the politics of identity can be introduced, the opponents to globalization may still find terrorism an attractive instrument.

If we turn to the reasons globalization has been occurring, we might find other reasons for it to accelerate. Improvements in technology might play a critical role in the future of globalization. If something like the development and adoption of containerization dramatically reduced the time it takes to load and unload ships, transfer cargo from ships to trains or trucks and vice versa, could have such a dramatic impact, what will happen with further digitization of cultural products? Have we seen the full impact of the Internet yet? Improvements in communication could cause further changes.

The Internet makes it possible to deliver products with speed and at low cost over great distances. In the information age, more and more products are purely service-oriented: they are ideas, not objects. The range of products that can be digitized has rapidly increased in recent years (from simple written material, such as a book, to music, to increasingly complex products that combine audio and visual aspects, such as DVDs). We have every reason to believe that more and more of the future economy will be made up of these products. The fuel driving globalization forward is far from exhausted.

Thinking about How States will Deal with Continued Globalization

If globalization is likely to continue, but opposition is also likely to arise, how will states respond? Our best guesses come from studying how globalizing finance has elicited state policies. Since the end of World War II, global finance has slowly slipped from the control of national regulations. Helleiner described this process well in *States and the Reemergence of Global Finance*.[9] His central thesis is that states chose this path. With financial and corporate actors facing different opportunities than their foreign competitors, and having trouble achieving other goals via regulations, some states decided to lower regulatory barriers on capital flows. The biggest surge came in the 1970s and early 1980s, led by the United States. Other governments, under pressure from their constituents, followed suit.

Changes include more than the stripping away of old regulation. Often, new types of regulation have to be put in place to foster the spread of new types of transactions or to endorse new financial instruments. Saskia Sassen notes that "A basic proposition in discussions about the global economy concerns the declining sovereignty of states over their economies."[10] She goes on to point out that states have elected to deregulate certain parts of the economy, but have also chosen to introduce new regulations that foster globalization. In particular, by introducing new laws and rules allowing the securitization of previously fixed (or nonliquid) capital, they make it easier to trade capital across borders.

States also choose to keep certain segments of the market under tight regulation, even as they loosen others. It seems unlikely that a single process is at work, undermining the state's power or abilities—otherwise we would see it losing its grip over most policies.[11] Since states are able to exercise control over certain aspects of globalization, when they choose to do so, we are led to focus more intently on why and when states have chosen to reassert their powers.

Louis Pauly agrees with these assessments, but provides a better way for us to think about the situation concerning international capital flows. As he notes, states remain capable of exercising their sovereign powers in ways that constitute re-regulation of international financial links. "In practical terms, however," Pauly writes, "there was no doubt late in the twentieth century that most states confronted tighter economic constraints—or clearer policy trade-offs—as a consequence of a freer potential flow of capital across their borders."[12] The notion that the trade-offs are more discrete or more severe is especially useful.

Better regulation of the international activities of banks illustrate how these trade-offs work. In the wake of the 1980s debt crisis, the Bank of International Settlements (BIS) helped establish widely agreed upon standards for accounting to be used when national authorities monitor and regulate the activities of banks. This helps control the competition between banks and among the various national regulatory schemes. The Basle Accords governing capital requirements for international lending are a very specific example of how globalization creates risks and problems, but also how states and private actors might come together to help control those risks.

Thus, we can consider the state still capable of asserting control over financial markets—even though international finance is the quintessential example cited by authors as the market most beyond state control. As Benjamin Cohen concluded in a recent book, "National monetary authority is undoubtedly under challenge, but it is not yet ready to be tossed into the dustbin of history."[13] An interesting contrast arises when we consider regulations on labour. The "race to the bottom" so many fear globalization generates is used typically to describe changes in the regulation of international capital flows, but also of domestic labour and environmental standards. What has been happening on those fronts?

INTERNATIONAL CO-OPERATION IN LABOUR AND ENVIRONMENTAL REGULATION

We have long had an international organization to deal with labour's issues: the International Labour Organization (ILO). The ILO has been in existence since the end of World War II—yet it enjoys none of the fame or notoriety of the IMF or other organizations. Partly, this is because it lacks enforcement powers, and few resources. Unlike the IMF, which has goodies to hand out, it has little to offer beyond advice and information.

The ILO's work is often unnoticed, and unappreciated as well. It has authored numerous conventions on labour rights, including recent ones regarding child labour. These conventions are only binding if a member country chooses to ratify them however. Yet its activities are discernible, though the real impact of these actions are difficult to measure. Supervisory actions by the ILO have led to observable changes in national laws some 2,000 times since 1964, according to one analysis.[14]

Labour regulations have not been lowered in significant fashion in any of the major economies in recent years. Wages and unemployment rates have moved both up and down, but there remain major differences from one national economy to the next. These characteristics reflect differences in the way national labour markets function; it would be very difficult to take all the evidence from the experiences of different countries and view it simply as a sign that international competition was eroding national standards. Countries continue to react to these pressures differently—due to differences in preferences, capabilities, and opportunities.

Turning to environmental regulation, we find several examples of spectacular international failures. Attempts to get meaningful international agreements on limiting greenhouse emissions, protecting biodiversity, and scaling back specific forms of pollution all have failed in some respects in recent years. The Kyoto Accord was recently undermined by the Bush administration's decisions to promote other goals and other policies than those initially agreed on. Yet, failure to make progress internationally is not the same as saying national standards are being degraded. Certainly more could be done, both nationally and internationally. Pressures from economic globalization may be slowing the development of more effective environmental regulations, but there is little to suggest that states have lost their capability to implement such rules. That is precisely why demonstrators continue to push for changes.

Edward Luttwak, whose discussion of "turbo-capitalism" emphasized how freer trade was leading to changes in business practices that would eventually lead to a major redistribution of wealth in society, remains confident that the economy can be re-regulated. Luttwak had emphasized how liberalized trade, as well as improvements in communication and transportation, made it possible for firms to rely on more outsourcing of inputs. Outsourcing could even be done internationally. This would allow firms to downsize, or use other strategies to put downward pressure on wages even as share values rose. Yet re-regulation could change businesses' practices and reverse some of these trends.[15]

Of the different scenarios described above, the most likely seems to be the second. Globalization is more likely to create some opponents. Governments are most likely going to seek to respond to these groups' demands, but not by abandoning participation in the global economy. They will seek some sort of balance—but how? What international policies offer a suitable way to temper globalization?

CO-ORDINATION BY GOVERNMENTS: HARMONIZATION, CONVERGENCE, AND CO-OPERATION

Opponents of globalization (or at least those who continue to have faith in national governments) recommend greater international co-operation, especially harmonization of national policies. Such efforts are usually viewed as attempts by states to bring greater efficacy to their policies. Ronald W. Jones, for instance, equates harmonization of national policies with collusion, i.e., that states currently harmonize policies in an effort to reduce or control the movement of factors of production.[16] Harmonization is attractive to states because it offers to lessen the degree of competitive differences; it tends to do so by making each participant compromise.

Because harmonization can be portrayed as a compromise between states, it can be sold politically to domestic publics. Harmonization eliminates the pressures for a "race to the bottom" so long as states adhere to their international commitments. It is easy to sell such agreements because it appears obvious that harmonization is better than variation in national policies, and certainly better than competition.

Yet harmonization does not always make states better off. One policy would hardly be expected to fit all states' needs. Countries with different levels of economic development have different requirements for growth and investment: countries differ in the needs of their population for education, in their savings in pension schemes, and so forth. It seems unlikely that a single regulatory scheme would be well-suited to a wide range of countries. Evaluating whether harmonization would make a country better off also entails understanding how harmonization would proceed. Harmonizing tax levels, for instance, would require some states to charge higher rates, others to charge lower, or some combination of changes. Since these states began with different rates for some reason, harmonization tends to sweep aside these reasons.

Harmonization will undoubtedly create more challenges for some states than for others. Much depends on where the convergence is—will it be at the bottom of regulation or somewhere higher up? William

Watson notes that Canada will have a much harder time converging to some international norm on regulations, or harmonizing regulations with its major trading partners, because it has historically used regulations more intensely.

> For most developed countries, the prospect of policy harmonization with many of the world's most competitive economies is harrowing enough, but for a country such as Canada, which for at least three decades has vested so much of its identity in greater use of government than its principal trading partner, it threatens, at best, a near-death experience.[17]

If Canada has to bring its policies into line with those of the United States and Mexico, for example, it probably will suffer substantial shifts.

What is often not appreciated is that there are very different consequences to harmonization, convergence, and the creation of a regulatory floor, depending on the process by which each is implemented. For example, in tax policy, if one adopts assumptions about business interests that stress agglomeration, the sort of competition that develops can reach quite different results.[18] The countries that already have industries can charge a high tax rate—yet they are constrained from charging a higher rate by the competition from countries that lack industry. The tax rate in the countries lacking industry is not constrained by competition. If the two sets of states use convergence or attempt to harmonize their tax policies, the result will be to lower rates in the countries with high taxes, making those worse off. The same is true for convergence in tax rates between the two sets of countries. When a tax floor is introduced, however, the high-rate countries can continue to charge a high rate, while the low-rate countries can increase the amount they charge.

Harmonization carries with it the implication of choice, and of positive connotations. After all, the end of the process of "harmonization" is harmony. Yet convergence is not seen in such a positive light. Some European writers—particularly those who belong to the *régulation* school—fear that national regulations are already converging. They are worried that national regulations soon will be similar, but their fear is not that these levels would be inappropriate for some states simply because states have diverse needs. Instead, the proponents of the *régulation* school fear that national rules are converging towards lower levels. This is the "race to the bottom" scenario once again. Existing and past regulation was based on the nation-state, but as fiscal restrictions cause the state to contract its welfare policies, and as other levels of government take on new powers, they argue that a similar trend seems to be emerging.[19]

What would these same writers think about harmonization? First, they probably would assume that harmonization means converging towards higher than average levels of regulation, which they would view as positive. Yet similarity in policies is not the focus of their attention, so much as the resulting level of state intervention. Much of this reflects concerns expressed in Europe. Many European states have well-developed social democratic practices, which hinge on extensive state services that developed over long periods of time. If competitive pressures do in fact undercut government revenues or otherwise require a reduction in those services, a number of politically stable arrangements may come undone.

The recommendations for policy-makers are twofold, and potentially contradictory. The first is for states to resist globalization as defense of national priorities. States therefore should feel free to opt out of international arrangements or organizations that challenge national policies. Second, if decision-makers do feel their country's policies are less effective, they may look to international co-operation to make their policies more successful. In this process, convergence due to market pressures might well encourage states to pursue co-operation internationally as a way to make their individual efforts more successful. The major economies already co-operate in a number of formal and informal forums, ranging from the G-7 summits to the WTO.

The contradictory nature of these recommendations can be seen in the policies of several countries, but especially France.[20] The French government rails against globalization, but also promotes development of the EU as a route to defending French interests and values. International organizations offer the possibility of defending French goals, including the maintenance of the state's role in the economy, and specific policies popular in France, but international organizations do not necessarily deliver such ends. In dealing with a number of issues, the French are quick to use the UN, because France can wield special power within that organization thanks to its seat on the Security Council. French officials see international organizations both as the proponents of globalization, and as possible tools for reversing globalizing trends they wish to resist.

WHAT ROLE WILL INTERNATIONAL INSTITUTIONS PLAY?

The French are not the only ones worried about how globalization is proceeding. The real source of the French fears is that American-style regulation will be foisted upon them. Similar concerns lay behind Canada's traditional reliance on multilateral institutions. Faced with the need to rely on international trade and investment, and on economic ties with the U.S. in particular, Canada's leaders have sought to control or manage their external relations via formal multilateral international institutions. These international institutions offer smaller, weaker states the opportunity to spell out their desires in explicit terms, employ sovereignty, band together in numbers to put weight behind their positions, and use international opinion in their favour.

International institutions can help protect national interests when such interests are embedded within international regulatory frameworks. Defense of national levels of environmental regulation could be placed within the overall NAFTA accords, for instance, by making regulations explicit, and a component of the broader agreement. Canadian officials would also argue that they have been doing the same thing in the GATT and WTO negotiations, as well as in contesting trade practices through tribunals over the years. By pursuing this strategy, the interests of a small state can be balanced against the interests of those with more economic or political power.

International institutions are often promoted by opponents of globalization as a better tool for achieving desirable goals. If the nature of the problem lies in the international dimension of economic activity, shouldn't the best instrument to resolve these problems also be found in the international arena? To turn this into a specific example, if global finance is outside political control, might not the best device for bringing this part of the international economy under control be an international institution? Should greater power be vested in international financial institutions?

The two most prominent IFIs, the World Bank and IMF, are not very popular, especially with those who oppose globalization. These institutions are already seen by the public as too much the servant of private financial interests. Some of this criticism may be warranted, since many IMF policies are geared to creating conditions favourable for international investors. Opponents of globalization also see these institutions as two of the loudest proponents of globalization. Could the proponents of globalization be entrusted with regulation of private international transactions?

Second, these institutions are now regularly charged in public with being "non-democratic." They are not considered accountable, and many now see them as illegitimate. Take for instance this description from Jeremy Brecher and Tim Costello:

> Like the absolutist states of the past, this new system of global governance is not based on the consent of the governed. It has no institutional mechanism to hold it accountable to those its decisions affect. No doubt for this reason, it also fails to perform those functions of modern governments that benefit ordinary people.[21]

This is a bit ingenuous, however, since these organizations are made up of the governments of the member states. Some states undoubtedly have governments that are not very representative of their citizens. Democracies have become more not less common in recent years. The IMF and other institutions have tried to promote the spread of responsible government, not block it.

Yet this criticism by Brecher and Costello points out a serious issue with the whole harmonization strategy. International institutions are only as effective as their own constituents choose to make them. Most international institutions have meagre resources at their disposal. They often rely on national authorities to carry out their decisions.[22] The organizations themselves are composed of national officials, with allegiance to their own countries. Politically, these sorts of international agencies are unlikely to prove any more useful than other routes to national co-ordination of policies.

Third, existing institutions are not in a position to carry out such a mission. They are intergovernmental in character. Rather than seeing them as the servants of business, they are the direct servants of governments.

> It [the IMF] has the most comprehensive membership [of any IFI], for nearly all states in the world are members. It also has the clearest legal mandate, the largest professional staff, and significant financial resources under its own day-to-day control. It nevertheless remains an intergovernmental institution, and its basic policies and functions mirror the intentions of its members, especially its leading members.[23]

If existing institutions are not suited to deal with emerging problems, does that mean we could not design better institutions to handle the issues wrapped up in globalization?

WHAT CAN NEW INTERNATIONAL INSTITUTIONS OFFER?

In the wake of recent financial crises, the inadequacy of international agencies to deal with current challenges, let alone the ones that may lie ahead, has been recognized. The international financial crises of the late 1990s were extremely complex, and developed very rapidly. The speed of the crises, and the connections between events around the globe, caught many people by surprise. These characteristics merely mirrored the speed and interconnections of the current financial market. The widespread practice of hedging via derivatives makes it difficult to head off crises once they begin. National regulations governing financial markets in many economically developing countries remain poorly developed, making some states more vulnerable than others. The IMF and World Bank are poorly positioned to do more than give advice, which they can only try to persuade governments to enact when those countries are most vulnerable to pressure—after a crisis has already occurred.

Some people have therefore argued that new agencies be created, with the sort of powers required to deal with aspects of recent crises. George Soros, an international speculator blamed for wreaking havoc on international financial markets, proposed the establishment of just such an agency. He opined that there should be an "International Credit Insurance Corporation" that could insure foreign loans up to a "prudent level." Risks would remain, but at least a portion of the risk could be reduced, thereby making creditors a little less quick to jump from a ship in trouble.[24]

Who would fund such a corporation? National authorities remain the source of most resources. They are unlikely to give up any resources without getting something in return. In finance, national practice is to provide aid and assistance in domestic financial crises, but only to those actors whose health is known, or whose behaviour has not been unduly reckless. (This is the problem referred to as "moral hazard." If insurance is given too freely, it actually encourages reckless behaviour.) Help in financial crises should hinge on regulation. To receive assistance, the national financial authorities need information assuring that lenders have complied with regulations meant to control their risk-taking. Insurance comes only at a price.

In international finance, the progress that has been made in recent decades has come through co-operation by national authorities. In the wake of the debt crisis of the 1980s, national financial regulatory authorities have come together to establish similar accounting rules, minimum standards of capital adequacy for participants in international lending, sharing of information on borrowers, and so forth. These outcomes show that national authorities can make great strides simply by using their existing powers, and co-operating. There are those who feel that the standards being applied have not been entirely fair,[25] and even with such agreements severe international financial crises have occurred. Yet much has been done on this front.

These examples from international finance can be matched by examples from trade. Many who oppose globalization were displeased with the shift from GATT to the WTO. The significant institutional changes concerned the creation of the WTO as a separate entity—the GATT had been more of a contract, a set of promises between members, whereas the WTO has its own institutional identity. GATT was more of a forum for its members to meet and discuss trade issues, rather than a separate institution. Also, the WTO introduced new dispute settlement mechanisms, and new techniques for disciplining the behaviour of members.

The shift in institutional arrangements also came with changes in the scope of the agreements. Trade no longer stands by itself. Brecher and Costello—who probably were not fans of GATT—were sharply critical of the move to the WTO. Rules on trade were linked to rules on intellectual property rights and investment. As they put it, the package of changes

> redefines "free trade" to mean the right of companies to go wherever they want and do whatever they want with as little interference as possible from anyone. Such "freedom" for corporations means restricting the freedom of governments and citizens.[26]

Their position probably overstates the situation, but certainly the general impression many have is that the voices of citizens are drowned out by the lobbying efforts of large corporations.

SUMMARY: HOW CAN GLOBALIZATION BE LIMITED?

International institutions, even more recently constructed ones such as the WTO, do not offer very many special attributes that might make them a particularly desirable tool for the future. If globalizing trends are to be countered through policy, the most effective policies remain in the control of states. Pauly, speaking of capital markets specifically, has stressed that states remain the centre of our focus when considering possible future scenarios.

> If effective governing authority has been usurped by global capital markets, or if such authority has surreptitiously been devolved to those markets by states themselves, surely questions are raised about the process by which such a shift has taken place and about the obligation of citizens to comply. There remains today only one place where such questions can be directed and satisfactorily addressed. And whether we conceive of it as an arena, a structure, or a set of institutions, that place is called the state.[27]

Of course, it is possible to dream up alternative outcomes. Brecher and Costello, coming from a leftist perspective, urge people to promote "globalization-from-below." So far, they argue, globalization has been implemented by corporations pursuing their own agenda through non-democratic means. "Globalization-from-below ... recognizes the need for transnational rules and institutions which may limit national sovereignty,"[28] but it is a little difficult to understand where they ultimately wish for political power to be located. Part of that confusion can be seen in some of their recommendations. Referring to GATT, the IMF, and the World Bank, they point out that these institutions "are formally accountable only to national governments"—but then go on to urge that these multilateral institutions "be made more accountable to the United Nations and to non-governmental organizations representing citizen interests."[29] Making them responsible to the United Nations makes no sense. At best it would make no difference, since the UN is composed of representatives from the same national governments in these other institutions. At worst, such a change would make the WTO or IMF responsible to national governments that had not committed themselves to the principles of these organizations.

Brecher and Costello are ready to trust NGOs to act in the public interest rather than elected governments. This is curious, to say the least. Some NGOs have carefully planned mechanisms making them responsible to stakeholders, but stakeholders are defined in a variety of fashions. Few have the elaborate processes of elections, let alone referenda or propositions, found in many political systems. Not all states practise democracy, of course, but currently, the majority do in fact have democratic procedures in place. This is especially true among the countries most involved in liberalized international trade.

We have identified a number of important trends for the future. Globalization is likely to continue. Its impact will be felt, creating a backlash. In democracies, governments will respond to that backlash—

but governments will respond by striking a balance between continuing globalizing processes, compensating those hurt by these actions, and seeking better control over the situation. Democratic states will have incentives to co-ordinate or harmonize their responses, both in creating or reshaping international institutions, and in implementing domestic policies. All of this suggests that a "re-embedding" of liberalism will take place. Yet the original "embedded liberalism" model emerged out of the fiasco of the Great Depression. Will it take another economic crisis of large scale to propel this set of changes?

Conclusions: What Does the Future Hold?

To a great extent we will pick our own future. Democratic nations are at the heart of processes of globalization; they are leading the way, both by example and by constructing international agreements to solidify globalization. If the populations of the most economically and technologically advanced states reject trends in globalization, the processes of globalization at the international level will be slowed, or possibly even reversed.

Many would not expect this to happen, however. Saskia Sassen, for one, expects trends to continue precisely because current globalization rewards particular segments of society and punishes others. The very processes comprising globalization are restructuring politics. By redistributing decision-making within the economy and society and by redistributing wealth (which can be translated into political power), globalization creates stronger and stronger support.[30]

On the other hand, this argument is reminiscent of one made by Ron Rogowski. In *Commerce and Coalitions*, Rogowski used the economic models to understand who won and lost economically when trade was liberalized. The new winners would naturally accumulate more wealth, which in turn would enable them to wield more political power. This pattern was not entirely self-sustaining, because there were numerous factors shaping the further liberalization of trade. Not least of these factors were changes in technology, but there also were exogenous shocks determined by the policies of other states (such as wars, depressions, and so forth).[31]

Political decisions remain central to understanding our future. Whether one recommends harmonization of national policies in the face of globalizing trends, or greater use of international institutions in the search for co-operative outcomes, or whether one rejects all these and wishes for each state to choose its own path, national politics remains pivotal. No matter how one thinks things will unfold, the connections between the international economy, domestic interests, and they ways these are filtered into national decision-making have to be the basis for our analysis. These help us understand how we got to where we are, and the same tools will help us figure out what future outcomes are most likely. Globalization probably will proceed in most places, but with opposition gaining the upper hand whenever communities find themselves too uprooted, or at least when their political leaders are motivated to convince them of that. It will only be reversed internationally if the major economies of the world lose interest in these trends—and that won't happen without a major economic crisis. Globalization can always be tempered, since states can still exercise quite a bit of control. That issue is the focus of our concluding chapter.

NOTES

1 Robert W. Cox, "Political Economy and World Order: Problems of Power and Knowledge at the Turn of the Millennium," in Richard Stubbs and Geoffrey R.D. Underhill, eds., *Political Economy and the Changing Global Order*, 2nd ed. (Toronto: Oxford University Press, 2000), 25.

2 A point made by Kenneth N. Waltz in "Globalization and Governance," *PS: Political Science & Politics* 32, 4 (Dec. 1999): 698.

3 Eric Helleiner, "Post-Globalization: Is the financial liberalization trend likely to be reversed?," in Robert Boyer and Daniel Drache, eds., *States Against Markets: The Limits of Globalization* (London: Routledge, 1996), 193-94.

4 The shift to floating exchange rates made it possible for states to employ monetary policy to gain some protection, in effect, however.

5 Helleiner, "Post-Globalization," 202-03.

6 Helleiner, "New Voices in the Globalization Debate: Green Perspectives on the World Economy," in Stubbs and Underhill, eds., *Political Economy and the Changing Global Order*, 2nd ed., 61.

7 Thomas Friedman, *The Lexus and the Olive Tree* (New York: Anchor Books, 2000), 348.

8 Ibid., 363.

9 Eric Helleiner, *States and the Reemergence of Global Finance* (Ithaca, NY: Cornell University Press, 1994).

10 Saskia Sassen, *Globalization and Its Discontents* (New York: New Press, 1998), xxvii.

11 Alan Scott, "Globalization: social process or political rhetoric?," in Alan Scott, ed., *The Limits of Globalization: Cases and Arguments* (London: Routledge, 1997), 13.

12 Louis Pauly, "Capital Mobility and the New Global Order," in Stubbs and Underhill, eds., *Political Economy and the Changing Global Order*, 2nd ed., 124.

13 Benjamin Cohen, *The Geography of Money* (Ithaca, NY: Cornell University Press, 1998), 20.

14 Jeremy Brecher and Tim Costello, *Global Village or Global Pillage* (Boston: South End Press, 1994), 129.

15 Edward Luttwak, *Turbo-Capitalism* (London: Weidenfeld & Nicolson, 1998), 232-33.

16 Ronald W. Jones, "Private Interests and Government Policy in a Global World," *Tinbergen Institute Discussion Paper* TI2000-051/2, 16.

17 William Watson, *Globalization and the Meaning of Canadian Life* (Toronto: University of Toronto Press, 1998), ix-x.

18 Richard E. Baldwin and Paul Krugman, "Agglomeration, Integration and Tax Harmonization," unpublished paper, draft of Sept. 2000, 19-22.

19 Alan Harding and Patrick Le Galè, "Globalization, Urban Change and Urban Politics in Britain and France," in Alan Scott, ed., *The Limits of Globalization: Cases and Arguments*, 190-92. They cite the works of Bob Jessop, Robert Boyer, and M. Aglietta.

20 I doubt that all French intellectuals or officials oppose globalization; I am sure many would endorse these same tendencies if French leaders or products played a more prominent role in these processes.

21 Brecher and Costello, *Global Village or Global Pillage*, 63.

22 This sort of argument was already played out in the 1950s, when some scholars believed that officials in the European Community would speak for Europe rather than their national governments, due to the international and technical nature of the problems they were tasked to resolve. This quickly proved not to be the case.

23 Louis Pauly, *Who Elected the Bankers?* (Ithaca, NY: Cornell University Press, 1997), 8.

24 Hirst and Thompson, *Globalization in Question*, 146.

25 Japanese banks, in particular, have had to adjust their accounting practices substantially.

26 Brecher and Costello , *Global Village or Global Pillage*, 58.

27 Pauly, "Capital Mobility and the New Global Order," 124.

28 Brecher and Costello , *Global Village or Global Pillage*, 78.

29 Ibid., 176.

30 See Sassen, *Globalization and Its Discontents*.

31 Ron Rogowski, *Commerce and Coalitions* (Princeton, NJ: Princeton University Press, 1989).

10 | Grasping the Consequences of Globalization

In this book, I have endeavoured to explore some of the most prominent causal linkages between globalizing processes and politics. Political outcomes are changing as globalization proceeds. Globalizing economic forces—in the forms of increased trade, greater international integration of production, and greater mobility of capital across borders—have some predictable effects; so do increased abilities to communicate internationally, and to travel. Each of these changes affects the opportunity costs of engaging in greater international economic intercourse. Simply, that means the political significance to ourselves of what is going on in other countries will rise—a point illustrated with devastating and dramatic impact on 11 September 2001. Specific policy decisions in foreign economic affairs will be much more important than before. Exchange rate policy, stability of the international financial system, a government's credit rating, and other factors will garner much more public attention than previously. This will be especially novel for the U.S., Japan, and some other countries.

Politically, we would expect these policies to be the focus of more attention, and perhaps more division. It is more difficult to predict how the changes in the importance of these policies for certain groups will work its way through different political systems. While we have posed questions concerning future support for or opposition to globalization, proposed answers lead us to many more questions. This is partly because these same changes will alter the degree of complexity in linkages between policies. Globalization blurs the distinctions between domestic and international boundaries, making it possible to use policies in one realm as substitutes for policies in the other. Decisions in one area will generate natural complements in the other. If the late nineteenth century provides us any clear lessons, it is that globalizing processes will offer political entrepreneurs new ways of constructing coalitions, and new ways of tying policies together. The complexity of these linkages gives entrepreneurs more room to manoeuvre, and conversely makes it harder for us to predict what precisely will happen.

The Causes and Consequences of Globalization

Globalization is blamed for a variety of ills, often incorrectly. Though his may be a disappointing discovery, Herbert Stocker's conclusions after he had examined some specific issues in the debates over globalization may have value. "Given all the attention that 'globalization' has received from scholars, international organizations, and the press, these calculations are a reminder of how modest the influence of globalization—at least on a very high macroeconomic level—still might be."[1] Of much greater import might be two trends that reversed in recent decades. One involved the high levels of debt governments everywhere seemed to accumulate between the 1960s and the 1980s, and the other encompassed the accumulation of state-owned businesses between the 1930s and the 1980s. Increasing international competition in trade and investment forced a reversal of these trends in the later 1980s and 1990s, as governments decided to stop borrowing so much and to begin paying their debts. Governments everywhere also privatized many businesses they had previously run as pressures to compete grew with the spread of liberalized trade.

International factors were critical in igniting the reversal of these trends, but it is also important to remember how much choice political actors retain. Very little in the preceding chapters left us with the impression that governments are being "railroaded" into anything. And as many states do reduce their debt burdens, the costs of pursuing diverse choices will go down. Citing James Rosenau, Sassen argues that states have chosen to narrow their sovereign powers. "This is not the end of states' sovereignty, but rather that the "exclusivity and scope of their competence" has changed, and that there is a narrowing range within which the state's authority and legitimacy are operative."[2]

At the same time, those limitations have been overemphasized by many who write on globalization. Alan Scott is critical of those who view globalization as "an unstoppable historical force in the face of which politics is helpless."[3] Instead, globalization should be viewed as merely the latest version of conflict between market forces and society (or the community). As Scott argues:

While globalization theorists have emphasized the complementary nature of globalization and fragmentation and of universalizing and particularizing tendencies, they may have fallen into an historicist trap by viewing this, to adapt another Polanyian metaphor "double movement" (or simultaneous de- and re-regulation) as something new or as itself evidence of globalization rather than simply a phase of the struggle between the opposing (but mutually interdependent) logics of the economic and the socio-political at a time when the balance of forces lay with the former.[4]

One thing seems clear: the economic misfortunes of some in the industrialized economies should not be blamed completely on the better economic performance of those living in less economically developed countries. Globalization is often employed as a scapegoat for unpopular political decisions. Politicians using this excuse are quick to suggest that globalization has an inevitable quality. Globalization may wrongly justify dismantling of the welfare state, as well as placing greater authority in international organizations.[5]

On the other hand, we need to be vigilant about the choices that are being made. As Louis Pauly put it, "Many people now fear 'global' finance, and their fear is not irrational. It is rooted in a dilemma of political legitimacy that deepens with each step towards markets that are truly integrated across national political borders."[6] Saying that globalization doesn't by itself undermine the welfare state as it was constructed after World War II cannot be taken as a reprieve for those arrangements. The post-World War II welfare arrangements are being challenged, but often for other reasons. The overall level of government debt, the availability of capital, and other factors also come into play. Underlying shifts, such as population changes or lower rates of inflation, have also had a profound impact on the welfare state. In the immediate post-war period, people didn't live long after retirement, economies were growing, and the working population was increasing at a rapid rate. These conditions are nearly reversed in most OECD countries.[7] Welfare arrangements could not be paid for in the same ways as before. Most governments tried borrowing to continue to pay for these benefits, rather than renegotiate the balance between payments and benefits. Large deficits prevented this option from lasting too long. Globalization is often invoked as a rationalization for change by politicians forced to reopen these issues.

Also, as Kenneth Waltz has recognized, although the evidence on convergence of state activities at a new, lower level appears to be quite weak, that does not discredit the arguments about globalization entirely. Arguments about a "race to the bottom" in regulation or taxation may not be a "statement about the present, but a prediction about the future."[8] Yet if one message comes through, it is that choices about the future remain. We can sustain a more reasoned discussion of how to handle these choices if we continue to learn about the specific composition of globalization, as well as appreciating some of the consequences of its different processes.

Choices for the Future

As French intellectual Daniel Cohen notes, one of the most interesting aspects of the debates on globalization is that people fear its consequences precisely because they fear that they cannot control or undo those outcomes.[9] The notion that globalization is fueled by a host of technological factors feeds into this imagery. Politicians reluctant to take responsibilities don't help to clarify the situation. It is not surprising, then, that fear of the unknown adds to the apprehension many feel about globalization. If we need to make decisions in this area, we should make them with as much knowledge as possible.

Politically, we can expect conflicts over globalization to continue, since the economic processes at work create winners and losers in material terms. In democracies, the winners and losers have to seek some method of ameliorating their differences. Economist Dani Rodrik, who has written extensively on globalization, provides a very insightful suggestion about political goals for the future. Although he has faith in the market's ability to deliver material benefits, he also recognizes the destructive power markets can wield. To offset social disruptions from market effects, he proposes the following objective: "The broader challenge for the twenty-first century is to engineer a new balance between the market and society—one that will continue to unleash the creative energies of private entrepreneurship without eroding the social bases of co-operation."[10]

This view is seconded by Thomas Friedman. After describing the sort of breakdown of authority that swept through Albania, the former Yugoslavia, and elsewhere, and the consequences of such a collapse, he concludes:

> Those people who warned or predicted that, because of globalization and the increasing irrelevance of borders, the nation-state would begin to wither away or diminish in importance are dead

wrong. In fact, they speak utter nonsense. Because of globalization and the increasing openness of borders, the quality of your state matters more, not less.[11]

The ability of governments to provide collective goods, develop infrastructures supporting society, and resolve dilemmas created by globalizing processes will continue to be part of the critical tasks they face. In processing the impact of globalizing processes, politics will become more important. What we need to do next is get a better grasp on how states currently are striking balances between their economic and political goals. Only then can we hope to understand and contribute to the political dynamics at work. The challenges for us, as political economists, are enormous, since the complexity of the ties between policies and actions become increasingly intricate. The issues raised in debates about globalization are too important to be left unquestioned or misunderstood.

Future research needs to look more closely at disaggregating globalization, but doing so in ways that allow us to see how different elements can be combined or pulled apart. Too often we have failed to see linkages between policies—even where such links were obvious. A case in point would be the close intertwining of tariffs, taxation, economic regulation, and monetary policies in the late nineteenth century. We haven't come to grips with the array of choices states faced in that previous era of globalization because we have broken these subjects into different fields that fail to talk to each other. The big picture has been lost. If we do not disaggregate globalization into its components, but then study how these components may or may not fit together, we will never be able to properly evaluate the possible ways to control or restrain globalization. We have to be able to do a better job on these tasks if we are to assess the political dangers and opportunities of pursuing different policies. Only then would real choices about how to participate in globalization be clearer.

NOTES

1 Herbert Stocker, "Globalization and International Convergence in Incomes," in John-ren Chen, ed., *Economic Effects of Globalization* (Aldershot, UK: Ashgate, 1998), 113.

2 Saskia Sassen, *Globalization and Its Discontents* (New York: New Press, 1998), 25. Sassen quotes Rosenau's phrase from "Governance, Order and Change in World Politics," in James Rosenau and E.O. Czempiel, eds., *Governance without*

Government: Order and Change in World Politics (Cambridge: Cambridge University Press, 1992), 1-29.

3 Alan Scott, "Globalization: Social Process or Political Rhetoric?," in Alan Scott, ed., *The Limits of Globalization: Cases and Arguments* (London: Routledge, 1997), 1-3.

4 Ibid., 15.

5 Daniel Cohen, *The Wealth of the World and the Poverty of Nations* (Cambridge, MA: MIT Press, 1998), 111.

6 Louis Pauly, *Who Elected the Bankers?* (Ithaca, NY: Cornell University Press, 1997), 2.

7 Cohen, *The Wealth of the World and the Poverty of Nations*, 112.

8 Kenneth N. Waltz, "Globalization and Governance," *PS: Political Science & Politics* 32, 4 (Dec. 1999): 695.

9 Cohen, *The Wealth of the World and the Poverty of Nations*, 103-04.

10 Dani Rodrik, "Sense and Nonsense in the Globalization Debate," *Foreign Policy* (Summer 1997): 36.

11 Thomas Friedman, *The Lexus and the Olive Tree* (New York: Anchor Books, 2000), 157-58.

Index